T0338226

Race and Work

Work & Society Series

RACE AND WORK

Persistent Inequality

Karyn Loscocco

polity

First published in 2018 by Polity Press

Polity Press
65 Bridge Street
Cambridge CB2 1UR, UK

Polity Press
101 Station Landing, Suite 300
Medford, MA 02155, USA

ISBN-13: 978-0-7456-9640-9 (hardback)
ISBN-13: 978-0-7456-9641-6 (paperback)

A catalogue record for this book is available from the British Library.

Library of Congress Cataloging-in-Publication Data

Names: Loscocco, Karyn A., author.
Title: Race and work / Karyn Loscocco.
Other titles: Race & work
Description: Malden, MA : Polity, 2017. | Series: Work & society | Includes bibliographical references and index.
Identifiers: LCCN 2017012650 (print) | LCCN 2017030940 (ebook) | ISBN 9780745696430 (Mobi) | ISBN 9780745696447 (Epub) | ISBN 9780745696409 (hardback) | ISBN 9780745696416 (paperback)
Subjects: LCSH: Discrimination in employment. | Sex discrimination in employment. | United States--Race relations. | Equality--United States. | BISAC: BUSINESS & ECONOMICS / Organizational Behavior.
Classification: LCC HD4903.5.U58 (ebook) | LCC HD4903.5.U58 L67 2017 (print) | DDC 331.60973--dc23
LC record available at https://lccn.loc.gov/2017012650

Typeset in 10.5 on 12 pt Sabon by Servis Filmsetting Ltd, Stockport, Cheshire
Printed and bound in the United Kingdom by Clays Ltd, St Ives PLC

For further information on Polity, visit our website: politybooks.com

Contents

Detailed Contents

Acknowledgments

I offer heartfelt thanks to the scholars whose work has inspired and informed my analysis of persistent inequalities in race and work. I hope I have done their important work justice. I am grateful to Richard Lachmann, Melinda Lawson, Hayward Horton, Christine Bose, and Carol Tye, who took time out of extremely busy schedules to read parts of the manuscript. Their suggestions and assurances were extremely helpful. Thank you to the Polity readers who provided insightful suggestions and pointed out blind spots. Special thanks to editor Jonathan Skerrett who wouldn't take "no" for an answer, launching me into a project that has expanded my horizons. During our journey together I have been consistently impressed with how good he is at his job. I also want to thank editors Rachel Moore and Susan Beer who ushered the manuscript into print with skill and patience.

I was fortunate to have the research assistance of Rachel Sullivan, Elizabeth Harwood, and Wen-Ling Kung at various stages of the research and writing of the book. Very special thanks go to Annemarie Daughtry whose excellent skills and impressive work ethic have been essential throughout the project.

I am grateful to my wonderful family and friends for showing interest in the book and for understanding when I disappeared. Additional thanks go out to Kecia Johnson and Dawn Knight-Thomas, who convinced me that I had a contribution to make, and to Dorene Earner for being my mirror and my anchor.

Thank you, again and forever, to my parents, whose generosity and sacrifices made it possible for me to do meaningful work. Thank you to my son Nicholas for letting me know (in his own way) that he values my work, and for being an enjoyable distraction. My biggest debt of gratitude goes to my life partner Larry, for his unflagging support and understanding. Thanks for keeping the home fires burning (and the house from burning down).

I dedicate this book to all of the people who have fought – in whatever ways they could – to create more racial equality. And to those who are part of the resistance now.

Introduction

Discussions of race and work are common at dinner tables, across campuses, and on social and news media pages. Social science corroborates what a cursory look at the content of those discussions shows: people from different race groups see things very differently. While some groups call attention to equal work opportunity as a key unfinished goal of the Civil Rights Movement, others are convinced that whites are now oppressed as much or more than blacks, Latinos, and Asians – particularly when it comes to finding and keeping good jobs.

There are many misconceptions about the economic histories of different racial and ethnic groups. There is confusion about the extent and content of racial disparities in the work realm. Finally, misleading and incorrect information about the *reasons* for race-based patterns in work and occupations abounds. In these pages you will find the evidence and conceptual building blocks needed for a more accurate discussion of race and work in U.S. society.

Sociology makes a unique contribution to the study of work and race systems because of its emphasis on structure. This is an important corrective to our cultural emphasis on "rugged individualism." People tend to look to individual behavior and attitudes for explanations, even when there are clear and consistent *patterns*. It is as though they focus in on the final frame of a video clip, instead of examining what came before. If they watched the whole video clip, their interpretation of the behavior of the person in the single frame might be different. While sociologists certainly acknowledge the important role of *agency*, or the self-conscious decision-making and actions of individuals, social context is particularly important to the study of race and work. That is because when we believe that work outcomes are the product of individual inputs, we conclude that we all get the work lives we deserve. This is a strong cultural value which can lead some people to overlook large amounts of data showing that structural forces channel individuals into work positions and affect attitudes and behaviors.

Because race and work developed together in the United States, work is an important focus for understanding race, and race should be front and center in the study of work. Society is built around the economy so the effects of racial inequities ripple out well beyond the workplace, into homes, communities, and futures. Work is likewise a key potential site for disrupting race-based inequities and tension. Of course work systems do not exist in a vacuum. Employment systems, occupations, and industries, and the ways they sort people by race, are intricately connected to other systems such as education, polity, and family. Though detailed discussion of other social institutions is beyond the scope of this book, you will see that race-based work and employment patterns affect and reflect patterns in other institutions.

The sociological study of race and work exercises the critical thinking skills prized in today's business and professional world. It pushes us to reject surface explanations; instead, we go deeper, excavating the sources and consequences of the intertwined work lives of people from various racial-ethnic groups. Though it is common to judge and reason from one's own limited standpoint, robust thinkers and leaders situate individuals, groups, and events in social context.

Thus, this book presents "the whole video clip" about how race and the U.S. economic system developed together, the role of race in propelling white ethnics into the middle class, the stubborn persistence of racial disparities in unemployment rates, how a racialized immigration process creates race disparities in occupations, and much more. My goal is to provide an unvarnished analysis of race and work in the United States. As others have noted, the language with which we often talk about both American history and race has been sanitized to hide prickly truths (e.g. Moore 1988; Loewen 1995; Bonilla-Silva 2001).

Even well into the second decade of the twenty-first century, there is a great deal of segregation by race in U.S. neighborhoods, schools, churches, and social organizations. The workplace is the single most common arena where adults from different racial and ethnic groups have close and continuing interaction (Estlund 2003). Employers seek job candidates who understand the role of race at work, whether visible or invisible. Perhaps that is motivation for reading this book. Of course it is more important than ever, in this age of constant information and opinion, to be an informed community member, parent, voter, and consumer of the internet. The race and work story told here provides framing, context, and information that contribute to that end.

As the title makes clear, the focus of the book is race. For that reason it does not provide a full analysis of how gender intersects with race to create unique patterns for women and men. Nor is there a full discussion of class variation within race groups. As I will explain a bit more in the next chapter, I made these choices to make the race story clearer. But I hope that readers will keep in mind that race is always created and experienced at the intersection of other major social statuses such as gender and social class.

In these pages you will find an analytical rather than a comprehensive review of research on race and work in the United States. The book would be far too long if I tried to include counter findings and critiques of every topic. That means that there is always other research "out there" and I encourage you to find it and evaluate it for yourself. I have chosen to highlight research that illustrates race inequality in the United States. Based on the preponderance of research evidence, I believe that our starting point should be to assume racism and disprove it rather than taking the more common route of having to prove it exists. As noted sociologist Barbara Reskin (2003) has pointed out, when elaborate statistical models show racial disparities the default hypothesis should be that racism is at work; researchers should reject that hypothesis only if they verify another causal mechanism. Further, even small statistical differences matter because racism is hard to measure and any amount can reflect important differences in people's lives.

The book begins with a brief introduction to the major conceptual tools that will be used in the chapters that follow. The next two chapters provide essential historical context. Chapter 4 presents data documenting systematic patterns as well as fine-grained detail about race and work. It is followed by an explanation for those research findings that uses many of the concepts from Chapter 1. Chapter 6 takes a look at current trends related to race and work. The book concludes with a sketch of how we might move toward greater racial equality in work opportunities and experiences.

I offer what follows in the spirit of deepening understanding and elevating the discussion of race, racism, and work in the United States.

1
Race and Work: Laying the Conceptual Groundwork

What is work? If you ask most Americans they would likely say something about employment. Yet there is plenty of work that goes unpaid, such as volunteer work and family work. During the 1970s researchers pointed out the illogic of considering activities done mostly by wives and mothers to be work *only* when women were paid to do them for someone else's family (Hall 1994).

The key thing that distinguishes work from other kinds of activity is that it results in something of value to other people. Whether you do something meaningful or menial, whether you define it as work or pleasure, if others gain from it, you are doing work. One of the clearest signals we are doing something useful is when someone pays us to do it.

Work done for pay is organized into specific jobs or occupations, and professions. Sets of work tasks and skills are bundled into occupations and we have a sense of what a person does when we hear that they are a doctor or a web designer, a child-care worker or a home health aide. Yet most jobs require a variety of types of activity and people with the same job title in different companies may be doing somewhat different things; this can happen even within the same organization. Professions are more formalized sets of activities and often require certification or advanced degrees. Careers typically refer to job sequences for which there are increases in pay and responsibility. These may unfold within occupations and professions or across companies.

The jobs we do and the careers we pursue serve as key mechanisms sorting us into "haves" and "have not's." Occupations vary not only in wages and salaries, but also in the value society accords to them.

When we hear what kind of work a person does we know more than what they do, because occupational groups are also status groups, sharing lifestyles and viewpoints.

The focus of this book is work done for economic gain, because it has been tied to race throughout U.S. history. In addition, working for pay is the central way that most people try to achieve the American dream of a comfortable life; if not for themselves, then for the next generation.

Keep in mind that jobs are vitally important not only as a source of income and the route to a better life, but also as a social anchor and a major potential source of self-worth and meaning. That is why people who are fired, chronically unemployed, or pushed to retire suffer not just a loss of income, but also blows to social status and well-being.

Our chances of getting the best jobs – or any job at all – may seem to depend on our own initiative. That is partly true. But volumes of social science research also demonstrate that our chances depend a lot on our race group membership.

What is race?

Many of us have been taught some version of "there is no such thing as race – there is only the human race." To eliminate the racial prejudice still very much on display during the Civil Rights Movement, there was an emphasis on universal humanity. Phenotype (e.g. facial features, hair type, and skin tone) or country of ancestry was deemed irrelevant. That was an important corrective. As careful scientific research has shown, people from diverse countries of origin are far more similar biologically than they are different.

It is also common to confuse race and economic or social class, because they are strongly associated with one another not only in the public mind, but also in statistical findings. Yet race exists outside of social class, as Omi and Winant's (2014) important analysis of racial formation demonstrates. Race has a separate meaning from class and is intertwined with social institutions in distinct, though often connected, ways.

> Race is a pigment of our imagination
>
> (Ruben Rumbaut)

Even though it seems that race has something to do with our physical selves, its meaning was, and continues to be, created by people. The ways we define and think about race and racial identities derive from political and cultural actors with conflicting interests and worldviews (Omi and Winant 2014; Bonilla-Silva 1997; Feagin 2004).

The illogic of racial categorization abounds, supporting the DNA evidence that race is not biologically based. For example, it is common to write and talk about skin color as a marker of race, but the skin color of Americans from India is often darker than that of African Americans; the first group is not classified as black while the second always is. It is common to view race as rooted in ancestry – but people with features that suggest some African heritage are classified as black even if many of their ancestors hailed from European countries. In the infamous Plessy v. Ferguson case, which made it legal to preserve public spaces for whites only, the plaintiff Homer Plessy was 7/8 European, but his 1/8 African ancestry mattered more. The "one-drop rule" that governed race categorization applied: a person with even a tiny amount of black or indigenous blood was never considered a kind of white person but always a person of color.

Some people reason that if race is a social construction then races are equivalent, and inconsequential, categories. However, race groups have never been equivalent. Race is vitally important because it has been woven deeply into the fabric of U.S. society and is used to pre-judge people. Race is one of the first things people know (or think they know) about others, because it has physical markers associated with it. The meanings given to race are in play all the time. Here is the bottom line: *we made race up, and we made it matter*. Once the concept of race was created, and people were sorted into different racial-ethnic groups, they did not have the same work opportunities and experiences

Race Hierarchy as an Engine of Economic Privilege

There was an economic motivation for race categorization. In competition for resources and rewards, there are always some groups who have an advantage. A society in which one racial-ethnic group benefits at the expense of others has a racist social structure (Feagin and Vera 1995; Bonilla-Silva 1997). The dominant group has the power and resources to create a race hierarchy that reflects its preeminence, ordering groups from best to worst, from valued to de-valued, from human to "other."

The most important thing about the social construction of race is that it took a hierarchical form. The notion that there were different human types, called races, that could be classified on the basis of physical characteristics "was not invented until the eighteenth century" by Europeans (Frederickson 2002: 53). The idea to rank people by race came out of pseudo-scientific work in the eighteenth and nineteenth centuries. Scientists applied their assumption that the natural world is hierarchical to their understanding of race, creating a race-based ranking system with white (European) at the top. Racial classification studies lent legitimacy to whites' colonization of people in Africa and Asia, and the subjugation of people of color in the United States (Wander, Martin, and Nakayama 1999). The groups "white" and "non-white" were defined as opposites and the notion of intellectual and moral superiority was a crucial component of the construct of "white."

The Racial Other

The group at the top of the race hierarchy maintains or improves its social and economic position by oppressing, or literally, keeping down (Frye 1983) people who have been relegated to the "other" racial-ethnic groups. The concept of "the other" is central to academic writing on inequality. The "racial other" is feared, exoticized, rendered invisible, and yet "sticks out like a sore thumb." The reaction of the dominant race group to the "racial other" tends to be full of suspicion, unease, and confusion. Perhaps most consequential is that the "racial other" is seen first and foremost as a racial group member, while their humanity and individuality are ignored (Madrid 1988). Whether it takes the form of hostility or avoidance, white reaction to the "racial other" leads to disparities in the world of paid work. People of color can also have these reactions to different race and ethnic groups, and even to people within their own group. That is the power of the race hierarchy, embedded at the core of U.S. social life.

The socially constructed notion of race conceived and imposed by whites began as a white/non-white binary in the United States (Corbas et al. 2009). People with roots in Asian and Latin American countries were racialized in relation to whites and blacks, and placed somewhere in between them on the race hierarchy. In the earliest days of immigration, most racial-ethnic groups began – socially and economically – somewhere near the bottom of the race hierarchy. Because race is a fluid social construct (remember, we made it up), not all of the groups assigned to the bottom of the race hierarchy stayed there. As succeeding chapters show, the Asian racial position has been a wedge between the top and bottom positions on the hierarchy, preserving white advantages (Kim 1999).

The privileges and oppression of the race hierarchy were built into all U.S. structures early on. They were expressed mostly in the realm of paid work though, because working for pay is so important, especially to the U.S. version of capitalism (Blauner 2001: 26). Work relationships are *central* to race processes such as how black and white America developed as connected but separate entities (Bennett 1975: 236). To grasp the connection between race and work, it is useful to know that jobs were also ordered on a hierarchy from best to worst. Then the two hierarchies were transposed onto one another. In any sorting of jobs or occupations, the best were reserved for whites at the top of the race hierarchy and the worst jobs were assigned to the "racial other": at first African Americans and American Indians, then immigrant groups such as the Chinese and Mexicans, who began at the bottom of the race hierarchy. The merging of race and occupation hierarchies helped it all seem natural.

Throughout history there have been people from every race group, including white, who have contested the organization of people into a hierarchy of unequal groups based on phenotype or country of original ancestry. It has also been typical for groups and individuals defined as the "racial other" to contest or reject that identity. Furthermore there are people from each and every one of the country's racial-ethnic groups who have achieved the American dream. Some descendants from the most oppressed groups enjoy work roles and standards of living that only the most optimistic of their ancestors could have imagined.

Yet the seeds of a race-based economy that were planted and nourished early in U.S. history bear fruit even today. In order to understand current race-based work inequalities, we have to uncover how and why race became essential to the American economic system. That is the subject of the next chapter.

Though many people think about individuals when they hear the term racist or racism, focusing on *systems* leads to deeper understanding of how work and race are connected. Replace the images of a hate-spewing malcontent who leaves nasty messages in a co-worker's locker, or even the mild-mannered vice-president of operations who doubts that Asians make good supervisors, with this: *racism is a system of white advantage* (Wellman 1993). This definition promotes much better insight into how race and work are intertwined than focusing on individual racists would.

THEORIES AND CONCEPTS

Theories are sets of ideas that help to answer both the why and how of racial-ethnic patterns of work. It is at the theoretical level that key concepts are developed, as well as hypotheses about how phenomena such as race and pay are linked. Theories guide analyses of historical and contemporary patterns of race and work, influencing what questions researchers ask, how they go about answering them, and what interpretations they give to their findings.

Any analyst must make choices from among the many theoretical perspectives available. Some key theoretical perspectives on work have not highlighted the importance of racism and white privilege, while theories of race and racism do not always give central emphasis to work. There are commonalities in the best sociological theorizing about race, as scholars build on the work of others, using a different focus or creating a new concept to expand or deepen understanding.

What follows is but a brief overview of the theoretical and conceptual tools guiding this analysis of how and why race and work matter to one another. These will be illustrated further in the coming chapters.

Systemic or Structural Racism

The central sociological insight into how race affects work is that race is an ongoing system or a structure built directly into society. Race categories are created and reinforced as an explicit strategy for gaining material advantages for some by exploiting others. Those with the power to do so claim more resources for themselves, manipulating ideas and messages to justify their dominance. Both because race is not natural and because it matters so much to work and other opportunities, its social construction is continually contested. Though structural theorists accentuate the oppression of people of color by whites, they also recognize the agency and resistance of those whose labor was exploited. Finally, theorists emphasize that racial inequality is created at all levels of society, from macro level institutions to micro-level interactions between individuals.

The capitalist economy that served as the engine of U.S. economic development is a significant part of the race and work story.

Marxist and Neo-Marxist Perspectives

Karl Marx's analysis of capitalism, developed during the transition to industrialization in the 1800s, continues to influence research on work and employment today. Volumes have been written on Marx's theory of the labor process and it has been thoroughly critiqued, amended, and revised. Here I touch briefly on some key ideas.

In a capitalist system the goal is to maximize profit, or what Marx called surplus value. This surplus value is the "extra" that workers generate after they have done enough labor to cover their wages. Under the feudal system of labor, serfs would work their lord's land for his benefit and then work for their own sustenance. The lord could see exactly how much work the serfs had done for him and when they were doing it. Under capitalism owners and workers meet in the labor market. Owners have what Marx called the means of production: the buildings and equipment needed to make products or supply services. Workers have only labor power, or the promise of their labor, to sell. Unlike the feudal lord, the owner or employer does not know when the labor of employees is creating profit. Thus owners want to squeeze as much labor as they can from the labor power they have purchased. Yet workers gain nothing from pushing themselves to the limit; in fact their health and well-being will be jeopardized.

Inequality is built into the capitalist system. The only way that owners make a profit – which is the engine of capitalism – is by ensuring that workers do not get the full monetary value of their labor (e.g. Bowles and Gintis 2002). Thus employers and workers constitute separate classes with opposing interests. To ensure profit, owners need to control the execution of the labor potential they have purchased, though it resides in the bodies and minds of employees who work for wages.

One way that owners have exerted control and maximized profit is by breaking down work tasks into smaller components. This was greatly facilitated by industrialization. Former artisans who knew the whole process were turned into easily replaceable cogs in an industrial machine. Capitalists also transformed the labor process such that the conception of work was separated out from its execution, creating two different kinds of work: mental and manual. Jobs requiring mental work were given more social value than those requiring physical labor, as the aim of those conceptualizing the work was to maximize the output of the now de-skilled manual workers. Capitalists seeking profit from the labor of workers gained even greater control by used technology to dictate *how* people do their work (Braverman 1998). Today, these principles are applied both to service work and prestigious jobs. Even physicians are timed, and their work has become narrower; more of their tasks are performed by technicians, nurses, and assistants who are paid considerably less.

Racialized Capitalism

Major theorists agree that the United States is a *racialized* capitalist society, though they vary in their language and emphases (e.g. Blauner 2001; Bonilla-Silva 1997; Feagin 2006; Glenn 2002). As discussed below, the racialized economy is also gendered.

There is a long and rich black intellectual tradition emphasizing the link between racism and the economic oppression described by Marx. Scholar and activist W. E. B. DuBois, writing in the late nineteenth and early twentieth centuries, was one of the first to articulate the connection, in addition to illustrating it through rigorous empirical work. Because DuBois was African American, the intellectual debt owed to him has been largely underestimated but his work was path-breaking (Winant 2000).

Confronting the view that race was a fixed, natural characteristic, DuBois conceptualized whiteness as a *social* category with economic consequences (Feagin 2010). He also contested negative white beliefs about African Americans. His writing and research, along with that of contemporaries Anna Julia Cooper and Ida Wells Barnett, supported his argument that race is a social force or process; the lives of African Americans could only be understood in specific socioeconomic and political context (Collins 1993; Feagin 2010; Young and Deskins 2001). DuBois was an intersectional thinker who recognized that a race category could not capture the variety of experiences of the people included in it. To help expose the arbitrariness of race hierarchy, he identified distinct classes of African Americans, with different circumstances, attitudes, and practices (Williams 2005). He also emphasized capitalists' use of race to obscure the exploitation of working-class whites (e.g. DuBois [1935] 1998).

Internal colonialism theory illustrates that communities of color in the United States are in the same position as the so-called Third World nations invaded or colonized by the Western world (Blauner 1972). Patterns of work and wealth cannot be understood without attention to the ways that race hierarchy, or stratification, *combines* with class position; race groups are sorted into "winners" or "losers," dominated or exploited. Internal colonialists focus on four economic classes within which race is used to designate "winners" and "losers": in addition to capitalists and workers, there are managers and supervisors who help capitalists control workers, and small business owners who control their own labor but do not have the economic or political power of capitalists (Barrera 1979).

Evelyn Nakano Glenn (2015) developed a settler colonialism model to better account for the specific experiences of the major racial-ethnic groups whose land and labor fueled U.S. economic development in various times and places. At the center is what Glenn (2015: 60) calls the English colonizers' creation of "a hierarchy of humankind" based on race and gender, which was then used to justify the "erasure" of indigenous people, the enslavement of blacks, the bonded labor of Chinese immigrants and the theft of Mexican land and wages. The belief in white (European) racial superiority dovetailed with "heteropatriarchy"' or the superiority of white men over women; property, governance, and wives should be under men's control. This model of "supreme white manhood" in which white men are leaders and protectors was built into social and legal policies and practices (Arvin, Tuck, and Morrill 2013; Glenn 2015: 60).

While Marx emphasized *a* labor market in which workers and owners meet to exchange labor power for wages, modern scholars contend that race (combined with gender) is used to maximize surplus value. They describe segmented industries and markets: there are desirable core and undesirable peripheral industries and split, or primary and secondary, labor markets with distinct pay scales, benefits, and working conditions. Though all workers meet capitalists in markets to sell their labor power, white men and men of color and white women and women of color compete in different realms.

The concepts of the dual economy and segmented labor markets emphasize that white (men) workers reap benefits in the creation of a tiered system which reserves the best industries and jobs for them (Bonacich 1972; Edwards 1980; Reich 1981). Capitalists gain because competition between race and ethnic groups masks the conflict between owners and workers and keeps the overall price of wage labor low. Different groups of workers can also be played off one another to break strikes or negotiate wage contracts, giving owners the upper hand.

Joe R. Feagin's prominent theory of systemic racism borrows Marx's notion of oppression as central to society, casting white racism as an ongoing conflict between those who benefit from racism and those who are held back by it. Just as owners and workers have contentious relationships because of their conflicting class interests, so too do whites and other racial groups clash over aspects of an economic system that is set up to the benefit of only one socially con-structed race group. This helps explain why whites have had a stake in denying that racism exists (Feagin 2010, 2014). The theory of systemic racism also adopts Marx's notion that capitalism has to get inscribed in institutions and systems, its workings rendered invisible, to hide the central conflict on which it is based. Racism, too, gains power from its invisibility.

Institutional Racism

Eduardo Bonilla-Silva's influential "racialized social system" perspec-tive calls attention to the ubiquitous nature of racism in the United States. Racial domination is continually created at the social and political, as well as the economic levels of society. It is woven into an elaborate tapestry of formal and informal rules that convey white advantage. Bonilla-Silva emphasizes that racism is not an aberration but a rational, ongoing process rooted in power differences. He added to Omi and Winant's racial formation perspective the important reminder that racial categories exist because whites benefit from them (Bonilla-Silva 1997; 2015). The domination of whites over people of color was built into the policies and practices of the web of institu-tions (and their organizations) connected to the economy – such as education (schools), politics (legislatures), and criminal justice (police departments and courts).

> White power secures its dominance by seeming not to be anything in particular.
>
> (Richard Dyer)

Critical race theory (CRT) came out of the work of legal scholars (e.g. Crenshaw 1993; Bell 1992) to expose supposedly race-neutral laws and policies as laced with racism. CRT explains race-based inequality by focusing on the power structures through which white advantage is embedded in the law and ignored by conservative and liberal think-ers alike. It has expanded to include economic and other social insti-tutions (Delgado and Stefancic 1999).

Intersectionality

Path-breaking work by feminists of color improved structural theo-ries of racism with the crucial insight that race combines with gender, social class, and other social status hierarchies to create intertwined systems of oppression and inequality. Crenshaw (1993) showed, for example, that black women were rendered invisible in class action lawsuits that conceived of women as white and blacks as men. Intersectionality theory directs us to both the similarities across systems of oppression and the unique features of each. It is particularly instructive for understanding work, because the economic classes of Marxist theory were not independent from the race and gender systems that facilitated capitalist growth (Acker 2006; Glenn 2002). Though earlier scholars "added" race and gender groups to neo-Marxist theories, intersectional theorists (e.g. Glenn 1991; Collins 1993; Walby, Armstrong, and Strid 2012) caution that the development of economic or class positions cannot be separated from the race and gender positions created through white racism and patriarchy (the domination of men over women).

Intersectional theorists encourage those investigating work inequalities to consider multiple levels of analysis. There is sometimes a tendency to reduce race, gender, and class to social positions or identities, but it is essential to place these in the framework of interlocking *systems* of race, class, and gender oppression (e.g. Belkhir 2001). As Patricia Hill Collins (1993) emphasized, people experience and resist oppression at the personal level of identity, the group level of shared membership in race, gender, and other social categories, and *also* at the system level of social institutions.

Racial Ideology

Those who study race inequality underscore the importance not only of physical or economic power but also cultural domination. According to many theorists of social inequality, the ideas and practices disseminated by families, schools, and media are those of a single dominant culture that is white, Anglo, Western, patriarchal, and nativist. As the U.S. economy developed, these white ideas and practices were asserted as superior and normal; all other groups were evaluated on the basis of how closely they fit (Dyer 1997; Collins 2000; Bonilla-Silva 1997, 2006; Feagin 2006, 2010).

Marx and DuBois underscored the importance of cultural ideologies, or belief systems, which serve to legitimate inequalities by providing distorted explanations of social reality. The process begins with categorization which will ultimately be used to parcel out resources (Tilly 1998). The categories we use and the characteristics we associate with them (stereotypes) are organized in cultural schemas that produce the scripts for social interaction (Ridgeway 1997; Kim 1999). According to Bonilla-Silva (2001; 2015) the cultural schemas include a "racial etiquette" that gets attached to positions on the race hierarchy and to the relationships between and among people sorted into those positions. In the United States the script says that American Indians, African Americans, and some Latino groups are lazy or irresponsible, justifying their high unemployment rates. The illusion of fundamental race differences – whether biological or cultural – infuses "lasting social meaning" into physical traits. Ideological fictions about race become a part of social reality, organizing interaction and providing sources of identity, despite their falsehood (Shelby 2003).

Feagin (2013) introduced the concept of the "white racial frame" to emphasize that white ideas and practices became the default. People from all racial-ethnic groups accept white elite definitions of what is appropriate. White racial framing includes not only stereotypes, but also language, images, interpretations, and narratives. Even emotions are racialized, as we are reminded every time there is a report of a non-threatening black man who was experienced by a witness or a police officer as dangerous. The frame has a powerful impact on thought and action, perpetuating systemic racism from one generation to the next (2010: 60).

Bonilla-Silva (2006) developed the notion of color-blind ideology to explain how racism has been hidden, normalized, and denied by the fiction that races are equivalent in the post-Civil Rights era. He and his colleagues note that people engage in color-blind racism when they fail to consider the existence of structured inequalities by race, attributing disparities to "anything but racism" (Bonilla-Silva et al. 2004). When scholars and opinion-makers report race patterns in work and employment without analyzing the racism at the core of those patterns they are not just doing bad social science or journalism; they are also justifying the racist structures that are responsible for those findings (Bonilla-Silva and Baiocchi 2008).

Bobo and colleagues (1997) have developed the similar concept of "*laissez faire* racism." The authors point to whites' professed support for racial equality since the Civil Rights Movement, a signal that race is no longer significant and work systems can be left to operate as they will. But they establish that attitudes are not consistent with behavior, and point to the racism embedded in institutions and organizations as an important site of inquiry irrespective of what white people say they believe.

Counter-Frames

To counteract the dominant cultural scripts that justify racial inequality, scholars study the perspectives of those whose lives are most constrained by those scripts. As DuBois put it, for example, though black folk are "shut out" from the white world by a veiled social structure, they are "gifted with second sight," seeing through the veil to "the workings of the white world" (1986: 364). A central premise of black feminist thought (Collins 2000) is that we can come closer to the truth by seeking knowledge from those whose marginalization gives them the clear-eyed view of race and gender structures that more privileged race/gender groups lack. Oppressed racial groups actively resist the negative images of their qualities and cultures. They develop positive counter-frames to navigate a world that has been set up for whites (Feagin 2010).

Presenting what they call counter-stories, CRT scholars ensure that the voices of oppressed and marginalized racial-ethnic groups are heard (e.g. Yosso 2006; Sue 2003). This project has also been taken up by historians and sociologists critical of "status quo" historical understanding. Their aim is to provide a more accurate record of the experiences and contributions of women and men of color, as well as the sociohistorical processes that created white advantage (Zinn 1980/1995; 2004; Takaki 2008; Glenn 2002; Amott and Matthaei 1991). Chapters 2 and 3 are delivered with these goals in mind.

The concepts of color-blind and *laissez-faire* racism highlight the attitudes and actions of policy-makers and employers, whose decisions contribute to race-based inequities in work opportunities. Yet analysts using such concepts keep the notion of systemic racism front and center. They note that decision-making and welcoming versus hostile actions take place in the context of work organizations built on racist economic foundations. Structural theorists view color blindness as problematic because it hides racism within the confines of culture (e.g. Bonilla-Silva 2006). Instead of culture being understood as a fluid entity, it is used as a new way to assert that there are essential differences between race groups. Thus the colorblind observer may acknowledge that African Americans, American Indians, Puerto Ricans, and Mexicans are not biologically inferior, but point to their inferior cultures as the reason these groups are at the bottom of the race hierarchy.

Thus to fully understand why race-based inequities in employment and wealth persist into the twenty-first century, we have to attend to the power of images and ideas about racial and ethnic groups written into dominant cultural scripts (Omi and Winant 2014; Bonilla-Silva 2015; Feagin 2010). We also need to showcase evidence from the lives of the "racial others" that directly contradicts those messages.

One final note about work organizations: they are affected by what goes on in the wider social and cultural world, as the institutionalist perspective on work highlights (e.g. DiMaggio and Powell 1991). This theoretical approach also encourages us to examine the "culture wars" that erupt in society, as challenges to elite white culture, and attempts to protect it, affect relations between labor and capital as well as dynamics within particular work organizations.

Social Interaction Perspectives

In reflecting on his internal colonialism model of race inequality in the United States, Bob Blauner cautioned against overemphasizing structure as impersonal forces divorced from people. He urged that we pay attention to the individuals who are crucial to supporting racism and also to getting rid of it (2001: 193). Luckily there are theorists who take their analytic lenses and zoom in on how social inequality is created through the actions of individuals. Social interaction (SI) perspectives on inequality lead us to the "relationships and practices" that create race-based differences in work and wealth (Schwalbe 2007). Like the structural theorists of racism discussed, authors in the social interaction tradition emphasize that people of color act against their oppression. For example, Roscigno (2007) has noted the vital role of resistance in shaking up racist social practices.

A noteworthy strand of this work focuses on the actions not just of employers but also of occupational gatekeepers and employees at all levels. For example, founding father of sociology Max Weber's notion of social closure, especially as developed by Parkin (1979), has been influential in attempts to understand how work inequities are created and maintained (e.g. Tomaskovic-Devey, 1993; Tilly 1998; Elliott and Smith 2001; Massey 2007). The central idea is that people who have the power to do so hoard resources and other opportunities for themselves, actively keeping others out. All manner of boundaries are drawn around whiteness, in order to protect the advantages of this race position.

Charles Tilly (1998) theorized that there are three major social processes thorough which dominant groups hoard resources. Dominants keep a disproportionate share of the value added by the labor of "racial others," actively deny equal opportunity, and use threats or actual violence to maintain control over key resources – among which good jobs are arguably one of the most important. These are the mechanisms behind owners' creation of segmented industries and labor markets discussed earlier, as well as white-only labor unions. These mechanisms also played out in white mob activity (often with tacit or overt support from the state) that eliminated other race groups from competition by driving them out of thriving Chinatowns or black communities (Glenn 2015). Jaspin's (2007) research shows that white mobs commonly flipped counties from black to white – and that many of them remain essentially all-white today.

Theories of cognitive processes help explain the staying power of color-blind racism. Aversive racism refers to the subtle psychological process through which people who have egalitarian views justify racial bias. They do so by ignoring both their own feelings and behavior as well as structures of racism. Well-meaning people might be uneasy, anxious, indifferent, or disgusted when they encounter a person who has been categorized as the "racial other" (Cortina 2008). If those feelings lead them to avoid co-workers of color, they explain it in other terms. Aversive racism allows people to view themselves as non-biased, reaping the rewards of race privilege without guilt (Dovidio and Gaertner 2004; Pearson, Dovidio, and Gaertner 2009). A key point is that they are often *unaware* that this is what they are doing. The notion of biased social cognition is at the heart of Loury's (2006) contention that stigma attaches to the "racial other" in U.S. society, such that people are likely to attribute negative employment outcomes or poverty to failings of the group rather than to structured racism. Feagin and Vera (1995) describe the importance of "sincere fictions" used by whites to define themselves as good people even as they enjoy the benefits of systemic racism.

The central takeaway from psychological theories is that even employers, union leaders, and co-workers who value racial equality express racism in indirect, subconscious, and disguised ways.

These are the main theories and concepts interwoven and elaborated throughout the book. Before we move on, though, I want to clarify some conceptual building blocks needed to make sense of the analyses of race and work patterns that follow.

Race and Ethnicity

One of the most confusing things about race hierarchy is the fact that some ethnic groups are treated as race groups. People who did not hail from Europe were placed on the race hierarchy in categories such as "Asian" and "Hispanic" or "Latino"; these categories were then used to sort people into different kinds of work. Again, note the arbitrariness of these constructions. How is it, for example, that Mexicans were legally defined as white up until 1930 when the Census created a separate racial category for them? How can it be that, even when they had legal whiteness, they were denied the "perks" that went with whiteness? (Foley 2008).

While all groups who hail from Asian countries are assigned the "race" of Asian, Latinos were eventually (in 1980) given both a race and an ethnic category; many forms we fill out now include choices such as "non-Hispanic white" or "Hispanic black." Research shows a lot of variation in whether and why Latinos identify as black or white (Golash-Boza and Darity 2008; Frank, Akresh, and Lu 2010) or "some other race" altogether. This last category was chosen by 42 percent of Hispanics in the 2000 Census (Tafoya 2005). Government classification of races has shifted over the years, often in response to pressure from groups who are unhappy with their position. As one example, the U.S. Census eliminated "Mexican" as a U.S. Census racial designation in 1940, after strong pressure from Mexican-Americans (Snipp 2003).

Still, in the United States, race trumps ethnicity. Being able to claim membership in the white racial group makes the difference when it comes to economic security and upward mobility, as the next chapter illustrates. The more secure a group's position in the white racial category, the less impact one's ethnicity has on access to good jobs. Though people of Asian, Latino, and African descent come from many different countries and cultures, they are often lumped together in a single race group, as the very different nations of indigenous Americans have always been. Their phenotypic and cultural distance from white on the race hierarchy will affect their work choices and experiences (e.g. Okihiro 2000; Cable and Mix 2003).

I use the term racial-ethnic a lot because it captures the reality that ethnicity is sometimes treated as though it is a race, that race ultimately references country and culture of ancestry, and that for some groups race and ethnicity have been lumped together. The term racial-ethnic denotes the slipperiness of the concept of race and its connection to ethnicity in the minds of decision-makers. It acknowledges that race categories erase ethnicity, which is arguably a more important source of identity for American Indians, Latinos, and Asians than for whites (Waters 1990). Though some who wish to downplay racism say that race groups are simply different cultural entities on a par with white ethnic groups, the social creation of people of color as "less than"

– less than American, less than trustworthy, less than employable – reveals the deceit of this notion. Equating race categories with ethnicity or failing to see when ethnicity is being treated as a race category does not lessen the impact of race-ethnicity on work and employment (Dalton 1995).

White Privilege

The concept of white privilege has been used to highlight the chances for better jobs that come from being at the top of the racial hierarchy. Its best-known depiction is an "invisible knapsack" filled with all kinds of benefits, which whites carry around wherever they go (McIntosh 1990). One major "goody" in that knapsack is that whites who are up for a promotion can be pretty certain they will be evaluated as an individual rather than by the actions of the last white person to hold the job. Another is that during a job interview whites can expect to be judged by someone who thinks positively of their race group – they get the so-called benefit of the doubt. Whites are highly unlikely to be harassed on the job or fired from it because they are white. That knapsack is fuller than many people realize.

White privilege is a concept that many whites reject. For instance, it is common for whites to say that their race position did not matter during their job searches (DiTomaso 2012). Some whites from poor or working-class backgrounds bristle at the idea that they have privilege over other race groups, and this is certainly understandable. Knapsacks of white privilege are not all filled to the brim, nor do they contain exactly the same items. White people in different class and gender positions carry different configurations of privilege in their knapsacks. Still, there is a large body of empirical evidence that whites of all backgrounds have advantages over people of color when it comes to employment and careers, as Chapter 4 shows.

Keep in mind that the concept of white privilege applies *only* to race. There are some things that whites can take for granted and one of them, *always*, is that they live in a society which places more value on whiteness than on any other racial position. White privilege accompanies them to job interviews, into work environments, and onto career paths. From a scientific perspective, it is important, *always*, to make an accurate comparison. It is absolutely true that many whites have difficulty finding and keeping good jobs and whites can be fired for petty reasons or be passed over for promotions. Yet it is unlikely that any of that happens *because* they are white. If you are thinking of a struggling white family, then comparing them to a middle-class black family does not tell you anything about privileges associated with race group membership. Instead, you have to do in your mind what social scientists do with their statistical models – hold constant all of the other variables that affect economic success and look only at whether the poor white person has a better chance of success than a poor black person. Studies tell us that the answer is yes (e.g. MacLeod 2009).

Even highly successful people of African, Asian, Latino, and American Indian descent do not get to carry that invisible knapsack of white privilege to their workplaces. Instead, people of color are carrying invisible but heavy knapsacks full of concrete, or the many challenges to their recognition as individuals and as equals. The weight of those bags differs by racial and ethnic group, and also by gender and social class. But every person of color hauls one to the labor market and the workplace.

Race, Gender, and Class: Intersections

As the discussion of intersectionality foreshadowed, gender and social class positions are also organized into hierarchies that intertwine with the race hierarchy in the development of the economy and the arranging of people into jobs and industries (Glenn 2002; Acker 2006). While people from the same racial-ethnic groups have some of the same experiences in the labor market, it is also true that race experiences differ for women and men. By the same token, the economic lives of women differ by racial-ethnic group and the work experiences of men from different racial-ethnic groups vary in common patterns. Even in the first decades of the twenty-first century white women do not enjoy the same work opportunities and pay scales as white men. Yet throughout history white women have gained economic benefits from their connections to white fathers, husbands, siblings, and friends that have been unavailable to most women of color (Hurtado 1989).

Race hierarchy has positioned some groups, such as American Indians and African Americans, in seemingly permanent positions of economic deprivation, yet recall that race does not determine social class. As Chapter 3 recounts, there have always been some people from oppressed racial groups who have achieved economic success – sometimes against all odds. Today the African American and Latino middle classes continue to grow, and those defined as black have attained all kinds of positions formerly closed to them, including the most prestigious job there is in this country: President of the United States. Throughout history poor and working-class whites have been oppressed by capitalists who owned the means of production. They have had much in common with their counterparts of color, although as a group they were always better off. It is also noteworthy that some Latino groups have experienced a lot more economic success than others, and that while "Asian American" conjures up images of accomplishment, some Asian groups are disproportionately poor.

Thus while race is the primary lens and the major organizing principle of this book, along the way I will show how race intersects with gender to create unique inequalities and cultural stereotypes, affecting employment patterns and work experiences. I will also note periodically that the experiences of women and men from different social and economic classes interact with race and ethnicity to complicate how, why, and when race matters to work. To keep the narrative clear and manageable, I zero in on racism and race groups. But underneath every such mention is the reality that racism intersects with sexism and other key systems of inequality and identity. Our lives are all lived at multiple intersections.

Sociohistorical Context (Equal vs. Fair)

One of the main differences in emphasis among studies of social inequality is the extent to which sociohistorical context is considered. The concepts of cumulative disadvantage – and its counterpart cumulative advantage – figure prominently in the work of scholars who take a longer and more nuanced view. The central idea, as most of us have experienced at some point in our lives, is that it is always harder to come from behind. Even small differences in starting points can lead to larger discrepancies between groups as time goes on, and those larger differences will have an even greater snowball effect as we acknowledge in the saying "the rich get richer."

In his classic study of race stratification in the United States, Swedish sociologist Gunnar Myrdal (1944) asked why such an "extraordinarily large proportion" of blacks were so poor. He noted how often responses to that question pointed to the concentration of blacks in the struggling agriculture industry or the fact that most black workers were in low-paid jobs, whatever the industry, or maybe to high black unemployment rates. Yet as Myrdal pointed out, those answers still begged the question of *why*. Why were blacks in farming, *why* didn't

The Footrace Metaphor: False Starts and Unequal Lanes

One of the most cherished American beliefs is that anyone can make it if they try hard enough. We tell ourselves that by "pulling themselves up by the bootstraps" – a metaphor for doing whatever it takes with whatever you have – people can secure better jobs and ensure upward mobility for future generations. There is certainly plenty of truth in that story. Everyone can think of groups who mostly started with next to nothing and mostly became financially stable or even highly successful. Yet there are also stories, not as readily told, of groups of people who worked exceedingly hard and found their success thwarted at every turn, as subsequent chapters demonstrate.

The metaphor of a footrace captures more of the truth. In a fair footrace, the parallel lanes are exactly the same and everyone leaves the starting line at the same time. Thus the different finish times of the runners are mostly a result of individual performance. We infer from the outcomes that the runners with the shortest times are the most talented and hardest working athletes. When there is a "level playing field," with everyone having the same chance to use their skills and hard work to achieve success, we are correct.

But now imagine the sprinters are competing in a meet that has been organized in a racist society. Some runners – let's call them the whites – get a false start, sprinting along well before others, such as Asians and many Latino groups, are let into the race. While the Asians and Latinos work hard to catch up, they find that their lanes are hilly rather than flat, and full of hurdles that slow them down – while the lanes of many white runners are free and clear. There are some runners from the white groups who do have hills to climb and hurdles to jump, but they are not as steep, high, or numerous. None of the whites have hurdles representing not being considered American; none are slowed down by racial stereotypes at every stage of the employment process.

American Indians and African Americans are begrudgingly let into the race when the contest is almost over, long after people from the white group got their false start. The lanes of former slaves contain not only the hurdles associated with being a "racial other" but also brick walls that are vestiges of a concerted effort to deny their humanity. Descendants of the Dakota and the Micmac, the Seminole and Shoshone, the Walla Walla and the Mohawk and all of the other groups indigenous to the nation face the giant brick wall resulting from their depiction as uncivilized nuisances in the way of capitalist progress.

Because American Indians and African Americans are the two groups who have been most oppressed and exploited, they have to work hardest to make it to the finish line. They have to stop and figure out what to do about the brick walls – will they scale them, try to get some help taking them down, or will they decide to give up on this race that is so clearly stacked against them? There are other groups – such as Puerto Ricans, Dominicans, Cambodians, and Vietnamese – who face lanes with hills and hurdles, though they do not have the history that created the brick walls.

If we look at the outcomes of the race, with no knowledge of when the sprinters started running and what their lanes looked like, we conclude that whites are the hard-working, superior athletes and that American Indians, African Americans, Puerto Ricans, and Cambodians have no aptitude for running or are just lazy or both. Within the various groups of color, those with the fewest economic resources will be held back even after their racial-ethnic group gets into the race and the obstacles in their lanes will be even more daunting. But under our assumption that everyone is running the same race, we will conclude that these people are unmotivated and incapable. Our grossly inaccurate belief that we can assess the motivation and talent of runners by how quickly they get to the finish line reinforces the "naturalness" of race hierarchy and the superiority of some race groups over others.

The more you know about the history of the racial-ethnic groups that make up the United States, the better you understand that the runners have not been in a fair competition. It is quite remarkable that some of the runners in the lanes filled with obstacles finish the race at all. Their success is a testament to their ability, their motivation, and their unwillingness to give up even when the odds are stacked against them. We can only imagine how much better they would have been able to run that race to economic success if they had been able to get into one of the lanes reserved for whites.

they have higher paying jobs and rates of employment? It is still common for employers and policy-makers to use the *outcomes* of racial disadvantage (such as high poverty rates) as explanations for racial disadvantage. Though such reasoning is illogical, it flows from the cherished American notion that people are responsible for their own economic fate. It reinforces race-based stereotypes as it draws on them, propping up the race hierarchy and furthering the disadvantages of blacks. This creates a "vicious cycle" that continues if there is no effort to stop it.

Foreshadowing Omi and Winant's argument that race and class are related but distinct, Myrdal noted the similarities but ultimate differences between poor whites and poor blacks. Poor whites are subject to the same incorrect and myopic view of the reasons for their plight. "Few people have enough imagination to visualize clearly what a poor white tenant or common laborer in the South would look like if he had had more opportunities at the start. Upper-class people in all countries are accustomed to look down upon the people of the laboring class as inherently inferior." However, he asserted that the poor black person is judged more harshly and looked down upon more intently, because of a race hierarchy that is far more rigid than the class system (Myrdal 1944: 209).

The following chapters dig down to the roots of racism, examining the role that racism and white privilege have played in the development of the U.S. economy, and documenting the uneven work outcomes for people of different racial-ethnic groups. There will be color conscious framing and interpretation throughout, as a race lens is held up to every topic – from unemployment rates, to labor organizing, to workplace dynamics, to trending economic patterns. I emphasize the role of context, aiming to unmask race-based advantage and disadvantage within even those structures and actions that appear to be race-neutral and reasonable.

2

The Roots of Race-Based Work Inequalities

It may seem that what happened over three hundred years ago (or even fifty) has nothing to do with work patterns today. Yet the construction of race hierarchy that drove early economic development in the United States was never dismantled. Thus historical developments, such as the industrial revolution, Reconstruction after the Civil War, or post-World-War II prosperity had an uneven impact on people of different racial-ethnic groups. There are many superb books that detail the history of race-based inequities in the world of work. What follows is a quick sketch done with broad brush strokes.

Race in the "New World"

Modern racism was born of western European attempts to colonize the rest of the world (Mills 1997). Developments in what would become the United States of America were part of this larger process. Before the eighteenth century there was no notion of sorting people by physical traits. Religion and nation or ethnicity mattered; these were the supposed sources of "inherited traits." The idea that there was a white racial category developed slowly (Frederickson 2002: 53–4). The earliest European colonizers' belief in the superiority of their culture – and their divine right to pursue economic gain – set the stage for the construction of race hierarchy in the United States.

To achieve their goal of advancing civilization and their own fortunes, the earliest arrivals to what are now U.S. shores first had to overpower the indigenous people – dubbed Indians – who were thriving on the land the newcomers wanted to own. The colonizers used their power, including that provided by their guns, to advance their interests. They took the land and its resources through slaughter, trickery, and theft. In 1623, for example, some Virginians negotiated a treaty with a group led by Chiskiack Indians. The British proposed a toast to their "eternal friendship" with the Chiskiacks, but they had poisoned the Chiskiacks' drinks; the Chiskiack chief's entire family, his advisors, and 200 others were killed (Wright 1981: 78; Loewen 1995). The British interlopers used harsh tactics even when faced with little resistance from the people who had already settled the land. Powhatan, who headed a large consortium of indigenous people, asked of Captain John Smith,

> Why should you take by force that from us which you can have by love? Why should you destroy us, who have provided you with food? . . . You see us unarmed, and willing to supply your wants, if you will come in a friendly manner and not with swords and guns, as to invade any enemy.
> (Blasdell 2000: 4)

Indigenous civilizations were decimated not because they didn't fight back or were "backward," as many history books would have us believe (Loewen 1995). American Indians were outfought and out-foxed (and ultimately outnumbered) by the British who used weapons and tactics unknown even among indigenous nations at war with one another. The British brought with them a pattern of depraved violence, originally directed toward the Irish (Dunbar-Ortiz 2014). When Narragansetts fought alongside the newly arrived Puritans against the Pequots, they were surprised by the level of brutality they witnessed. At the end of the war, the small fraction of Pequots still alive were starving, defenseless, and no longer fighting; the British burned them alive or slashed them to pieces according to Puritan William Bradford's account (Grenier 2005; Dunbar-Ortiz 2014).

The people of the many Indian nations who made treaties with the British, and then Americans, expected the treaties to be honored rather than brazenly broken. They did not know at first that the colonizers and their descendants aimed to eliminate American Indians and their culture. There would be dire consequences for American Indian well-being for generations to come (Deloria 1988; Blauner 2001; Fixico 2006; Austin 2013; Dunbar-Ortiz 2014).

Historians have established that American Indians "thrived for millennia" before their lands and economic livelihood were wrested from them (Dunbar-Ortiz 2014: 27). According to Weatherford (1988) American Indians had spent those millennia becoming the world's greatest farmers and pharmacists; but Europeans were amassing the world's greatest arsenal of weapons. "The strongest, but not necessarily the most creative or the most intelligent, won the day" (p. 252).

Having seized prime land from indigenous people, the English elite set about trying to develop commerce. They did so largely through the indentured servant system, drawing mostly from Europe, though also from the African slave trade. Before race was institutionalized, there were men and women from Ireland, England, and Africa working side by side clearing land, building infrastructure, harvesting tobacco and providing personal service to white elites (Bennett 1975). Their labor power was sold (by themselves or others) as part and parcel of their bodies rather than in return for wages and they did not retain ownership of it until their contract was up and they paid "freedom dues."

On the basis of his research of original documents and early accounts, Lerone Bennett Jr. concluded that the first Americans of African descent were free men and women bound to service, mostly sharing the same plight as their co-workers from Europe. The greatest divide was between those who had control or ownership of land and other resources and those who did not, irrespective of country of origin. For instance, there were people of African descent who had indentured servants or slaves of their own, and some of those servants were of European origin (Bennett 1975; Walker 1998).

The Invention of the Race Hierarchy and Racist Ideology

Thus unfree white labor preceded unfree black labor. The colonial belief in European superiority surely meant there were biases against Africans, but "there is world of difference" between biased individuals and "a social system institutionally committed" to racial bias (Bennett 1975: 18). Moreover there is evidence of harmony, friendship, and marriage among Africans, American Indians, and European servants. Unlike the English, American Indians had a long practice of adopting into their midst any person captured through war – on equal terms. This is shown clearly in reports of whites and blacks who had been captured by or fled to American Indian communities and became chiefs (Nash 1974: 284).

Though they were pitted against one another by elite whites, American Indians and African Americans often supported one another. In 1676 white servants and laborers and black slaves joined together in what has been called Bacon's Rebellion. It was quashed but raised fears among white elites, helping to propel the move to use "color" as the basis of hierarchy; even white servants were given advantages denied to their black counterparts (Allen 1976).

It is in the shift to a two-tiered system of unfree labor at the end of the 17th century that race is built into the U.S. economic as well as political and social systems. For those of European ancestry, bonded labor continued. However the Africans kidnapped from their home country or ships at sea were assigned servitude for life. The colonizers discovered that it was easier to enslave people by uprooting them, stamping out the material and cultural resources for resistance that might be available on one's home turf (DuBois [1924] 2009; Blauner 2001). The physical severing of ties to Africa was accompanied by vigorous attempts to eradicate African culture. One major tactic was to break up families; another was to force slaves to adopt the language, religion, and habits of their owners.

It was also easier to make the system work if slaves could be easily distinguished from free laborers. With physical markers of their social position such as skin color and facial features, runaways could be spotted easily, slaves and servants could be kept separate from one another, and enforcing race boundaries was simpler.

Though children born to indentured servants were free (Morgan 1975), legislation that decreed that the offspring of slaves were also slaves ensured the permanence of the social and economic status of blacks; there was no way up or out. Along with the rule that any African ancestry at all made one black, the legislation ensured a ready supply of slave labor. As African nationality became synonymous with slave, and slave was defined as the antithesis of northern European intellect and virtue, the race hierarchy began its influential role in American labor and social history.

The Puritan belief that wealth was a symbol of worth in God's eyes fueled interest in slavery. In a letter he wrote in 1645, Massachusetts Governor John Winthrop noted that importing African slaves would create more profit than British servants because it would be cheaper to "maintain" the slaves. He went on to express his view that "prosperity from the slave trade and slave-produced commodities affirmed one's godliness as a Christian" (Walker 1998: 22).

Though slavery waned a little after its introduction, and was outlawed in the north, the invention of the cotton gin in 1793 promised an opportunity for tremendous profit if a ready supply of cheap labor could be secured. The African slave trade presented just such an opportunity. Thus it was that slavery became essential to the southern economy, solidifying the oppression of people of African descent as a core feature of the entire American economy and society. Keep in mind that most people in the south did not own slaves and that many northern entrepreneurs profited directly or indirectly from the slave trade (DuBois [1924] 2009; Allen 1976; Cable and Mix 2003).

> Black labor became the foundation stone not only of the Southern social structure, but of Northern manufacture and commerce, of buying and selling on a world-wide scale; new cities were built on the results of black labor.
>
> (W. E. B. DuBois)

White workers in the north as well as the south benefitted from the national economic prosperity generated by slaves' toil. Immigrants from Europe gained from the permanent spot that people of African descent were given at the bottom of the race hierarchy, and therefore, the occupational ladder. This was the beginning of a very effective "divide and conquer" strategy that would contribute to the exploitation of white as well as workers of color throughout U.S. labor history. As former slave and prominent abolitionist Frederick Douglass (1857: 310) observed:

> The slaveholder ... by encouraging the enmity of the poor, laboring blacks, succeeded in making the said white man almost as much of a slave as the black man himself ... The slave is robbed by his master ... and the white man is robbed by the slave system ... because he is flung into competition with a class of laborers who work without wages.

The Ideology of Racial Superiority

It is a lot harder to massacre and enslave people who you recognize as equals. The definition of American Indians and Africans as "savages" who were less than human made white dominance seem reasonable and even natural. Also, stripping other people of their land, the fruits of their labor, their culture, their dignity, their humanity, and their lives calls out for some kind of justification. This is particularly necessary in a society that has defined itself as an incubator of liberty and equality (Fields 1982; Leach 2002; Sue 2006).

Thus as Marx would predict and DuBois would underscore, white elites developed compelling ideology. Think of it as a massive public relations campaign that stretched from pulpits to newspapers to minstrel shows, books, and then films. Whites claimed superiority in intellect, work ethic, morality, and every other characteristic deemed important to the advance of the country. To do so, they depicted other race groups as ignorant, sexually depraved, and uncivilized. Such ideology was rife with contradiction, illogic, and falsehood but whites had the power to define these "racial others." Thus American Indians were demonized by religious leaders such as Cotton Mather who argued that "The Devil decoyed those miserable savages [to New England]" and Increase Mather who proselytized that Indians were "Devil-driven" and their deaths a triumph (Takaki 1993: 41–2). Minstrel caricatures of African Americans as simple buffoons content with plantation life supported the propaganda that slavery was actually a good thing for them (Loewen 1995).

White elites also had the power to control the lives of American Indians and African Americans, denying them the resources to demonstrate the lie in their definition as "less than" whites. Thus there were *laws* to keep slaves ignorant. This one is from the Statute Book of South Carolina:

> And whereas, the having slaves taught to write, or suffering them to be employed in writing, may be attended with great inconveniences . . . that any person who shall teach any slave to write or to employ any slave as a scribe in writing, shall forfeit 100 pounds.
> (Hurd 1858: 304 quoted in Lerner 2004: 17)

The fact that African American bodies became property made their situation unique; live property required absolute control because it was not at all the natural state of affairs. The historical record offers first-hand accounts of the brutality visited upon slaves to keep them in bondage and get as much labor out of them as possible. The cultural fictions developed to justify the intense and harsh supervision of African American slave labor had to be strong, persuasive, and widely disseminated. White elites were so successful in embedding those fictions in cultural schema that the myths about blacks continued to influence labor market (and other) opportunities long after slavery was abolished and citizenship granted to Americans of African descent.

To "seal the ideological deal" so to speak, white superiority was written directly into the country's founding documents. The self-evident truths of the Declaration of Independence and the protections of the Constitution did not apply to African Americans, American Indians, or other groups of color. They were not entitled to the liberty, equality, and opportunity promised to "We, the people . . ." For major political figures of the early republic – including Abraham Lincoln, Thomas Jefferson, James Madison, and Andrew Jackson – the "ideal

America was a white republic." That is why they supported creating colonies for blacks outside of the country. President Lincoln went so far as to summon black leaders to the White House to urge them "to encourage their people to emigrate" (Foner 2000: 3).

Race Stratification in Labor Markets and Jobs

Racism was also institutionalized in the occupational hierarchies and segmented labor markets of an economic system fueled by conflict and competition. To wring as much profit as possible from workers, capitalists found it useful to pit them against one another, placating some groups with slightly higher wages and a false sense of superiority while offering other groups just enough to survive. Throughout U.S. history, race and occupational hierarchies have reinforced one another. For example, Mexicans contested their racial status in court. But the concentration of Mexicans in the menial jobs at the bottom of the occupational ladder solidified Anglos' sense that, no matter what the courts said, Mexicans were decidedly not white (Glenn 2002).

The work experiences of all other racial-ethnic groups would be shaped by the contours of this economically driven race hierarchy that placed northern Europeans at the very top and indigenous people and African Americans at the very bottom. Immigrants who hailed from regions beyond Europe were denied "the perks" of whiteness; in the case of Chinese this included citizenship. Using race as a reason to deny citizenship rationalized occupational hierarchies. It seemed "natural" to reserve the best jobs for citizens and channel non-citizens (no matter how long their families had been productive members of society) into lower paying, less desirable jobs (e.g. Lowe 1996; Tuan 1998; Takaki 2008; Glenn 2002).

The original work relationships forged between white elites and the "racial other" were continually reinforced. Each group that entered the United States in search of a better life was placed somewhere on the pre-existing race hierarchy and soon learned that one's race position had significant consequences. The definition of American as "white" reverberated through the work and occupational histories of immigrants from regions beyond Europe for generations; it is still felt today, as Chapter 4 will show.

While it is easy to see that the earliest, most powerful whites benefited directly from the ways they used American Indians and African Americans, there are four additional points that are not as obvious. The first is that many immigrant groups were able to achieve the

American dream only because the race hierarchy ensured that there were other groups cemented at the bottom of the occupational ladder, their labor easily exploitable by property-owning white men. The second related point is that although white workers did not have nearly as much power as white owners, there were real (as well as imaginary) racial dividends for even the least privileged white workers, including women. Because the race hierarchy permeated all aspects of society, it was relatively easy for powerful whites to manipulate poor and working-class whites into trying to protect their white privilege, even when it prevented them from getting better working conditions and fairer pay (Edwards 1979; Reich 1981; Kushnik 1996).

The third often unacknowledged point is that the economic advantages whites gained from exploiting other racial-ethnic groups did not disappear when the major activity, such as slavery, genocide, land theft, or denying a living wage was abolished. Instead, the race hierarchy at the center of U.S. economic history lived on. Usurping of land, segmented and dead-end labor markets, legal discrimination, and denial of economic opportunity through law, violence, intimidation, and discrimination continued.

The final point is twofold. The American cultural and political systems were well suited to the rapid development of capitalism and also to the use of systemic racism as a mechanism for capitalist expansion. As Bennett (1975: 41) notes, the British colonialists brought a "spirit of adventure and ruthlessness that included a certain contempt for all human beings and a willingness to use any and every expedient in the search for gold, glory, and conquests for God." Kovel claims that "material success led to material expansion and the gradual gathering of all white Americans into a cult of property and ownership" (1984: 24).

The next sections delve deeper into these four important points.

POINT 1. WHITENESS IS THE KEY TO UPWARD MOBILITY IN AMERICA

Many Americans take pride in the fact that they live in a country made up of people who have come from all parts of the globe to seek jobs that would ensure better lives for their families.

It is still common for thoughtful people of European descent to wonder, if their own ancestors started with so little and landed solidly in the middle class or beyond – why is it that more African Americans and Latinos have not done the same? It is typical but incorrect to draw parallels between the white immigrant and African American or American Indian work experiences. It is also incorrect to equate the work opportunities of Asian and Latino immigrant groups with the experiences of ethnic groups from Europe. The reason is this: European immigrant groups were able to claim whiteness while groups from regions beyond Europe were not. Many whites are not aware of the benefits that being classified as white had on the work experiences and successes of their European ancestors because they think in terms of ethnicity rather than race. They refer to themselves as "Polish" or "Irish" or "Italian" rather than white. This happens because they can now take for granted their status as whites. Yet many of those European ancestors were not considered white when they first arrived in the United States.

European Immigrants and African Americans: Apples and Oranges

Industrialization required more workers, fueling immigration to the United States. For the great waves of immigrants from eastern and western Europe during the 1880s to the 1920s "becoming white" was essential to upward mobility (Barrett and Roediger 1996; Kushnik 1996). Because American Indians and African Americans anchored the bottom of the race hierarchy, immigrant groups were able to claim key perquisites of the white race category, such as getting jobs that led to upward mobility, ensuring better lives for their children. These newcomers were the beneficiaries of laws and practices that gave advantages to white ethnics and kept blacks and other people of color "closed out" (Allen 1994; Barrett and Roediger 1996; Brodkin 1994; Ignatiev 1996; Franklin 1997).

The case of Italian Americans illustrates how the *process* of race construction operated (Loscocco 2009). Because mainstream scientists held that only northwestern Europeans were truly white, and therefore American, (Wander et al. 1999; Brodkin 1994) race-based exclusion applied particularly to Italians. Poor, uneducated Italians came in large numbers, mostly from southern Italy. Their physical features, cultural practices, and desire to stay connected to one another set them apart from "white" Europeans. Instead, they were linked to African Americans in the public imagination and in practices of exclusion. Violence and discrimination against Italians was commonplace; according to one report, they were lynched more than any other European immigrant group (Puleo 2007).

It took Italian immigrants longer to move out of poverty than was true for other Europeans (Parrillo 2009). The Irish, who had physical features and cultural practices more similar to the Anglo Europeans, acquired whiteness more quickly. Still, by the 1950s Italians had begun to populate suburbs, signaling their arrival in, or at least their proximity to, the middle class (Alba 1985). Within a few generations Italians were living the American dream. They had largely overcome skill and resource deficits, and curtailed cultural practices at odds with mainstream capitalism as they rose.

Yet the American dream might have remained elusive for a lot longer if Italians had not ultimately been accepted as white, even if it sometimes seemed begrudging (Loscocco 2009: 247). The homes in the suburbs that gave their children access to better schools and better jobs were largely made possible by federal housing and loan programs denied to African Americans (Brodkin 1994; Franklin 1997; Cable and Mix 2003). At workplaces and union halls across the country, their newfound whiteness gave Italian Americans a foot in doors that were still slammed in the face of African Americans.

Italians, like the Irish who had come just before them, were transformed from a non-white group into a kind of white people who would continue to distinguish and distance themselves from African Americans, in particular (Brodkin 1994; Ignatiev 1996; Loscocco 2009). When Italians and all the other European immigrants were pulling themselves up by their bootstraps, they were doing so *as whites* and at the expense of blacks (Barrett and Roediger 1996; Lipsitz 1998; Loscocco 2009).

The In-Between Immigrant: Not White, But Not Quite Savages Either

Immigrants from countries outside of Europe, who were "in-between" the top and bottom rungs of the race hierarchy, were not able to attain whiteness and thus were closed out of the best work opportunities.

Asians

Early Asian immigrants – valued for the work ethic and compliance tied to their spiritual beliefs – found that this was not enough to grant them status as Americans. Asians began as "near blacks" (Okihiro 1994) situated on a bottom rung of the race and occupational hierarchies. Most came as bonded or contract labor, in debt to their employers until they could pay off the cost of their passage and whatever else was stipulated. While contract laborers were formally free, their employers held tremendous power over them. Thus early Chinese immigrants had severe constraints on their freedom, which helped to solidify white superiority (Chang 2010: 69). Because they were not descendants of American slaves the Chinese escaped the lowest rung of the racial ladder, but they were often lumped together with blacks to facilitate resource hoarding by whites.

The first waves of Chinese immigrants were men recruited in the mid 1800s to the west coast to build railroads, cultivate the land, work in mines, and perform manual labor in manufacturing and service industries. The Chinese migrants, who were fleeing economic and political turmoil, were welcomed as docile workers well suited for the hard physical work needed to continue the U.S. advance toward its "destiny" (Blauner 2001; Glenn 2002; Takaki, 2008). Later, immigrants from other Asian countries colonized by Europeans (such as India and the Philippines) worked in gangs on western farm factories (Blauner 2001: 52). Asian immigrants encountered harsh working conditions in the jobs reserved for them, and they received lower pay than whites even when they managed to get the same jobs.

The ideology of Chinese inferiority vis-à-vis whites was disseminated in fiction, political cartoons, ad campaigns, and pronouncements from politicians and labor leaders. In the late 1800s laws prohibiting Chinese immigrants from owning land marked them as inferior to whites because property ownership was a defining perquisite of white colonizers (Glenn 2015: 67). Research documents that white mobs eliminated competition from the socially constructed "Chinese other" by driving them out of more than 200 Chinatowns (Pfaelzer 2007: 253–54; Glenn 2015: 67).

From the beginning of their economic history in the United States, Asians were used by white elites as a wedge to preserve white advantage and keep blacks "in their place" at the bottom of the race-based economic and social hierarchies (Kim 1999; Okihiro 2000; Lowen 1988). For example, as the largest early group of immigrants, the Chinese were pitted against black and white workers alike (Takaki 2008). After the Civil War, plantation owners sought out Asians to punish and control former slaves (Loewen 1988; Kim 1999). As the governor of Arkansas articulated: "Undoubtedly the underlying motive for this effort to bring in Chinese laborers was to punish the negro for having abandoned the control of his old master, and to regulate the conditions of his employment and the scale of wages to be paid him." Chinese immigrants were described as "new and essential machines" to replace blacks, who "have been destroyed [or are] wearing out, year by year," as one official put it (Okihiro 1994: 68). Black wages could be kept down and their demands for better working conditions ignored if there were other supplies of cheap and easily controllable labor, as Chinese labor was perceived to be.

Japanese immigrants worked sugar plantations in Hawaii under oppressive conditions. As of 1910, over half of the Japanese field workers were women and children. Japanese women were clearly not thought to be subject to the same physical limitations as white women. Whites in Hawaii (Haoles) apparently believed that Asian women, like their black counterparts, "were inherently suited to labor that would have broken most white men." (Glenn 2002: 213)

Latinos

Latino immigration patterns have largely mirrored U.S. economic needs throughout history. Mexicans and other ethnic groups have been used as part of what Marx called a "reserve army," to be alternately attracted and repelled depending on the needs of capital. For example, with whites struggling to find work during the Great Depression and therefore willing to work for low wages, 500,000 Mexicans were deported – many of whom were U.S. citizens. But after World War II, the *bracero* program recruited Mexicans for seasonal agricultural work; it continued in various forms until 1965 (Gonzalez 2001: 103; Hondagneu-Sotelo 2002).

Mexicans figured prominently in the economic history of the southwest. That history began when Anglo land barons took land from Mexicans using many of the techniques that had been used to appropriate American Indian land, including government-sanctioned violence and trickery (Feagin and Feagin 2011). By the 1920s in the Rio Grande Valley, "Mexicans comprised more than 90 percent of the population, but the white majority controlled most of the land" (Gonzalez 2001: 102). The Mexicans and Mexican-Americans who created the lucrative agriculture industry in the southwest were typically "bound to contractors, owners, and officials in a status little above peonage" (Blauner 2001: 52). As Glenn (2015: 65) points out, Mexican Americans also faced attempts to eradicate their culture. Children were sent to Anglo schools with the goal of getting "the Mexican" out of them and preparing for the low-level jobs reserved for them in racialized and gendered labor markets.

Like European immigrants, Mexicans distanced themselves from African Americans in their quest to claim whiteness. Yet they had an additional hurdle. Because the Spaniards who had conquered Mexico had intermingled with Africans and indigenous people (Brodkin 1994; Foley 2008) Mexicans were not viewed as white even when the courts declared them to be. As a "conquered people" the Mexicans of the southwest were not considered American either. They were forced to work on land that once belonged to them in an occupational system created and reinforced by white capitalists, managers, and workers who actively hoarded resources for themselves, closing Mexicans out. Within the separate occupations and industries created for women and men, there were different wage scales for Mexicans and whites. A "fundamental principle" organizing work in the southwest was that "in no case should a Mexican have authority over an Anglo" (Glenn 2002: 153).

Because Mexicans were viewed as an inferior race, it was deemed natural and reasonable to keep them in subordinate work positions doing menial tasks; this is a view that has been applied to poor Latinos throughout U.S. history (Amott and Matthaei 1991; Foley 1997; Glenn 2002; Feagin and Feagin 2011).

POINT 2. RACE TRUMPS CLASS: OR HOW POWERFUL WHITES SUCCESSFULLY USE RACE TO MAXIMIZE THEIR PROFITS

Because owners purchase the *potential* to work in a capitalist economic system, it is more profitable to organize work along "hierarchal rather than cooperative lines" (Reich 1981). By using race to order and divide workers, white capitalists kept all wages lower (e.g. Foley 1997; Cable and Mix 2003; Marable 2015). The existence of a caste of black workers at the bottom of the hierarchy – an outgrowth of the equation of "slave" with "black" – spurred a *white* working-class consciousness. Defining their own economic interests in racial terms, whites had no qualms about oppressing blacks to gain a better work position (Kelley 1993: 100). Although white workers often acted counter to their economic interests in their collusion with white capitalists, the advantages of whiteness, permeating as they did every aspect of social life, were more compelling to them (DuBois [1935] 1998; Roediger 1991; Kelley 1993; Lipsitz 1998).

Segmented Labor Markets and Occupational Castes

The concentration of capital made possible by industrialization (monopoly capitalism) reinforced the race hierarchy (Edwards 1980; Roediger 1991; Reich 1981). With so much economic power in their hands, major capitalists could easily manipulate workers from different racial and ethnic groups. In the early 1900s, company owners often chose blacks as strikebreakers, drawing on and intensifying racial animosity. Chinese workers were used as strikebreakers to quell the demands of both white and black factory workers (Amott and Matthaei 1991; Takaki 2008).Though some early white labor leaders recognized that they would gain leverage by including other race groups, the desire to protect white advantage kept them focused on people of color as competition they should not have to face. This deflected attention from the white corporate owners who were the source of their low wages and harsh working conditions (Foner 1974; Edwards 1979; Zinn 1995; Takaki 2008).

By maintaining race-based labor markets, white capitalists provided the white working class with an opportunity for social closure. White men and women could hoard better wages and working conditions within occupations that were also segmented by gender. Split or segmented labor markets also perpetuated the illusion that the race position white workers shared with capitalists was more consequential than the class position they shared with African Americans, Asians, and Latinos. People of color were crowded into peripheral industries and secondary labor markets where the worst jobs were offered, reinforcing their economic disadvantage and the better position of whites (Edwards 1979: 194).

Chapter 1 noted that segmented labor markets diffuse conflict between workers and owners by fomenting racial and ethnic tensions. White workers' ability to command a higher price for their labor power is threatened by the willingness of their counterparts from other race and ethnic groups to work for less. (This is the very point that Frederick Douglass made about slave labor). What appear to be ethnic antagonisms are actually masking class conflicts at the center of capitalism. According to Edna Bonacich: "cheaper labor does not intentionally undermine more expensive labor; it is paradoxically its weakness that makes it so threatening, for business can more thoroughly control it" (1972: 554). The author suggested that capitalists benefit most when white workers respond by keeping other racial-ethnic groups out of their labor markets. Bonacich argued that a more effective response would be to form cross-race and cross-ethnic coalitions (1975), to be discussed below.

Racial-ethnic occupational castes and niches were the norm, however. There could be elaborate hierarchies, as in pre-war Hawaii. There whites held the best jobs, and Hawaiian and Portuguese workers got the next-best positions. The Japanese were on the rung below, while the Filipino workers were at the bottom of the occupational hierarchy (Jung 2006: 185).

The job segregation begun when slave labor was equated with people of African descent was not dismantled after the abolition of slavery; in fact, it was fortified (Cable and Mix 2003). Blacks' status as suited for backbreaking, subservient, and menial work carried into labor markets everywhere. With what remained of the American Indian population mostly sequestered on reservations, blacks anchored the bottom of the occupational hierarchy wherever they went. Southern blacks jumped at the chance, ushered in by the industrial revolution, to move out of agriculture. Still, the "economic imperatives" to create profit kept segmented labor markets firmly in place (Cable and Mix 2003). Even when African Americans migrated to the north to pursue manufacturing jobs, they found themselves locked into an occupational caste system similar to that of the southern coal mining, steel, and iron industries (Reich 1981). They could get only the jobs rejected by whites: the jobs that were the most taxing, the most menial and the lowest-paying (e.g. Franklin 1997; Collins 2000). The power of white capitalists and workers in a racist society is palpable in the creation and maintenance of occupational stratification by race. As historian John Hope Franklin (1993) highlighted, people of color were completely locked out of some jobs and industries; these practices constituted affirmative action for whites.

Gender and Race Combine

Capitalists also used gender very effectively as part of their divide and conquer strategy and the labor of black women has been "super exploited." Though white women and black men did not have the same gender and race privileges as white men, they could advance at the expense of black women, who were in the bottom-most position of the occupational hierarchy. Through intersectional quantitative analyses, Enobong Branch (2011) established that there was a measurable negative impact on black women's work opportunity over and above that of being a woman or black. Her study of the years between the end of the Civil War and the beginning of the Civil Rights Movement revealed that black women were restricted to the kinds of jobs that other groups escaped as soon as they had the chance. They worked in low paying jobs that were dangerous, stressful, demeaning, and tiring (Jones 1986).

Intersectional studies of what Marx called "reproductive labor" – the work that is needed to ready the proverbial factory worker for a hard day's work and the work needed to raise the next generation of factory workers – have established this work as the purview of women of color. From the slave "mammy" to the immigrant nanny, domestic work was defined largely as the work of women of color (Collins 1993; Hondagneu-Sotelo 2001; Branch 2011). Evelyn Nakano Glenn (1992) showed that even as the model of reproductive or domestic labor changed from one of servitude to one of service work, it remained largely the work of women of color, though some jobs such as cleaning offices and (later) preparing food opened up to men from the same racial-ethnic groups (Duffy 2007).

Race-Ethnicity as a Source of Division

The rigid segregation of labor unions contributed to the occupational caste system. Some leaders and reformers understood that whites were paying a high price for their relative privilege but this awareness was not widespread (DuBois [1935]; 1998). Early efforts to organize workers across race groups failed largely because of racism in the labor movement. Opportunities for potential victories went by the wayside because white workers and their leaders so often rejected or ignored their counterparts of Latino, African, and Asian descent (Trumpbour and Bernard 2002; DuBois [1935] 1998; Takaki 2008). During the Great Depression Mexican agricultural workers organized major strikes on the west coast. They were backed by some AFL personnel but received little support from key leaders (Trumpbour and Bernard 2002).

Irish shoemakers in New England attempted to organize the Chinese who had been brought in as strikebreakers. But they also took out their anger on them, and made it clear that they saw the Chinese as inferior. Mexican and Japanese workers, widely stereotyped as compliant, created the Japanese-Mexican Labor association in 1903 and went on strike to protest cuts in their wages. They gained a victory, yet Samuel Gompers, head of the American Federation of Labor at the time, would only issue a union charter to the organization if the Mexicans agreed to deny union membership to Japanese and Chinese workers. The Mexicans did not agree, and without the AFL affiliation, the organization died out within a few years (Takaki 2008: 175).

Whites were not the only ones opposed to multiracial labor unions. According to Cable and Mix (2003: 189) many black leaders saw strikebreaking as the only way blacks could get access to skilled jobs. Others suggested that union membership would decrease blacks' chances for jobs because unionized black workers would no longer be able to work for lower wages than white workers – and they understood that this was the only incentive employers had for hiring blacks. They made choices severely limited by a racist capitalist system (cf. Marable 2000). Similarly, in pre-war Hawaii, Portuguese, Hawaiian, Filipino, and Japanese workers were divided by "the qualitatively different racisms they encountered" (Jung 2006: 185).

Many of the white male "captains of industry" recognized that workers of all racial-ethnic groups could wield considerable power if they banded together. Hence they balanced the workforce among different racial-ethnic groups to keep them off balance. The steel strike of 1919 is a prime example. The main strategy of the steel companies, when faced with the first major attempt to organize skilled and unskilled workers into unions across an entire industry, was to use the race hierarchy. They had tried to pit native-born and/or English-speaking workers against the immigrants from many different nations, but most newcomers were eager to support union efforts. Ultimately, employers broke the strike by exploiting racial divisions (Brody 1987; Reich 1981). Labor groups seemed more concerned with protecting their white privilege than gaining a bigger piece of the expanding profit for all workers.

Capitalists' ability to squelch even the combined efforts of different racial-ethnic groups also hindered the development and growth of multiracial unions. In fact, employers responded particularly strongly to multiracial labor protests, with "maximum force and violence" (Glenn, 2002: 81). As but one example, black coal miners in Alabama led a strike in 1920. State troopers beat and arrested thousands of black members of the United Mine Workers. "Coal company executives vowed to . . . crush the UMW, a union guilty of 'associating the black man on terms of perfect equality with the white man'" (Cayton and Mitchell 1939 quoted in Marable 2015: 31).

Chinese immigrants were propelled by a hostile labor market toward self-employment, and their race position as intermediaries between black and white contributed to their success. Small business activity was also a means for Chinese men to be reunited with their families, as once they were "established merchants" they could send for their wives and children (Amott and Matthei 1999: 206). As a group, the Chinese began to experience noticeable upward mobility and were defined as "ambitious, unknowable, cruel, violent, and thoroughly mendacious" (Chang 2010: 221). One response was "ethnic cleansing," as whites literally ran the Chinese out of town using brutal and extreme violence similar to that directed toward American Indians and African Americans (Courtwright 1996; Glenn 2015). In 1882 legislation restricted further immigration from China (Blauner 2001; Glenn 2002, 2015; Takaki 2008) and later from "the Asian Pacific Triangle" (Ngai 2004: Glenn 2015: 68).

The debate over the legislation showed white elites' careful maintenance of racial boundaries to elevate working-class whites over Chinese workers, while amassing wealth from the labor of both groups. The manager of the Central Pacific Railroad argued before a legislative committee that having a ready supply of Chinese laborers for the menial work had moved whites into supervisory positions. He used racial ideology to make sense of this – arguing that menial work was suited to Chinese, but that whites should not be "subject to a position which they have outgrown." The fact that the Chinese had been used to quash the largely Irish workforce's demands for higher wages and better working conditions was hidden in a trickle down argument: the lower wages paid to the Chinese workers would mean cheaper goods for white workers, so their wages would go further (Takaki 2008).

Eventually the Committee for Industrial Organization (CIO) courted black members from all racial-ethnic groups and worked to change racist white workers, though racist practices persisted (Foner 1974; Edwards 1979; Reich 1981; Jung 2006). The International Longshore and Warehouse Union (ILWU) in Hawaii, along with the CIO, promoted and elected leaders from various racial-ethnic groups and printed materials, made broadcasts and held meetings in many languages. The CIO explained that owners wanted to weaken worker power by keeping racial and ethnic antagonisms alive. Progress was not linear; some attempts to ensure racial unity fueled racial-ethnic conflicts, at least in the short term. But the ILWU went on to a major successful strike, demonstrating the viability of a multiracial union (Jung 2006).

Given their more tenuous economic position, blacks benefitted even more than whites from being in a union. For example, there was a larger wage advantage between unionized and nonunionized blacks. Yet the seniority system central to labor unions meant that African Americans were still the first fired because they had been the last hired. After 1948, as the labor movement lost momentum, its commitment to racial equality went by the wayside. In the 1950s African

Americans were still trying to get into the better lanes they knew were available to unionized whites. The Negro-American Labor Council worked to make racially segregated local unions illegal and to force all-white craft unions to open their doors to blacks (Marable 2000).

Family Wage: Whites Only

With industrialization, households were no longer productive units and a "separate spheres" model of work and family life emerged. Men left the home to do the wage-earning, which was more highly valued than the work activities of women's domestic sphere. The notion of a family wage emerged – actually a "man's wage" – which needed to be high enough to support wives and children. This clarified why women should be paid less, even when they did the same tasks or had the same levels of productivity as men (Kessler-Harris 2003; Glenn 2002).

However the notion that men, as designated breadwinners, were entitled to a family wage did not apply to families of color. The wages of men of color, it was argued, did not need to be as high as white men's because the women in their families should be working for pay as well. Throughout labor history women of color were held to different gendered work norms, in keeping with their definition as "less than" white women. Further, past practices and racial ideology made it seem "natural" that white families should have a higher standard of living than other racial-ethnic groups (Collins 2000; Glenn 2002: 82; Landry 2000).

POINT 3. THE PLAYING FIELD DOES NOT GET LEVELED: CUMULATIVE DISADVANTAGE IN THE WORK HISTORIES OF AFRICAN AMERICANS AND AMERICAN INDIANS

> There has always been racism in the United States, even though it has not always been the same racism.
>
> (George Lipsitz)

Racial inequalities in labor markets and wealth accumulation continued after the most obvious and egregious exploitation stopped. Long after slavery was abolished (by the 13th Amendment to the

Constitution in 1865) and even after The Civil Rights Act in 1964, policies and practices granted advantages to whites denied to people of color (Lipsitz 1998). The equation of "slave" with "black," and the creation of the race category of "white" proved to be of tremendous and lasting importance. There have been periods of relative gain for the groups near the bottom of the race hierarchy but those gains erode with changes in the economy and the political climate. Much of the race discrimination after the 1960s was the color-blind kind, folded into what appear to be race-neutral labor policies and practices. This discrimination is so deeply embedded in ongoing social practices that it often goes unnoticed, which contributes to its power (Bonilla-Silva 2006; Feagin 2006).

An economic and social system built on a foundation of racism does not crumble when some aspects of the system are changed; it would take a concerted effort to repair the damage and overhaul the system. Without that, racial advantage and disadvantage accumulate, passing from one generation to the next. This is partly because it is nearly impossible to catch up in a foot race your ancestors were not in, even if you have now been allowed to enter it. White elites and white workers aggressively hoarded land, profit, jobs, and money. They did so through genocide or ethnic cleansing, mob violence including lynching, laws that restricted and excluded groups of color, cultural erasure, and segregated jobs with subsistence wages. They used these techniques over and over again (cf. Glenn 2015).

Because of exploitation and exclusion, whites accumulated more wealth than people of color at every historical juncture. They have passed what they stockpiled to their children, so that more whites start each generation with a relative economic advantage (DiPrete and Eirich 2006). But whites also got more wealth because race-based oppression and white privilege continued, as many studies have shown (e.g. Feagin 2014; Oliver and Shapiro 2006).

The cumulative disadvantage of African Americans and American Indians has been greatest. Though early European and Asian immigrants bonded to English masters were not free, they were never defined as chattel or real estate (DuBois [1924]2009), the way slaves were. Though Mexicans and Puerto Ricans were colonized, and suffered physical and cultural erasure, the experience of American Indians was more extreme.

The two groups whose super exploitation fostered unprecedented economic growth, the effects of which would accumulate far into the future (Moore 1996), were also the two groups who would swell the ranks of the poor and unemployed into the twenty-first century. The benefits of their labor went to other groups and there was never a serious attempt to make up for their early exploitation. Instead, processes of exploitation and political disenfranchisement simply changed forms (Marable 2000: 2).

African Americans

> Racism, although the child of slavery, not only outlived its parent, but grew stronger and more independent after slavery's demise.
>
> (George Frederickson)

As history (and the next chapter) show, Americans of African descent – whether slaves, servants, bonded, or free – showed a strong desire to improve their economic circumstances. Yet slavery mostly denied African Americans the fundamental building block of the capitalist system – the ability to use one's body or mind to create and exchange something of economic or "use value." Most slaves were also denied control over their human capital, those skills and abilities that are exchanged in the labor market. The attitudes and desires of their masters constrained slaves' efforts to better themselves.

If after emancipation men and women of African descent had been given the "forty acres and a mule" suggested, the economic history of black Americans would have been radically different. This promise of land, and therefore, self-sufficiency, was first decreed in Union General Sherman's Special Field Order No. 15 during the Civil War, after consultation with a group of black ministers. They recommended that the land be set apart from whites because, as their spokesperson said, "there is a prejudice against us in the South that will take years to get over" (Gates 2013).

Imagine for a moment that the nation had taken what DuBois called the "path of wisdom and statesmanship," making it possible for former slaves to achieve according to their ability and hard work. Suppose society had protected freed women and men from violence and oppression, "encouraging them, educating their children, giving them land and a minimum of capital, and thus inducting them into real economic and political freedom" (DuBois [1935] 1998: 88). It would have been a major re-set to the economic disadvantage they had been accumulating.

This is what some whites, such as politician Thaddeus Stevens, understood. He argued before the legislature that former slaves needed *economic* freedom and that it was up to the government to provide the tools to ensure that freed slaves could succeed. He cautioned against leaving freedmen to "the legislation of their late masters" which would replicate the system of slavery (DuBois [1935]1998: 266). To make the economic playing field more level would have required the kind of "billion dollar reconstruction and development program" that the United States provided to other countries, including former enemies, whose economies were shattered by war (Walker 1998: 180).

Less Than Nothing

Instead President Andrew Johnson and other politicians, ignoring calls for fairness and reason, "did less than nothing," as DuBois put it. Because of his belief that blacks were inferior Johnson *opposed* efforts to provide them with the land or education that would improve their economic position. Above all else, Johnson fought against blacks' right to vote, which might have given them the political power to improve their economic circumstances through legislation (DuBois [1935] 1998: 280). Former slaves eagerly moved to the so-called "Sherman land" and they ultimately settled 400,000 confiscated acres. But President Johnson overturned the order and gave the land back to the planters after the war ended (Myers and Dobbs ([2005] 2016).

The Homestead Act signed by President Lincoln in 1862 enabled the government to give away, practically for free, close to 250 million acres of (stolen American Indian) land, but almost all of it went to whites. Author Trina Williams estimates that as many as 46 million people today are descendants of those who got the land (Feagin and Feagin 2011: 181).

Even if the Freedman's Bureau established by the federal government had been left alone to help newly emancipated women and men rebuild their lives, the economic situation of African Americans would have improved. Instead, the Bureau, which was tasked with making and enforcing wage contracts, was actively resisted and undermined by many southern whites. Northerners were also unwilling to support the bureau for the amount of time it would have taken to get former slaves into the metaphorical footrace toward economic success (DuBois [1935] 1998).

The fact that "color" had become enmeshed with the mark of inferiority meant that there was no serious effort to make up for what had gone before. There was also a concerted effort – of fraud, violence, destruction, and flouting of the law – to continue to keep African Americans "in their place" at the bottom of the social and economic hierarchies. Without property or equipment most blacks in the post Bellum period of U.S. history remained economically dependent on the people they had served as slaves before the Civil War (DuBois [1935] 1998; D. Franklin 1997: 30). The Emancipation Proclamation gave slaves freedom, but not equality, and not even full humanity. This key point helps explain why black economic history looks different from that of white ethnics and other groups of color.

Reconstruction and Jim Crow

After the Civil War, there were some positive developments for southern blacks, who showed eagerness and capacity to flourish. According to DuBois, during Reconstruction there were "a tremendous series of efforts to earn a living in new and untried ways, to achieve economic security and to restore fatal losses of capital and investment" by people who had endured "three awful centuries of degradation" and yet "staggered forward" ([1935]1998: 347).

For instance, by 1880 South Carolina had yielded somewhat to pressure and 33,000 plantations had been divided among 93,000 farmers (DuBois [1935]1998: 416). Many former slaves who continued to work for plantation owners were able to cut back on their work hours and some managed to do their work in self-directed teams rather than the harshly supervised slave gangs of the plantations. Black women moved out of the ranks of field hands to take on the work of the home (Glenn 2002: 100–1). Against extremely difficult odds some blacks did manage to purchase farmland – typically by dint of hard work and sacrifice by everyone in a household. The land that blacks could purchase was inferior and sold at inflated prices (Glenn 2002: 100). This ensured that even these extraordinary families would be unlikely to profit from their labor to the same extent as their white counterparts.

Yet southern landowners fought hard to preserve their economic exploitation of freed black women and men all the same. DuBois chronicled the "desperate effort of a dislodged, maimed, impoverished, and ruined oligopoly" to regain economic control "by force, fraud and slander, in defiance of law and order ([1935] 1998: 347)." When Reconstruction in the south ended in 1877, and federal troops were withdrawn, work opportunities, among other things, got a lot worse for blacks. The vast majority of blacks were sharecroppers – a system only slightly different from indentured servitude – tying black agricultural workers to the whims of white planters and merchants (Reich 1981). Thirty years after Emancipation, most blacks were making just enough money to survive (Woodward 1955; Reich 1981).

In 1896 the Supreme Court ruling (Plessy vs. Ferguson) that racial segregation was constitutional engendered Jim Crow laws in the south; these formal and informal norms were the heart of a system of racial apartheid in work and every other social institution. The segregation of blacks from whites was chiefly about maintaining white superiority. As Glenn observes, when it seemed that whites' power was being diluted or that shared spaces might imply equality, communities would go to great lengths – for example, duplicating services – in order to make the race hierarchy clear (2002: 118).

Thus by transposing the race hierarchy onto the occupational hierarchy, and using white culture and its courts to justify it, U.S. society cemented blacks into menial and low-paying jobs. This guaranteed that Americans of African descent would remain at the bottom of the social hierarchy – in keeping with the original definition of slave as black and black as inferior to white.

The Twentieth Century

Though other parts of the country did not have the overt system of racial oppression represented by Jim Crow laws, the race hierarchy was embedded in labor markets associated with industrialization, as well as in workplace norms and federal policies throughout the nation. When southern black women and men left their homes and families in search of better jobs to ensure better lives, just as all of the immigrant groups had done, they found few opportunities. Employers preferred immigrant groups to blacks stigmatized by the racial ideology of slavery, so immigrants got the jobs rejected by white natives. Perpetual newcomers in their own country, women and men of African descent were left with the most arduous, low-paying, and de-valued jobs (Franklin 1997; Cable and Mix 2003; Branch 2011).

Even when the words of officials called for justice and equality, their deeds were often in direct conflict. As one example, President Woodrow Wilson proclaimed in 1912 that blacks should be given full justice and that it should not be "mere grudging justice" but full of "cordial good feeling." Yet he gave federal officials in the south the right to fire or downgrade a black employee for any reason they chose; the employee would have no recourse. When black leaders met with Wilson to protest this development he was offended, and sent them away (Kovel 1984: 31).

American legislative history is full of instances in which politicians left out as many African Americans as possible, even long after they had gained rights to citizenship. The framers of these laws or provisions did not specifically say that African Americans could not be in unions, or entitled to minimum wages and reasonable work hours, or ineligible for Social Security benefits. What they did, instead, was to say that the benefits would not be made available to members of certain occupations. Thus people who held farm and domestic jobs – the only jobs available to many African Americans in 1930 – were written out of legislation that substantially improved the work lives of most whites (Katznelson, 2005: 22; D. Franklin 1997).

Mexicans were often lumped with African Americans in policies protecting whites. In the early part of the twentieth century (during what is known as the Progressive era), Mothers' Pensions for widows became available in many states, because of concerns that women could not earn enough to support their families. Yet black and brown mothers were typically denied this benefit because of the belief that they could find work (Goodwin 1995). The Federal Emergency Relief program used an "employable mother rule" and as long as there were domestic service and agricultural jobs available in a locality, African American and Latina mothers would be refused support (Mink 1995; Glenn 2002). In 1915 the Supreme Court upheld a law protecting workers that specifically excluded women harvesters, who were disproportionately Mexican (Glenn 2002: 85).

Federal programs of the early 1900s, created to distribute material benefits, likewise gave whites an economic advantage. It was almost impossible for people of color – African Americans and American Indians, in particular – to obtain the mineral rights, airlines routes, radio and TV frequencies, and other important resources available from the government (Feagin and Feagin 2011: 180). Franklin Delano Roosevelt's 1930s New Deal instituted a bundle of white advantages, solidifying residential segregation and educational disparities that would reverberate in labor markets for generations (Lipsitz 1998; Franklin 1997; Cable and Mix 2003).

World War II seemed to hold out the promise of greater racial equality as it expanded the economy and necessity outweighed prejudice. There were soldiers drawn from every racial-ethnic group, including Japanese Americans who enlisted from the camps where they were held by their suspicious government. There were nine hundred thousand African Americans in the military, though they were kept separate from whites and relegated to some of the most difficult tasks (Takaki 2008). Blacks also filled critical jobs left by white soldiers.

One might expect that fighting or doing factory work to support the war effort would finally propel African Americans off of the racial hierarchy's bottom rung. Instead, World War II illuminated the paradox upon which the United States was founded: democracy and freedom, yet racial inequality and oppression. Though men and women from all racial-ethnic groups demonstrated their strong work ethic and abilities and their belief in their nation's stated principles, whites remained firmly positioned at the top of the occupational hierarchy.

Post World War II

Developments after World War II were very different for blacks and whites, solidifying a two-tiered nation – separate and unequal. The GI bill propelled many white families into solid middle-class lives with its occupational and educational opportunities. According to Brodkin (1994: 77), those families enjoyed "what was arguably the most massive affirmative action program in U.S. history." Though blacks were technically entitled to GI benefits, they were often denied them – and they certainly could not use the benefits in the same way that whites did. For example, black colleges and universities could not accommodate all black veterans who wanted more education, and most white colleges and universities did not welcome African Americans. Drawing from a study by Walker in 1970, Brodkin reports that some twenty thousand black veterans had attended college by 1947, but almost as many were denied a place. Black women had difficulty getting into training programs or discovered that their training didn't change employers' preferences for whites (Franklin 1997). More blatant forms of discrimination also reappeared. One striking example: federal agencies that had actively recruited black women for clerical jobs during the war began advertising clerical jobs for 'whites only' (Newman 1978).

Race and gender continued to combine to keep black women at the bottom of labor queues. For instance, the war had made it possible for African American women to get out of domestic work as industrial jobs opened up to them. Yet Branch's (2011) analyses show that even when their work lives were improving, black women remained at the bottom of the occupational ladder. Black men got better factory jobs than black women, and white women were the primary beneficiaries of expanded and "feminized" occupations. Other women of color also had a hard time getting the new jobs set aside for (white) women, but they, too, were higher up in the labor queue than black women.

In 1930, for example, 25 percent of employed white women held clerical jobs compared to 12 percent of Chinese women and less than one percent of black women (Amott and Matthei 1991: 208). By 1960, 33 percent of employed white women workers were doing clerical work but only 8 percent of black women held these jobs. It was not until the demand for clerical workers outstripped the supply of whites that "clerical and kindred workers" became a major occupation for black women (Branch 2011: 107–9). Even so, they had the worst and lowest-paying jobs (Posadas 1982) and were twice as likely as whites to be poor (Branch and Hanley 2014).

Between 1930 and 1950 the unemployment situation of blacks compared to whites, including immigrants, had worsened (Lieberson 1980). By the 1950s the relatively favorable educational position of blacks compared to immigrants had pretty much disappeared (Franklin 1997: 113). Keller's (1983) study of labor market shifts in what would become Silicon Valley depicts how having access to the GI bill reaped substantial labor market advantages for whites. As the post World War II semi-conductor industry transformed, the growth was in white-collar rather than blue-collar jobs. The white men who had been production workers in the 1950s were able to fill technical and professional jobs largely because of GI benefits allowing them to take advantage of new training programs at junior colleges. The blue-collar jobs abandoned by white men were filled mostly by low-paid African-American and Latina women.

Over the course of the twentieth century the economic fortunes of black men and women improved considerably during periods of economic growth and race consciousness. But economic and racial justice downturns eroded those gains. During the Great Depression, for example, African Americans in urban areas had far higher rates of unemployment than whites (Wolters 1970). As employers and politicians grappled with the Depression, blacks were simply let go in some industries to make room for whites. In other industries technological advances created better jobs which were offered to whites rather than to the blacks who were already working there (Wolters 1970). When prosperity returned, whites did not cede ground gained and there was no way for blacks to make up what they had lost (Myrdal 1944: 207).

After the racial apartheid system was struck down in the 1954 Brown v. Board of Education ruling and the 1960s Civil Rights Movement achieved key victories, there were more and better job opportunities for all groups of color (Cable and Mix 2003). The 1960s was a period of tremendous economic, social, and political gain, lifting many working-class families into the middle class. Yet those who could not grasp the new opportunities plunged into poverty where a disproportionate share of black families had been all along (Collins 2000: 66). Class mobility was used to justify intensified racial inequality. If some blacks could make it, there had to be something wrong with those who did not. Yet there is racial bias at all levels of the occupational hierarchy as Chapter 4 documents.

American Indians

What about American Indians, the descendants of those who were the first to cultivate what would become U.S. soil? From soon after their first encounter with the white colonizers, the indigenous people and their ways of life were under attack.

The dominant white cultural value placed on ownership, individualism, and economic gain was at odds with the values of most indigenous nations. White elites denigrated American Indians for their disinterest in exploiting the land, and their tendency toward sharing and collective ownership rather than profit-seeking. Government policy aimed to change the relationship of indigenous peoples to the land, whether by tricking or forcing them to sell, or redistributing land from an American Indian nation to individual families (Deloria 1988; Weatherford 1988; Takaki 2008; Dunbar-Ortiz 2014). These practices persisted long after the first encounters between the colonizers and indigenous people.

Appropriating Land, Expelling Indian Nations

As the founding of the United States approached, brutal attacks on indigenous nations, often sanctioned or carried out by the government, continued; they were aimed at physical annihilation and cultural extermination. In 1775 George Washington ordered a peremptory strike against all of the Haudenosaunee (the Six Nation Iroqouis), some of whom were allied with the British monarchy in the hopes of better treatment. He instructed the officer in charge "to lay waste all the settlements around . . . that the country may not be merely *overrun* but *destroyed* . . . [Y]ou will not by any means, listen to any overture of peace before the total ruin of their settlements is effected" (Dunbar-Ortiz 2014: 77).

In mid 1780 the Cherokee nation had recovered from earlier attempts to crush their resistance, so they raided some of the squatters in their midst. In response, North Carolina sent five hundred mounted rangers to raze Cherokee towns. During the winter of 1780–1 the Cherokee were again under severe attack. A letter sent to Thomas Jefferson, then a delegate to the Continental Congress, described the complete destruction of towns and villages, and murder and theft aimed even at those fleeing the scene (Dunbar-Ortiz 2014: 75).

When Jefferson became President in 1801 he argued that appropriating their land was good for American Indians; it would "civilize them." He commanded agents to pressure Indians to sell and "let it be known that threats, intimidation, and bribery were acceptable tactics to get the job done" (Perdue and Green 2007: 31).

Military action against the first nations continued during and after the Civil War. In Nevada and Utah, a militia of California volunteers "massacred hundreds of unarmed Shoshone, Bannock and Ute people in their encampments." There were "scorched earth campaigns" and "search-and-destroy" missions against the Apache in New Mexico and the Navajos in Colorado. In 1864, 8,000 Navajo civilians were forced on a 300-mile march to a military concentration camp. A quarter of them died of starvation in the camps. (Dunbar-Ortiz 2014: 138–9).

The Dancing Rabbit Creek Treaty

Perhaps the greatest betrayal of Indian people was the treatment accorded the Choctaws. Treaty after treaty was signed with the Chocktaws, one of the so-called Five Civilized Tribes (because they were so like white men), until the final treaty of Dancing Rabbit Creek forced them across the Mississippi to the parched plains of Oklahoma. The Choctaws stubbornly resisted each encroachment but were finally forced to make the long trek westward.

In an earlier treaty, ten years prior to Dancing Rabbit Creek, the Choctaws had asked for a provision guaranteeing that the United States would never apportion the lands of the tribe, as they preferred to hold their lands in common. So in the Treaty of January 20, 1825, Article VII, the United States provided that "the Congress of the United States shall not exercise the power of apportioning the lands."

Just prior to the admission of Oklahoma as a state, the lands of the Choctaw were allotted, although a minority opinion in the report on the Dawes Allotment Act stated that perhaps the Choctaw method of holding land in common was superior to that of the white man because there was so little poverty among the members of the Five Civilized Tribes.

Today the Choctaws and people of the other "civilized" tribes are among the poorest people in America.

(Quoted from Vine Deloria, *Custer Died for your Sins*, pp. 42–3)

American Indian nations were under attack until the end of the century; prominent Civil war generals led the "army of the West," including Philip Sheridan who reportedly said, "The only good Indian is a dead Indian" (Dunbar-Ortiz 2014: 139). As Wilma Mankiller (Cherokee) wrote: ". . . during the administration of Thomas Jefferson, it was already cruelly apparent to many Native American leaders that any hope for tribal autonomy was cursed. So were any thoughts of peaceful coexistence with white citizens." She identified the nadir of government-sanctioned "genocide, property theft, and total subjugation" as the point in 1830 when President Andrew Jackson called for "forcible removal to expel the eastern tribes from their land" (1993: 51).

White Values: Private Ownership

The Dawes Act of 1887 doled out parcels of American Indian land to individual families and the rest of the land was made available to whites to buy or rent. The American Indian nations fought to preserve large community-owned reservation lands that had special status. Documents compiled by Francis Paul Pruch showed that during this period the Supreme Court made it *legal to defraud Indians* if Congress ratified the move; this was the infamous "Lone Wolf Decision" (Moore 1996).

The aim of the Dawes Act was to acculturate Native Americans to the "selfishness" necessary to be civilized, defined as exploiting the land as much as possible. The government turned American Indians away from the agriculture that had sustained their communities for so long, changing them into individual property owners and ultimately into low wage earners.

The legislation cleared the way for railroads to go through American Indian land and for whites to maximize profit from the land. Though the paternalistic language of the time suggested that American Indians would be better off if they shed their culture and adapted to the ways of white culture, it was whites who benefited at the expense of Native Americans (Takaki 2008: 222–3).

Deloria writes of a 1928 Meriam Report showing that "there had been no progress of any kind on the reservations since they were set up. The people were in the final stages of demise" (55). A 1933 assessment by the federal government showed that almost half of the Native Americans living on reservations that had been part of the allotment program of the Dawes Act had *no land at all*. They had lost about 60 percent of the 138 million acres of land that had belonged to them. "Allotment had been transforming Indians into a landless people" (Takaki 2008: 224).

In 1934, when the New Deal was ushering working-class whites into the middle class, the Indian Reorganization Act ended the land allotment program and permitted American Indians on reservations to organize and govern themselves. This was a major positive development for indigenous nations. Yet the government still inserted itself in their commerce. For example, the Indian Affairs Commissioner asked that the Navajo reduce their stock of sheep and goats. The government was concerned about soil erosion that might damage Boulder Dam as well as studies showing that the Navajo lands could not support all of the sheep they had. Raising sheep was a way of life and livelihood for the Navajo and they resisted. They contended that overgrazing was not connected to soil erosion. But their stock was reduced, and more Navajos had to become wage earners in order to support themselves and families. "The stock reduction program had reduced many Navajos to dependency on the federal government as employees in New Deal work programs." Scientists discovered later that the Navajo had been correct; overgrazing had not led to the soil erosion (Takaki 2008: 230).

Studies in the late nineteenth and early twentieth centuries show that in areas such as the Great Basin and California, many American Indians left their land to become wage laborers. In addition to doing menial farm and domestic work, they also held occupations such as ranchers, mine workers, bricklayers, masons, and carpenters. Still, they entered segmented labor markets, filling unstable, low-paid niches in every field. American Indians "built the mining structures but did not generally mine, laid the flooring, but did not set the tile, or performed rough carpentry but did not do finished carpentry (Albers 1996: 252–3).

World War II and Beyond

American Indians enlisted during World War II and worked in war industries at least partly because it was a good economic decision; there were few jobs on reservations. But they also supported the war effort by buying war bonds with their meager savings (Dunbar-Ortiz 2014). The Navajo played a key role in World War II, demonstrating their sense of themselves as loyal Americans. As some of the sounds of the Navajo language were unique and the grammar was extremely complex, Navajos were uniquely poised to be effective code talkers; anything intercepted would be incomprehensible to the enemy. Yet they returned from the war to low wage jobs or unemployment. A year after the war, for example, a New Mexico report showed that the average earnings of a Navajo man on the reservation was less than $100 a year. The population had far exceeded the numbers that the land allotted to them could support (Takaki 2008: 371).

Thus American Indians were largely left out of the post-war prosperity. During the 1950s there were many so-called termination programs. These represented long-sought independence for indigenous groups but also meant fewer funds for economic development, pressure on nations to liquidate their assets, the loss of land-based communities, and a possible end of indigenous status. Termination policy was "disastrous" for American Indians (Deloria 1988: 54–77). Twenty years of "collective Indigenous resistance" led to the defeat of the federal termination policy in the 1970s. Yet because proponents of termination hope to cancel all treaties and eliminate American Indians' special status, the idea reappears in Congress periodically (Dunbar-Ortiz 2014: 191).

The Indian Relocation Program encouraged indigenous people to move to particular cities where they competed with poor blacks, Mexicans, and whites looking for jobs (Deloria 1988; Berger and Dunbar-Ortiz 2010). Though urbanites fared better than their counterparts on reservations, they lagged behind other groups working in cities. As the 1960s began, the average American Indian family earned $1,500 a year while other families averaged $5,000. A number of initiatives stemming from President Johnson's War on Poverty improved the economic situation of American Indians (Fixico 2006: 22–4) but "[b]eing Indian in the 1970s meant being poor in general" (p.25). In response to American Indian activism, the government finally stopped termination in the 1970s as just noted (Dunbar-Ortiz 2014).

After World War II, the treaties that had assured American Indian nations on the Pacific coast "perpetual fishing and hunting rights as long as they agreed to remain on restricted reservations" were broken. Fishing became more of a leisure time activity during post-war prosperity for the white middle class and treaty fishing rights were routinely ignored by state Fish and Game Commissions. There were protests by smaller indigenous groups in the area but they did not get enough support to create change (Deloria 1988).

The President of the Manitoba Indian Brotherhood spoke about the difficulties faced by American Indians as the 1960s came to a close:

> Paternalistic programs of the past, based largely on the idea that we must shelter and protect the ignorant savage, have created complex problems to those who want to shelter and protect themselves . . .

We know that we can't live for long in a wilderness that is fast being ransacked of fish and fur to feed and clothe the luxury-minded dwellers of the city. So, we too must enter the confines of the city and try as best we might to make our way.

But understand, oh white man; understand lovely lady dressed in fur! It is hard, very hard to know that the land that once was ours will never ever again be our hunting grounds. It is hard to bear the crime-filled streets and the liquor selling bard where once was only peaceful grass and sobriety. We understand that we must change – and we are changing – but remember: it once was our land, our life, and it is hard.
(Leading Thunderbird quoted in Rosensteil 1983: 173)

American Indian fishing rights were still an issue into the 1980s. Though vigorous activism in the 1960s and 1970s led to some court victories (Dunbar-Ortiz 2014), Vine Deloria wrote, "Indians may have to starve so whites can have a good time on the weekends if present trends continue" (1988: 23).

In the twenty-first century, the cumulative disadvantage of the first nations is apparent; American Indians remain at the bottom of economic and occupational hierarchies.

POINT 4. RACISM AND U.S. CAPITALISM GO HAND IN HAND

Racism and U.S. capitalism were well-suited to one another. Getting people to compete for jobs is a sure path to the maximum profit capital seeks (Fletcher and Agard 1987), and using physical and cultural differences as a way to foment competition was very successful. That capitalists knew exactly what they were doing (e.g. Reich 1981; Blauner 2001; Zinn 1995) is shown by the particularly harsh and swift response of owners to multiracial strike or protest activity mentioned earlier. Woven into the fabric of the society, racism was a thick and ever present screen, hiding the exploitation of white labor and the fact that capitalists benefitted far more from racism than working-class whites ever would.

A big part of U.S. economic history centers on the seemingly single-minded pursuit of material gain. The French sociologist Alexis de Tocqueville, who made a study of the fledgling United States in 1831, was struck by how important advancing their economic position was to Americans. He also noted how hard Americans were willing to work to make that happen and how much the desire for independence was tied up in the quest for a secure economic position. Tocqueville saw a frenetic quality to American work and life (Glenn 2002: 59). This is likely because markers of economic (and social) success are ever changing, requiring increasing wealth and material possession. In a society whose greatest priority is money, there is always more to be made.

The American emphasis on money and possessions as measures of social status underlay capitalists' oppression of the proletariat – whose only means for a better life was working for someone else. Many owners were compelled by the *laissez faire* approach to capitalism to exploit and intensify race divisions as a means to amass as much profit as possible.

But capitalism itself is not the culprit; instead, it is *unchecked* capitalism that results in the consolidation of capital in the hands of fewer and fewer people who gain tremendous economic and political power (Edwards 1979). The U.S. capitalist system is precisely the kind of capitalism Karl Marx worried about. His image of capital with a "werewolf hunger for profit" seems to have roamed through American economic history, aided and abetted by social and political institutions.

> As one digs deeper into the national character of the Americans, one sees that they have sought the value of everything in this world only in the answer to this single question: how much money will it bring in?
>
> Alexis de Tocqueville

The notion of U.S. citizenship included an obligation to work hard to make money. Anyone able to work should do so, no matter how low the wages or how harsh the conditions. Vagrancy laws, strengthened in both the north and south after the Civil War, were a means to shore up labor supply. These laws were popular throughout the south in the late 1800s as a means to supply white owners with black labor. Local officials could hire out any person who appeared to be without work at the going wage rate. They could also send anyone convicted of misdemeanors (such as swearing) and unable to pay the allotted fine to sign a labor contract with the city or an owner who paid the fine. The debt would continue to rack up, keeping the black workers in a form of coerced labor (Glenn 2002).

When domestic servants were in short supply vagrancy laws were used to round up black women who were defined as idle if they were working in the home. The claim by some that the police officers and the owners were in cahoots is also quite believable (Glenn 2002: 104). Later vagrancy laws were applied to Mexicans in the southwest and the west. In the early 1900s in Texas, for example, vagrancy laws were invoked during cotton-picking season to force Mexicans into the fields. When large numbers of Mexicans began to leave Texas in search of better work opportunities, a Farm Placement Service "stationed uniformed officers at major intersections to stop vehicles carrying workers and to direct them to farms that had requested workers" (Glenn 2002: 157).

In a society driven by the desire for economic gain above all else and the belief that individuals have a right to make as much money as possible without interference it is not surprising to find a robust race hierarchy. The race hierarchy was institutionalized in service to capitalism. It was continually reinforced by social policy that tied what some other countries consider basic human rights – such as health care, family leave, and a living wage – to having a good job, and then denied entire groups of people access to good jobs. People of color were particularly useful as "reserve armies" as Marx put it, their labor power readily available when white capitalists needed it and left idle otherwise.

American Indian nations rejected capitalist ideals, but powerful white elites refused to allow this crucial cultural difference. American Indian children were removed from their communities and sent to boarding schools to replace indigenous ways of thinking with "white men's beliefs and value systems." Chief among the lessons was "the importance of private property [and] material wealth." They were taught "possessive individualism," which emphasized judging oneself by what one owns. This went against the fundamental American Indian belief in communal ownership of the land. It was not until 1978 that American Indian parents gained the legal right to keep their children out of such schools (American Indian Relief Council 2016).

Deloria's discussion of Canada's approach to dealing with indigenous groups illustrates a different path. In Canada, he notes, every province has Indian reservations and Indians have been able to retain their basic forms of government without interference. Canadian Indian land was not allotted to individuals and "then stolen piece by piece from under them." Deloria argues that the U.S. government could have continued to provide special legal status for American Indians rather than forcing them to convert to the dominant white capitalist way of life. "There was no need for the government to abruptly change from treaty negotiations to a program of cultural destruction, as it did in 1819 with its Indian assimilation bill" (1988: 49).

There is so much more to tell about the race, gender, and class oppression at the center of U.S. history. However there is also an important counter narrative. It is the story of the tenacity, intelligence, work ethic, and entrepreneurial spirit of race groups whose labor and humanity were exploited so that others could prosper. There were also white women and men who joined the struggle against the sweeping, powerful, and violent tide of racism. These are the topics of the next chapter.

3
Activism and Entrepreneurship

It would take an entire book to begin to do justice to this part of the race and work story. I hope to whet your appetite for more, which can be found not only in the excellent works cited here, but also in the ever-growing canon that revises dominant narratives of U.S. socioeconomic history. The chapter serves as an important reminder that *people* are at the center of that history. Powerful white men created racialized and gendered social systems that furthered their own economic gain, but those structures were continually challenged. Groups whose land, bodies, and labor were super-exploited fought back. Though their culture and humanity were constantly under attack, they found ways to preserve both. The work lives of people of color were severely constrained, yet they made tremendous contributions to American life. Further, there were always people of white race privilege who rejected their advantage or used it to work for equality.

As Chapter 1 showed, race gets attached to everything and everyone in a racialized social system – even to something as personal as what and how one sees. As DuBois depicted so vividly in his writing on the souls of black and white folk, the oppressed have a more clear-eyed vision of the structures of their oppression. They see what is invisible to or denied by the privileged. Those at the top of the race hierarchy develop attitudes and behaviors that reinforce it, while those at the bottom develop attitudes and behaviors that challenge it (Bonilla-Silva 2015: 77).

RESISTANCE STRATEGIES

The following material serves as a critical race counterpoint to the common tendency to assume that the groups at the bottom of the race and occupational hierarchies belong there. It is directed at the gnawing suspicion that some of those negative stereotypes about groups of color really do explain why they were not able to achieve greater wealth. As you read, you might think back to the footrace metaphor and key concepts discussed earlier: for example, the "racial other," racial ideology, social closure, and invisible knapsacks full of either white privilege or concrete blocks of race discrimination. Mark, if you will, all of the ways the information below contradicts the cultural scripts used to impugn the intelligence, values, and work habits of people of color in order to justify their economic circumstances. Notice the agency and "counter framing" of people of color resisting oppressive white racial frames (e.g. Feagin 2010; Chou 2012).

The facts are that racial–ethnic groups actively denied full participation in U.S. economic and political life fought vigorously to improve their lot. Against nearly insurmountable odds, American Indians, whose lives and culture were under attack, and enslaved Americans of African descent, who were "real estate" or chattel, continually searched for ways to break down the brick walls and jump the hurdles put there to give the white colonizers a chance to sprint past them.

Native Americans would find ways to cultivate the increasingly inferior land onto which they were pushed as their numbers dwindled. They adapted to unfair and harsh government dictates with tenacity and creativity (Dunbar-Ortiz 2014). Even slaves, whose bodies were turned into white property, their every move controlled closely, found ways to resist. Many adroit slaves played into owners' compulsion to view their slaves as happy and compliant in order to "shroud their subversive plans" (Takaki 2008: 107).

Violence

Enslaved Africans and embattled American Indians fought back frequently and consistently against the white colonialists. They fought for their lives and their land, for the freedom to chart their own paths, to preserve their values, to claim their humanity, and to ensure a better future for their children. In 1606 indigenous people successfully fought off an attempt by Samuel de Champlain to establish a colony in Massachusetts. The next year Abenakis helped to expel the first settlement of the Plymouth Company in Maine (Loewen 1995).

Sometimes indigenous groups who had been enemies would band together to try to root out the English intruders. Metacom's War (often referred to as King Phillip's War) is perhaps the best known of these offensives to take back land, crops, and the right to live in peace. Young Wampanoag males were ready for battle, refusing to accept the previous losses of their fathers. "Unwilling to face a life-time of submission to an alien culture and rankling with the thought that so much had been sacrificed in order to accommodate the white invader, they girded themselves for battle. Revitalization of their culture through war was probably as important a goal as the defeat of the white encroacher" (Nash 1974: 125)." During the battle, which began in 1675 and lasted over a year, the Wampanoag sachem Metacom and members of several other indigenous groups attacked 50 Puritan towns and completely destroyed 12 of them, killing 5 percent of the New England population.

American Indians, their black slaves who historians say were accepted as equals, and independent former slaves joined forces in the "longest and most expensive of all Indian wars against the government" in the so-called Seminole Wars. Government authorities tried to separate Indians from Africans. In 1818 President Monroe ordered Andrew Jackson (an army general at that time) and 3,000 troops to "crush the Seminoles and retrieve the Africans among them" (Dunbar-Ortiz 2014: 102). "The Indian chiefs contemptuously refused the bait and reaffirmed their commitment to their black allies" (Bennett 1975: 105). The second war erupted after the U.S. took over Florida and tried to force the Seminoles, along with many other indigenous groups, west of the Mississippi. According to Bennett (1975: 105) the main reason the war went on so long was the participation of blacks, whose lives were positively intertwined with those of American Indians, including through marriage. Though some Seminoles were forced to Oklahoma in 1832, the Seminoles "were never conquered" and their descendants remain in the Everglades today (Nash 1974; Dunbar-Ortiz 2014: 102).

There were many, many slave revolts – some small, some aborted, but each one was an attempt to secure freedom at all costs. One historian identified two hundred and fifty planned or accomplished rebellions by enslaved blacks (Aptheker, 1983: 67 cited in Feagin and Feagin 2011: 171). Perhaps the most famous was organized by Nat Turner against Virginian plantation owners in 1831. Indigenous people, whose numbers had been decimated by disease as well as war, and slaves, whose every move was watched carefully, were outmatched by the whites. They suffered swift and serious recriminations. But they went down fighting.

Some of the violent resistance against slave owners came from individual slaves reacting to the immediate circumstances of their oppression. They burned crops and destroyed animals, machinery, and farmhouses. They killed their owners and themselves (Bennett 1975; Feagin and Feagin 2011; Marable 2000). Slaves who tried to escape were tortured as a threat not only to the runaway but also to anyone else who might be thinking about it. Yet slaves often tried to escape. From memoirs, diaries, letters, and newspapers we have eyewitness accounts of the depraved brutality at the heart of slavery. The accounts of torturous punishment are bone chilling and stomach wrenching. Sometimes just staying alive was an act of resistance.

Education at all Costs

Most white plantation owners prohibited slaves from learning anything beyond what would enhance profit. Slaves who tried to learn to read and write did so knowing they would likely face punishment and that it could be brutal. Given that white culture painted people of African descent as animalistic and incapable of learning, one might wonder why it mattered whether they tried to learn? The answer, of course, is that slaveowners recognized the falsity of their claims. They knew that slaves had the potential to better themselves, which would interfere with the economic benefits derived from owning a source of labor that knew of nothing else. Formal and informal norms forbidding slaves to study or learn were a form of social closure.

The story of Frederick Douglass' life demonstrates that there were whites who made a positive difference in the lives of slaves, and that other whites made it difficult for them to do so. Whites were constrained from helping to blur the race hierarchy through law, social norms, intimidation, and violence. Douglass' story also shows that getting a glimpse of life off the plantation was important. It was when he was moved to a master in Baltimore that Douglass learned of the possibility of freedom from white workers there and used his contact with poor white boys as a conduit to learn to read and write. Though Frederick Douglass was clearly an exceptional person, we have no idea how many more "Douglasses" would have emerged if they had had similar formative experiences.

The Extraordinary Education of Frederick Douglass

According to Frederick Douglass (1845), who escaped slavery and would eventually write about his life, learning mattered because whites knew that knowledgeable slaves would not be as easy to control. New to her position as a slave owner, Sophia Auld, the wife of an early master in Baltimore, helped young slave Frederick Douglass to learn to read simple words. But when her husband found out, he ordered her to stop. Douglass, he said, "should know nothing but to obey his master – to do as he is told to do." If Douglass were taught to read, he argued, "there would be no keeping him. It would forever unfit him to be a slave." Young Frederick continued to educate himself, though he was watched carefully for any sign that he was trying to read. Sophia, settling into her life as a slave mistress, would angrily confiscate anything she caught him reading.

Even though he was very young, Douglass understood from Mr. Auld's words that knowledge was connected to freedom and he set about with tremendous determination to learn as much as he could. He carried a book and bread with him when he went out, and he made friends with the poor white boys he encountered. Young Frederick got the boys to teach him to read in exchange for bread. At the shipyard in Baltimore, Douglass studied the 4 or 5 letters that were used to mark boards. He recounts: "when I met with any boy who I knew could write, I would tell him I could write as well as he. The next word would be, 'I don't believe you. Let me see you try it.' I would then make the letters which I had been so fortunate as to learn, and ask him to beat that. In this way I got a good many lessons in writing, which it is quite possible I should never have gotten in any other way." When Frederick was a little older, he attended a Sunday school, run by a young white man, for slaves who wanted to learn to read the bible. But after a few lessons a group of men, headed by two community leaders "came upon us with sticks and other missiles, drove us off, and forbade us to meet again."

Later Frederick would be sent to a "slave breaker" who whipped him weekly, worked him unmercifully, and broke him temporarily: "my intellect languished, the disposition to read departed . . . and behold, a man transformed into a brute!" Douglass did eventually escape, of course, and passed on this important eye witness account of how the institution of slavery kept an entire group of people from developing the most basic elements of human capital.

Organizing and Speaking Out

In the fight for economic opportunity, "racial others" were also working to overcome the stereotypes that justified their exclusion. History is full of examples of activists from all racial-ethnic groups who struggled to change white opinion or law – from the periods of indigenous genocide to slavery, through recent U.S. history.

Frederick Douglass went on to prominence as an abolitionist and a political leader. His keen intellect was evident in poignant writing and electrifying oratory. He was an advisor to President Lincoln during the Civil War, working to convince Lincoln that slavery was the real reason for the war (King 1968). Frederick Douglass also fought for women's rights and helped pave the way for blacks to gain the right to vote.

Black women played vital roles in the abolition movement. As intersectional and critical race perspectives emphasize, black women's position at the nexus of race and gender oppression gave them a uniquely perceptive view of the two systems. Though the words and actions of Harriet Tubman and Sojourner Truth are now well known, there were many others who made their voices heard, whether in large venues or small church meetings.

Maria M. Stewart was a domestic worker who is reported to be the first woman of any race to speak publicly to a group of men and women. In addition to speaking out against slavery she also wrote for *The Liberator*, a newspaper founded by white abolitionist William Lloyd Garrison. Frances Ellen Watkins Harper was renowned at the time for anti-slavery speeches given with "passionate eloquence and musical voice." A white contemporary wrote of Watkins: [she] "speaks without notes . . . Her manner is marked with dignity and composure" (Flexner 1959: 97). Mary Ann Shadd Cary was free, but fled to Canada after the 1850 Fugitive Slave Act which prompted whites to kidnap free blacks and sell them in the south as runaways. Cary published her own newspaper *The Provincial Freeman* and traveled back to the states periodically to give speeches (Flexner 1959: 98).

In Philadelphia Grace Douglass, her daughter Sarah Mapp Douglass and several women from the Forten-Purvis family were among the founding members of the Philadelphia Female Anti-Slavery Society. They worked with white feminists such as Lucretia Mott and the Grimké sisters: organizing, writing, and giving speeches. They also urged white organizations to embrace black abolitionist viewpoints. This women's society broke through cultural scripts and social practices constraining women's activity and voices. It "emerged as an aggressive, persistent force "(Sumler-Lewis 1981: 283).

Sarah and Angelina Grimké were rich southern white women who abhorred the violence and degradation of slavery they witnessed on the plantation and in the community where they were raised. They went into exile in the north out of desperation and as public protest against slavery (Lerner 2004). Because of their second-class gender status, the many white women who fought against slavery were limited in what they could accomplish as abolitionists. They realized they had to fight for women's rights in order to make more headway (Lerner 2004; Amott and Matthei 1991).

Historians show that the founding fathers and the women around them grappled with the hypocrisy in their fight for freedom while they steadfastly denied it to others. Abigail Adams wrote to her husband John in the autumn of 1774: "It always appeared a most iniquitous scheme to me to fight ourselves for what we are daily robbing and plundering from those who have as good a right to freedom as we have" (Aptheker 1993: 98). In the end of course, the framers of the Constitution put aside any qualms and institutionalized race hierarchy. There in the Constitution of the new republic, white superiority is affirmed and the humanity of blacks and American Indians is erased. DuBois provides a fascinating historical footnote: the first draft of the Declaration of Independence "harangued King George III of Britain for the presence of slavery in the United States." ([1924] (2009: 61).

David Walker, who was born of a free mother and a slave father in North Carolina, published an influential work on the topic. This is a paragraph from it:

> Do you understand your own language? Hear your language proclaimed to the world, July 4, 1776 – 'We hold these truths to be self-evident – that ALL men are created EQUAL!! That they are endowed by their Creator with certain unalienable rights; that among these are life, liberty, and the pursuit of happiness!!! Compare your own language above, extracted from your Declaration of Independence, with your cruelties and murders inflicted by your cruel and unmerciful fathers and yourselves on our fathers and on us – men who have never given your fathers or you the least provocation!!
>
> "Now Americans! I ask you candidly, was your suffering under Great Britain one hundredth part as cruel or tyrannical as you have rendered ours under you?
>
> (DuBois [1924] 2009: 73)

Slowdowns and Other Hidden Resistance

On the sugar plantations of Hawaii Japanese employees would slow down their work pace, hide from their supervisors' view, and even pretend to be sick. Some would drink soy sauce to raise their temperatures (Takaki 2008). A particularly savvy slave woman feigned a longstanding illness in order to make dresses to sell to other slaves (Walker 1998: 69).

Mexican and African American laborers who toiled in fields and on plantations were often labeled as lazy or unintelligent by the whites who sought to gain from their labor. Yet their different work patterns were the result of resistance to the demands and value system of the Europeans (DuBois [1929]; 2009; Glenn 2002). The laborers valued family and relaxation; they did not necessarily feel the need to prove their worth through work the way the Europeans did. Why, they might wonder, was that such a great way to approach hard physical labor under harsh working conditions? Nor were they interested in contributing to the profits of bosses who treated them as machines. The hoe was a common tool in Africa, but some slaves refused to use it properly (Walker 1975). DuBois said of those whose labor was most exploited: "All observers spoke of the fact that the slaves were slow and churlish; that they wasted material and malingered at their work. Of course they did. This was not racial but economic. . . . They might be made to work continuously but no power could make them work well" (DuBois [1935] 1992: 40).

There were many ways that men and women working in factories resisted their exploitation by greedy owners and malevolent supervisors. Nannie M. Tilly (1948) told of black women in tobacco factories who, forbidden to associate with one another, would communicate through songs – the lyrics of which were often critical of their working conditions (Glenn 2002: 135). Others protested through sabotaging equipment, stealing material, not coming in for work, and using company time for their own use or enjoyment, among other tactics. These acts of resistance were also used by working-class whites, but they did not have the same connection to civil rights. There is evidence that a collective understanding of race-based oppression infused the labor activism of workers of color. For example, in tobacco factories when black women who were stemmers could not keep up with the pace, the black men (called handlers) who sent them the tobacco would pack the baskets more loosely (Kelley 1993: 90).

The types of resistance available to oppressed race groups helped feed stereotypes of people of color as lazy or unintelligent (Kelley 1993; Glenn 2002). As Kelley notes, however, groups of black workers would demonstrate a strong work ethic when it seemed that it might improve their work lives – proving the stereotypic slow and lazy "Sambo" image to be a response to circumstances rather than the innate quality that white elites depicted it to be (1993).

There is much historical evidence that blacks and other maligned "racial others" were willing to do whatever it took to lift themselves to a better economic place. The next sections provide a glimpse.

Leaving

During the period of contract labor in Hawaii, many Japanese laborers left for the mainland as soon as their contract was up; others fled beforehand, in the hope of evading agents sent by owners to bring them back (Tamura 1994). After the 1857 decision in the Dred Scott case confirming that blacks were without rights, thousands moved to Haiti, Canada, and Mexico (Sterks 1972). As soon as there was a glimmer of opportunity in other parts of the United States, blacks vacated the racially oppressive labor markets of the south. During the Great Migration periods of the early to mid twentieth century, approximately seven million African Americans journeyed to the north, midwest, and far west in search of better jobs for themselves and better education for their children. Many emigrated to Africa or the Caribbean for the same reasons, as well as the chance to live in a place where Africans and African Americans had power (Kelley 1993: 95; Franklin 1997).

Labor Organizing

Amid hostility from employers and the white workers who were struggling against those employers, many groups of color created organizations to help one another and to fight for work equity. When early immigrants from China and Mexico found themselves locked out of most white labor unions, they organized themselves. Chinese garment workers, for example, created guilds patterned after those in their home country. They were successful in gaining greater job security protections and almost double the wages from both white and Chinese employers (Amott and Matthaei 1991: 197). In the early part of the twentieth century, Mexicans developed mutual benefit societies, challenging discrimination in the courts and instilling pride in Mexican culture (Gutierrez 1995).

Though capitalists fomented divisions among different racial-ethnic groups, they were sometimes thwarted by those who saw through these tactics and recognized the common plight of workers who were not considered white. For example, shortly after the establishment of the Brotherhood of Sleeping Car Porters in 1925, the

Pullman Company replaced African American attendants and cooks with Filipinos, relegating the group who had been train attendants for 50 years to lower status porter positions. The initial reaction of the Brotherhood was to try to have the Filipinos removed, but they came to recognize that the Filipinos were being used as a wedge and made it known they had no animosity toward them. A statement proclaimed that the Filipinos "have been used against the unionization of Pullman porters just as Negroes have been used against the unionization of white workers." The Brotherhood invited Filipinos to join with them to secure better wages and working conditions for both groups (Posadas 1982: 363; Okihiro 1994).

The national Congress of Industrial Organization in the south typically required local affiliates to include blacks, who were "encouraged to participate in local union decisions" (Marable 2000: 35). The United Mine Workers Union set a standard for ensuring that whites shared leadership with blacks and it was emulated by a few other southern unions (Tindall 1967; Marable 2000).

Writing in 1935, a white organizer for the Southern Tenants Farmers' Union noted that they had 10,000 members, half of whom were African American and that some of their best leaders were black. During their eight months of organizing, he reported, "we have had practically no friction within the union over the race question." He went on to point out that blacks' experience in churches and community organizations proved very useful in running effective meetings, while whites' Ku Klux Klan activity had not provided "training in correct procedures at meetings." He went on to say that white sharecroppers had begun to realize they shared a common lowly position with blacks:

> The only explanation I have for sharecroppers joining our interracial organization who used to show their race prejudice by being members of the night-riding K.K.K., is that they have learned that both white and Negro sharecroppers are the victims of the same system of exploitation. . . . Both races have been driven down to a low economic level of bare subexistence. The white sharecropper also is discriminated against and insulted.

Organizers successfully persuaded both whites and blacks that if either group organized separately, the plantation owners would evict the race group that organized and replace them with the other. "In spite of terror," the organizer wrote, "the Union grows" (Rodgers 1935: 168).

Strikes, Protests, and Boycotts

Though employers had many more resources at their disposal, often including the backing of the federal government, workers from all racial-ethnic groups fought for safer, more humane working conditions and reasonable wages. The odds were against them. Still, many labor organizations were formed and there were many successful strikes and protests.

In Puerto Rico, whose land and economy was taken over by the United States in 1898, workers created a strong labor movement to fight the low wages and inferior work that ensued. Puerto Rican women and men created the *Federacion Libre de Trabajadores* (Free Labor Federation) in 1899. The ensuing loss of agriculture required women to work alongside men in low wage factory jobs. This led to more egalitarian views about women, which in turn helped to spur men and women to fight jointly for better work lives. Women leaders were not uncommon in the Puerto Rican labor movement (Rivera 1986; Amott and Matthaei 1991: 46).

In the 1930s Puerto Rican needle workers in Mayaguez went on strike. As was a common employer response to strikes, the police were called in and the women who were striking fought back, hurling stones at the police officers and the factory. The bravery and militancy of the women inspired other workers and led to a lot more union activity, and a year later more than 75 percent of garment workers had union representation (Amott and Matthaei 1991).

Though Asian immigrants were stereotyped as meek and compliant workers, they have flexed their collective muscles throughout U.S. history. Approximately 7,000 Japanese workers were involved in a major strike in 1909. They were fighting aggressively against the backbreaking labor conditions and paltry wages of their work on the Hawaiian sugar plantations. Plantation owners pressured the government to arrest the strike leaders and hired workers from other racial-ethnic groups; after four long months, the Japanese workers went back to the plantations. However, they came back to higher wages and a system that no longer paid them less than those from other groups (Takaki 2008: 243–4). In the 1980s Chinese and Korean women took their grievances to the streets of New York City, pushing for the protections of a union contract which was ultimately ratified. They gained job security as well as pension and medical benefits (Amott and Matthei 1991: 213).

African Americans have a very long history of creating resistance groups. Immediately following the end of the Civil War, freed blacks began to fight for their rights as workers (Bennett 1975). During the Depression a group of black tenant farmers in Alabama organized the Share Croppers Union with the assistance of the Communist Party to fight widespread evictions that were part of New Deal policies (Allen 1969). Even isolated black domestic workers in the south united early on to fight the capriciousness of their employers and low wages of their jobs, though the collective nature of the many individual acts of resistance or sabotage were hidden from their employers. They coordinated their actions and established lists of employers to be avoided (Kelley 1993). The organizing of black workers did periodically force changes in the unequal distribution of work and wages by race. Blacks were especially successful at strike activity in the jobs in which they were segregated (Glenn 2002).

An example comes from the tobacco industry where black women and men tobacco workers worked under extremely harsh plantation-like conditions. Black women had the worst situation; they endured sexual harassment as well as segregation in the most tedious tobacco work of all. As Mrs. Harris, a leader in the movement in Virginia said, "It took me just one day to find out that preachers don't know nothing about hell because they ain't worked in a tobacco factory." When the Tobacco Stemmers' and Laborers' Industrial Union went on strike in 1938, they were joined on the picket line by members of the white garment workers union. As Mrs. Harris reported, the (white) police officers were "salty as hell" that white women were "out here parading for black women," but they did not intervene (Holt and Brown 2000: 227).

During their conflict with the British-American Tobacco company, the Tobacco Stemmers' and Laborers' Union listed, among their key demands, that workers be addressed with the title of Mr. or Mrs. instead of their first names or the racial put-downs and epithets which sprang from slavery and Jim Crow era norms (Fletcher and Agar 1987). Through organized protest, African American workers were working to undo the continued dehumanization of blacks emanating from the racial hierarchy and white racial frames.

Writing in the 1970s Newman emphasized the success of the over two million black trade union members, a small group of whom formed the Coalition of Black Trade Unionists to bypass the constraints of an organized labor movement that did not fully represent them. Newman argued that all "black unionists had won themselves a privileged position" and "expanded job opportunities for all black workers" by establishing that black workers were entitled to pay scales and benefits that had been formerly reserved for whites (1978: 58).

Mobilizing for Migrant Workers

Mexican Americans Dolores Huerta and Cesar E. Chavez were young when they cofounded the United Farmworkers of America to improve the work lives of Mexican and Filipino migrants on the west coast. One tactic they used was to put pressure on legislators. For example, when Ronald Reagan was governor of California he vetoed (3 times) a bill that would give farm workers insurance. The UFW leaders organized farmworkers throughout California to help put supportive legislators into office. In 1975 the legislation passed (Aledo and Alvarado 2006).

Chavez and Huerta are perhaps best known for organizing a national boycott of table grapes and Gallo wine in the late 1960s. Their goal was to gain the right to union representation in order to secure better wages and working conditions. According to one estimate, seventeen million Americans were participating in the boycott in 1969. The boycott was considered a success when many companies gave their workers contracts (Global Action Nonviolent DataBase 2016).

There would be other boycotts to follow and much more work to do, but the young Mexican Americans had the nation's attention. Interviewed in 2006, Huerta noted her pride in having helped to get migrant workers medical benefits and unemployment insurance as well as cleaner and safer working conditions (Aledo and Alvarado 2006).

More recent labor history shows that workers who appear to have little leverage against powerful capitalists still take action to try to improve wages and working conditions. In the 1990s workers of Guatemalan origin who had been actively recruited by plant officials were being paid less than promised in high-injury, dehumanizing working conditions.

Workers staged a "militant campaign" for union representation at a poultry plant in North Carolina. Though their employer responded aggressively, they went on a series of strikes, picketed company sites in other states, and protested in front of the Bank of New York, the company's biggest source of loans. They won a union election. The company fought back and "refused to bargain in good faith." North Carolina was (and still is) a right-to-work state, which typically signals a hostile environment for unions. After six years, the union left, but the workers continued to fight for safe and humane working conditions. There was another union vote in 2005, which did not succeed.

Most recently, Guatemalan workers have joined with whites and Asians in work stoppages, petitions, and fighting against unfair labor practices, such as the firing of leaders of the stoppages. Their resistance has met with some success; the lines were slowed down, and more workers were added to facilitate breaks and safety (Gonzalez 2001: 146; Risso 2010).

Psychological and Additional Forms of Hidden Resistance

People of color have also used many less visible forms of resistance to the injustices built into the U.S. employment system. There have always been people of color who have found ways to climb over or knock down the brick walls in their way. They have ripped off the labels attached to them by dominants. Many developed their own understandings of their racial position and multiple strategies for dealing with racism in labor markets and workplaces. Sometimes they would withdraw, sometimes try to educate others; sometimes they would confront, and other times they would seek redress even if it seemed futile (Feagin 2010).

People whose intelligence and character were maligned to justify closing them out of decent jobs have always engaged in what DuBois called double consciousness, seeing clearly how they were viewed by white employers and co-workers but knowing full well that the images were false. This often meant wearing "the mask" or hiding their true feelings and selves to protect themselves from exploitation, workplace bias and racial harassment. This theme threads together the lives of "mammies" who pretended to be happy slaves (though note that many did not), domestics who did not respond overtly to their dehumanization by white housewives, and top professionals who "got along" though they felt their second-class status (Rollins 1985; Bell and Nkomo 2003; Collins 2000). It has often meant summoning the strength to keep from acting on feelings of rage. Many people of color rely on a similar range of strategies to cope with racism at work today (Feagin 2010; Durr and Wingfield 2011).

As Patricia Hill Collins argues, psychological and other private forms of resistance are likely just as important as "visible confrontation with institutional power" in a white racist system (2000: 217). Using the example of African American women, she points not only to their rejection of negative stereotypes or "controlling images"(p.216) but also to the work they did in their homes and communities to lift up their group and undermine structures of oppression (p.219). The history of black women's clubs and associations documents the variety, continuity, and passion of activity aimed at community uplift (e.g. Giddings 1985; White 1999). Whether they worked for the abolition of slavery, women's suffrage, or education for their children, black women activists were working for the economic freedom that had been denied to their families and communities.

As they fought for economic opportunity, "racial others" had to fight the racial ideology that justified their exclusion. There is a rich history of such activism, from the periods of indigenous genocide to slavery and throughout U.S. history, in the fight for equality of opportunity. For instance, in post-abolition America black women spoke out with eloquence and insight about how the job of domestic servant set them up to confirm the negative stereotypes used to confine them to such work. They noted that the jobs in private homes put young women's "virtue" in jeopardy, which was then used to reinforce the white view that black women were loose, amoral, and untrustworthy (Giddings 1985; Landry 2000).

In 1893 speakers Fannie Barrier Williams and Anna Julia Cooper felt compelled to address the topic before an overwhelmingly white audience. Cooper said it was not that young black women succumbed to temptation; instead the issue was "the painful, patient, and silent toil of mothers to gain title to the bodies of their daughters" (Giddings 1985: 87). Williams underscored white men's sexual violence toward black women, a theme echoed later when she wrote:

> It is a significant and shameful fact that I am constantly in receipt of letters from the still unprotected women in the South, begging me to find employment for their daughters . . . to save them from going into the homes of the South as servants as there is nothing to save them from dishonor and degradation.
>
> (Giddings 1985: 87; Landry 2000: 59)

During the 1960s women and men from all racial-ethnic groups fought against the systemic racism that stereotyped and marginalized them, excluding them from the economic equality that could only come from racial equality and justice. They did so in small acts of resistance that accumulated in large-scale social movements. Those who led the Black Civil Rights Movement, the Chicano Civil Rights Movement, the Asian American Civil Rights Movement and the American Indian Movement used the power of their words and actions to mobilize for large-scale and immediate change. Victory was not assured, and progress was not steady, but all of those who participated in movements for racial-ethnic equality made a difference.

ENTREPRENEURSHIP AND THE MODEL MINORITY MYTH

Entrepreneurship has often provided a way to sidestep the race-based biases of employers and the race-based antagonism of white co-workers. Racism in the workplace strengthened, and has been strengthened by, racism in neighborhoods throughout U.S. history. Thus many people of color started small businesses in their communities providing the services and products that their neighbors could not get easily elsewhere.

Among the early waves of Chinese immigrant men kept out of decent jobs, there were many who became independent contractors or set up their own businesses. They were able to bypass the low wages and harsh working conditions of agricultural, mining, railroad, and factory work by crossing into industries associated with women. Chinese men capitalized on the shortage of domestic servants in California by opening hundreds of small laundries, for instance (Amott and Matthaei 1991: 199). Writing at the time, Chin Foo Wong noted that men who could avoid the laundry industry did so, because of "fear of losing their social standing" (Wong 1888 quoted in Takaki 2008: 185). As a by-product of their entrepreneurial success, stereotypes of Asian men as being "too feminine" were reinforced.

Entrepreneurship has proved much more viable for some racial-ethnic groups than others (Waldinger, Aldrich, and Ward 1990; Light and Rosenstein 1995). As Max Weber emphasized in his classic work, aspects of white Calvinist religion encouraged the accumulation of wealth and therefore entrepreneurship. Portes and Bach (1985) stress that the cultures of the large waves of Jewish immigrants who arrived in the late 1800s and early 1900s likewise emphasized accumulating capital and seeking out business opportunities. Some racial-ethnic groups had better access than others to start-up and growth capital, small business role models, and a steady supply of reliable and reasonably priced labor.

Entrepreneurs who served as intermediaries or "middlemen" between whites and the "racial other" were particularly successful in industries such as retail, personal services, restaurants, and banking. According to "middleman minority" theory (Bonacich 1973; Bonacich and Modell 1980), variations in both cultural practices and sojourner status explain why some racial-ethnic groups more often responded to a lack of good jobs by establishing businesses, propelling their families into the middle class and beyond.

They went to the United States expressly to make money and return home – and provided goods and services to other groups, who like them, were considered the "racial other." They would fill in for the white man, distributing their goods or providing services (such as collecting rent) to segregated communities (Bonacich and Modell 1980) while those of European ancestry worked for pay or ran businesses in white areas. The middlemen helped whites to maintain the boundaries around whiteness, reinforcing racial segregation and difference in the process of propelling themselves up the economic ladder.

Many "middleman minorities" did not return to their countries, of course, and as immigration patterns and the statuses of racial-ethnic groups changed, the concept of the "ethnic entrepreneur" emerged (e.g. Light and Rosenstein 1995). While "the middlemen" tend to come from a different ethnic group and neighborhood than their customers, ethnic entrepreneurs operate in "ethnic enclaves" where recent immigrants from their group cluster.

There are still business owners serving as middlemen today, yet they are far less likely to be sojourners with strong ties to their homeland than was true for the groups about which Bonacich wrote. For instance, there are many Korean shop owners who serve predominantly African American and Latino groups in New York City and Los Angeles.

The middleman entrepreneur is another version of the wedge role that Asians have traditionally filled on the race hierarchy. As long as the face of capitalism is Chinese or Korean, for example, the Puerto Ricans, Dominicans, or African Americans they serve vent their frustrations at those groups, rather than the systemic racism that keeps them from similar successes. Ethnic entrepreneurship is also thriving among some groups. Cuban entrepreneurs in Miami who operate successful businesses in areas where Cubans predominate (though they are increasingly joined by other Latino ethnic groups) are perhaps the quintessential example (Douglas and Saenz 1999).

While self-employment has been critical to the success of some Asian and Latino groups, it has been less useful for others. A study by Herring and colleagues (2002) showed that black and Mexican entrepreneurs made less money than comparable members of their respective racial/ethnic groups who worked for pay. Yet among whites, it was the entrepreneurs who had higher personal incomes than the wage workers. Some Latino groups, such as Cubans, have been far more successful at business ownership than Mexicans and, especially, Puerto Ricans (Stepick and Stepick 2002).

Model Minorities

Asian and Cuban entrepreneurial success has been central to the myth of the "model minority." This is a key construct that supports the American dream, or the ideology of meritocracy, making the racial hierarchy seem natural and logical. Opinion-makers hold up the success of Korean, Asian Indian, and Cuban entrepreneurship and suggest that other racial-ethnic groups could be successful if they were willing to work as hard or if they had more business savvy in their cultural DNA. They reason from *outcomes* rather than causes or context.

The case of Cuban entrepreneurship in Miami provides an important corrective to this kind of thinking, when it is put in sociohistorical *context*. The first generation of Cuban immigrants to Miami enjoyed exceptional success. The elite or "Golden Exiles" (Portes 1969) from Cuba grew the first businesses in what would become a thriving ethnic enclave economy. The Golden Exiles were from the upper tier of society bringing skills and resources with them. They were the first to arrive in the United States because they had the most to lose from the socialist revolution. They were able to offer employment to later Cuban arrivals from more modest backgrounds and to support budding entrepreneurs. The entrepreneurs and their counterparts in the professions established themselves as the most successful Latino group in U.S. society (Portes 1969; Stepick and Stepick 2002).

But Cuban exceptionalism is not only the result of the skills and capital this group of immigrants brought with them. It is *also* because they were received willingly. As political exiles from a socialist country they enjoyed a warm welcome from the U.S. government. Those first Cuban immigrants benefited from programs aimed at disadvantaged racial-ethnic groups. Because of their advantaged backgrounds, they were poised to compete effectively and to make the most of these benefits. More than any other immigrant group, the Cubans received direct and indirect assistance, from small business loans and contracts to laws that encouraged bilingualism (Pedraza-Bailey 1985; Stepick and Grenier 1993). They also profited from the fact that they were viewed as white (Stepick and Grenier 1993). They had both the ancestry (mostly European rather than African or indigenous ancestry) and the resources to be viewed more as another white ethnic group than as "near black."

It has been more difficult for the racial groups without the resources of the Cubans to use entrepreneurship to propel them into the middle class and beyond. However it is certainly not because of cultural deficiencies as some suspect. The fact that there were early entrepreneurs even among the non-capitalist American Indians and many examples of thriving enterprise in traditional indigenous communities belies the conclusion that their culture is not compatible with business ownership (e.g. Champagne 2004; Deloria 1998). Extensive research on African Americans and entrepreneurship also reveals the falsity of such arguments (Bennett 1975; Butler 2005; Walker 1998). African-Americans have typically had strong interest in starting their own businesses, and their start-up rates in the past several decades have been higher than those of white men and women (Butler 2005).

Instead, the difficulties for the "non-model minorities" lie in resource deprivation, the fact that they were not accepted as middlemen and that the enclaves (reservations and ghettoes) where they have been concentrated are some of the poorest in the country. Among African Americans, even middle-class small business owners are continually hampered by structural obstacles, mingled with aversion and hostility on the part of consumers, as well as outright discrimination (Butler 2005). The most successful businesses are well capitalized, and African Americans have less access to capital than whites because of persistent economic disadvantage. Many small business start-ups are self-funded or draw from community pots of money, the scarcity of which is a legacy of generation after generation of discrimination (e.g. Oliver and Shapiro 2006).

Recent figures show that black business owners are charged a higher average interest rate on their loans than is true for white owners (Hu et al. 2011). Another study showed that if credit lines for African Americans were determined in the same way as for whites, their lines of credit would more than double (Henderson et al. 2015.) The historical record shows a strong current of entrepreneurship among the two groups at the bottom of the racial hierarchy.

African American Entrepreneurship

The original entrepreneurial activity of blacks in the United States was the purchase of their freedom. The first African Americans were keenly aware of the necessity of securing their own economic liberation and engaged in entrepreneurial activity well before slavery was abolished. They built businesses despite laws and local sanctions, including violence, prohibiting such initiative. They engaged in enterprise even when they were prohibited from learning to read or write or gather together. Throughout history entrepreneurs saved for family and community, to build and support churches and schools (Walker 1998: xix).

Craftsmen and artisans, many of whom had brought their skills from Africa, were most able to use profits from their own labor power to secure their freedom (Walker 1998). Still, there were people like Free Frank, who had nothing but his ability to do hard physical work on the plantation. He became a slave entrepreneur hiring out his own time, returning some of the profits to his owner, and keeping the rest. During the War of 1812 Free Frank established a mining and manufacturing business that became very successful. He also managed his owner's farm and established his own. Though his second owner charged a hefty sum, Free Frank made enough money to purchase his wife's and then his own freedom (Walker 1998: 59).

Women slaves were also successful entrepreneurs. According to a study of Petersburg, Virginia, increased white hostility and new legislation in 1806 made manumission (the freeing of slaves) more difficult, particularly for women. When women were freed during this period it was usually because of their own efforts. For example, Jane Minor gained her freedom after caring for prominent citizens during an epidemic in 1825. She did not stop there, however, using her medical talent to become the most successful black emancipator in Petersburg, Virginia (Lebsock 1984: 96). Aletha Turner sold produce from her own garden in Washington, D.C.; some of her customers were major political figures of the early nineteenth century. Though it took twenty-five years, she used her profits to purchase freedom for herself and twenty-two others (Walker 1998: 69).

After slavery ended, African Americans continued to open businesses even though new laws and ordinances were created to keep them out of industries in which they had gained a foothold. Many black entrepreneurs provided services to prosperous whites. The number and variety of black-owned businesses in the post Civil War south speaks volumes about the creativity, intelligence, and work ethic of black men and women. They had to muster "a shrewd and calculating tenacity" (Walker 1998: 103; 151) because of the white social closure that confronted them at almost every turn. With the advent of Jim Crow laws separating blacks from whites, black-owned businesses catered to "their own" and flourished. The number of businesses owned by blacks doubled between 1900 and 1914 (Marable 2000: 144).

In the early twentieth century national leaders such as W. E. B. DuBois and Booker T. Washington urged a kind of ethnic entrepreneurship, encouraging the development and patronage of black-owned businesses. To combat the economic oppression that kept blacks from achieving their true potential and their fair share, DuBois urged African Americans to construct a self-supporting economy. "We can work for ourselves. We can consume mainly what we ourselves produce, and produce as large a proportion as possible of that which we consume" (1986: 1237). They were joined by local leaders. After a major "race riot" in Chicago in the summer of 1919, Minister Lacey Kirk Williams encouraged his congregants to quickly "build up our own marts and trades so we can give employment and help to provide against such a day as we are now experiencing" (Spear 1967: 221). Washington established the National Negro Business League and both he and DuBois supported education for future business leaders. Their efforts clearly bore fruit, as the period from 1900–1930 is considered the golden age of black business (Walker 1998), which was also a period of extreme segregation (Marable 2000).

The lie in the cultural scripts that depicted blacks as less than human and whites as morally superior is perhaps most evident in the story of what has been called Black Wall Street. In 1921 the Greenwood neighborhood of Tulsa, Oklahoma was a thriving business and cultural community. Enterprising blacks had taken the opportunity offered by Tulsa's oil boom and their successes created an area that was "modern, majestic, sophisticated, and unapologetically Black" (Pickens 2013). The streets were lined with banks, theaters, libraries, newspapers, hotels, and nightclubs. There were two hospitals and a better school system than those in nearby white districts. Original footage from resident Solomon Jones at Yale provides a rare glimpse into African American prosperity during overtly racist times. (You can see what Solomon Jones captured on film at: https://www.youtube.com/watch?v=wi79YfLRqmE.)

Then it all disappeared in a matter of about sixteen hours. Mobs of angry whites, reportedly assisted by government forces, burned businesses and homes to the ground. Thousands of African Americans were instantly homeless and police arrested the majority of blacks who lived in Greenwood though there were few or no white arrests. The official (white) description of the incident was that it was a "race riot" but the evidence, some of it relatively recent, suggests that it was "a terrorist attack on an affluent black neighborhood" (Weber 2016).

The reason the story is so illustrative is that Greenwood residents rebuilt their community (Ellsworth 1982). After having been burned out of homes and businesses, robbed of their belongings, arrested, placed in internment camps, and policed by angry whites, black Tulsans rebuilt. Despite active sabotage on the part of white leaders, black Tulsans rebuilt. Many were prohibited from rebuilding on their own land. White leaders denied them money offered by sympathetic communities and organizations. A coalition of whites decided that the city should purchase what remained of Black Wall Street to build a railroad station. Whites blamed black Tulsans for the riot which justified, in their minds, the harsh treatment of these thriving property owners who had homes and livelihoods – millions of dollars' worth – yanked away from them (p.94).

Yet the once-thriving black community rose from its literal ashes. They did so, as African Americans have always done, by relying mostly on themselves (p. 103). A black law firm successfully fought the ordinance that would have permitted the land appropriation. The Greenwood residents used their own funds (some deposited in white banks, some loans from other communities) and their own labor to create, in the words of eyewitness Henry Whitlow, "an even more prosperous" business district. He reported new developments including a Greenwood Chamber of Commerce, a directory of black businesses, and a black-owned bus system (p.108). Greenwood prospered until the 1950s when highways and "urban renewal" pushed most black residents further north and desegregation diluted the economic and social strength that came from spending within one's community (Ellsworth 1982; Weber 2016; Montford 2014).

American Indian Entrepreneurship

Native American Indians engaged in entrepreneurship almost from their earliest encounters with the white colonialists. They became dependent on the goods the Europeans traded, leading some to have to hunt for furs to have enough to swap. Yet if European traders increased the number of goods they would trade for a fur, it did not compel American Indians to hunt for more furs to get more goods; instead, they would bring in fewer (Uhler 1951; Champagne 2004). During the height of the fur trade from about 1600 to 1840, there were no major entrepreneurial figures. Even Native American middlemen did not accumulate profit, purchasing only enough to get what they needed from a trading post (Champagne 2004: 314).

In the late 1800s Navajo women in the southwest created woven items to supplement the family income which came from tending sheep. Historians estimate that 100,000 Navajo women produced one million textiles. The woven goods, including rugs and saddlebags, fetched a hefty price for the white traders who brought the goods to market (Fixico 2006: 18).

There have always been American Indian entrepreneurs who responded to the constraints placed on them by the U.S. government by making a go of participating in "mainstream" capitalism rather than staying tied to their tribal lands. As Champagne (2004: 316) notes, after the Indian Territory governments of the Cherokee, Choctaw, Chickasaw, Creek, and Seminole were abolished in 1906, many entrepreneurs moved out of tribal affairs and into the heart of Oklahoma business arenas. In succeeding years, most American Indian entrepreneurs built their businesses off the reservations.

At the same time, what Champagne calls "tribal capitalism" has also developed. For example, the Mississippi Choctaws are highly successful manufacturers. Their businesses are profit-making and market-oriented, yet the tribal government manages the jobs and the profit for the benefit of the entire community. This type of entrepreneurship does not collide with, but instead upholds, the goals and values of American Indian nations (2004: 323).

According to Vine Deloria (1988: 21–2), the American Indian groups who stuck to native ways have generally been more successful at entrepreneurship than those who tried to adapt to the dominant white value system. As evidence, he points to the Pueblos of New Mexico who have preserved traditional ways of life and have integrated college-educated generations into the community. The result has been large-scale development projects and "a sense of tribal purpose and solidarity." He also discusses four groups of successful southwestern Apaches who adhered to their traditions and did not have high rates of education. "Without the benefit of the white man's vaunted education, these four Apache groups have developed their reservations with amazing skill and foresight" (p. 22). He notes their lucrative ski resorts, shopping centers, cattle farming, and tourism.

In 1988 gambling became legal on American Indian lands and casinos have been one of the most successful ways for Native American communities to develop economically (Jorgensen 2000; Champagne 2004: 310). Casinos are not a panacea. They may undermine Indian culture and create other problems. At the same time, casinos provide an ethnic niche for American Indian employment. There is also some evidence that the gaming establishments have a "multiplier effect," spawning additional economic opportunity for American Indian nations. Those involved report that revenues are used for higher education, infrastructure, medical facilities and a safety net for the poor (Jorgensen 2000: 102–3). The law that made gambling possible protected American Indians from control by non-indigenous corporations or organized crime bosses who might have felt kickbacks.

Perhaps the greatest testament to the success of American

Indian-owned casinos is that more states have legalized gambling on non-indigenous lands. This poses a serious threat to thriving American Indian establishments. As they have had to do throughout U.S. history, American Indian nations are fighting the encroachment of whites on their territory. Too many casinos in a region will seriously undermine profits. Capitalists who want to get in on gaming pose additional obstacles to American Indian economic development. As one example, a white casino developer challenged the Wampanoags' right to land in Massachusetts they claimed was owed to them by the federal government as he sought to establish a casino twenty miles away (Brennan 2016). But in New York the Schaghticoke Tribal Nation teamed up with "gambling giant" MGM Resorts International to protest the awarding of rights to the development of a third casino in nearby Connecticut to two nations who already have casinos there (Gosselin 2016).

As this discussion shows, American Indian economic development is closely tied to self-determination, while lack of economic success is a result of the wider economic and political context in which American Indian access to capital and jobs has been severely restricted (Jorgensen 2000).

Economic Contributions

Evelyn Nakano Glenn (2002) has written that the United States is the only rich nation that got that way by relying heavily on the labor of people from three non-white continents: Africa, Latin America, and Asia. People of color built infrastructure and facilitated the rise of industry. Slavery was an extremely lucrative enterprise, protected by the government, which propelled the United States into a major force in the industrial world. Whilst their land and labor was being squeezed by powerful white male capitalists to create tremendous profits, women and men of color (and white working-class women and men) were fighting for a fairer price for their labor power. They also battled for humane and safe working conditions.

Despite the racism that permeated every aspect of society, people of color created goods and services that improved lives and made money. We cannot know the true extent of their achievements, as racism limited their chances of getting their products made and put on the market. For example, whites often held patents for items that were invented by blacks. White elites "borrowed" ideas, strategies, and items from indigenous people as well, without request or attribution.

Thus the list of items invented by people of color is surely underestimated. George Washington Carver is one of the best known of the early African American inventors. He was taught to read and write by a white woman named Sally Carver who, along with her husband, raised George and his brother when their mother was kidnapped. Carver developed hundreds of products from peanuts and sweet potatoes; the most famous, of course, was peanut butter. Garrett Augustus Morgan is known for inventing both the traffic signal and the gas mask. You may have heard of Madame C. J. Walker, who invented a line of beauty products during the early twentieth century, catapulting her to millionaire status.

But did you know that African-American men and women were the inventors of an internal combustion engine spark timer, lawn mower, rotary engine, flag-making equipment, railway switching device, car coupler, locomotive smoke stack, and elevator? How about patents for a golf tee, egg beater, envelope seal, window cleaner, folding bed, portable pencil sharpener, umbrella stand, bicycle frame, and horseshoe? These are only some of the many items credited to African American inventors during the 1800s, when the institution of slavery was thriving or recently abolished, and racism was encoded in law (Butler 2005; Wilson and Wilson 2003).

Benjamin Banneker was a self-educated contemporary of Thomas Jefferson who published a book full of useful scientific facts for farmers. Jefferson was reportedly so impressed with "Banneker's Almanack" that he sent it to French scientists. Banneker, who also included anti-slavery essays in the almanacs, counseled Jefferson to work for abolition. He was living proof of the falsehood of the racial ideology used to justify the enslavement of fellow black Americans. He argued that Jefferson, who was a slaveholder, should "readily embrace every opportunity to eradicate that train of absurd and false ideas and opinions which so generally prevail with respect to us [African Americans]." Banneker made the point to Jefferson that if more blacks were free, there would be many others who could make key contributions to society (Katz 1995: 42–3).

American Indians are perhaps best known for the many crops they cultivated. They also created leisure activities now enjoyed by many: canoeing, ball games, lacrosse, snowshoeing, and tobogganing. They made many impressive discoveries in medicine, dental hygiene, and contraception. The Iroquois Great Law of Peace was used as an example for the U.S. Constitution (Keoke and Porterfield 2002; Dunbar-Ortiz 2014).

Evocative evidence that the depiction of American Indians as backward and uncivilized was fabricated comes from the historical record of life before the British colonizers arrived. There were farms, towns, nations, and networks of roads. American Indians had set up various forms of government and had "sophisticated philosophies of diplomacy" as well as international policies. Had it not been for the civilization of indigenous nations, the European colonists likely would not have survived (Dunbar-Ortiz 2014: 46). Instead, the British "stole already cultivated farmland and the corn, vegetables, tobacco, and other crops domesticated over centuries, took control of the deer parks that had been cleared and maintained by Indigenous communities, used existing roads and water routes in order to move armies to conquer, and relied on captured Indigenous people to identify the locations of water, oyster beds and medicinal herbs" (Dunbar-Ortiz 2014: 46).

American Indians made noteworthy contributions to the infrastructure of the northeast by developing an occupational niche in the steel industry. Mohawk ironworkers began in 1886 as menial day laborers transporting materials to the site of a railroad bridge. But they moved up, figuratively and literally, to work on the bridge; many were hired by the company. The Mohawk "skywalkers" quickly gained a reputation for their skill at this dangerous work (and they were eventually joined by other Iroquois – the Onondaga, Seneca, and Tuscarora). Skywalkers contributed their talents to many well-known high steel projects; a short list includes the Empire State Building, the George Washington Bridge, the Triborough Bridge, the Henry Hudson Bridge, the World Trade Center, the Waldorf-Astoria, and also San Francisco's Golden Gate Bridge (Fixico 2006: 21–2). They continue to do this work today.

Our brief look at agency and initiative on the part of people of color ends here. There were people from every racial-ethnic group who resisted their exploitation in big, public ways and small, almost invisible ones. There were also people from every rung of the race hierarchy who became capitalists themselves, bypassing the harsh and unfair labor system, and sprinting more easily toward achievement of the American dream.

"Racial and ethnic entrepreneurship" has been celebrated and criticized. Prominent writers and orators have pointed out that ownership often requires exploiting one's own and one's family's labor and treating co-ethnics only marginally better than they would be treated by whites. Further, it creates the adoption of a capitalist mindset in solidarity with white elites, helping to perpetuate race and class inequality. Thus entrepreneurs of African descent could also be considered a model minority, separate from poor or working-class blacks (Marable 2000). Though DuBois saw the benefits of black entrepreneurship, for instance, he also urged owners to work toward economic uplift for all African Americans, rather than seeking maximum profit (Marable 2000: 147). In the 1960s Martin Luther King Jr. echoed DuBois when he voiced concerns about a capitalist system that bred excessive materialism and extreme poverty (Harding 2010).

The intertwined histories of exploitation and resistance, of white racist practices and people of color's perpetual resistance, activism, and initiative, are the backdrop to race and work patterns in the twenty-first century. Contemporary race and work patterns will be investigated next.

4

The Past is in the Present: Persistent Work Inequalities

Many popular pundits, talk radio personalities, and internet posts give the impression that people of color are getting jobs and promotions more easily than whites. Perhaps that is why research reveals that many whites believe they are at a disadvantage in labor markets and work settings (Bonilla Silva, Forman, Lewis, and Embrick 2004; Norton and Sommers 2011; DiTomaso 2012). People point to affirmative action, vaguely understood as everything from quotas to hiring an unqualified person of color over a white candidate. Yet careful and detailed studies show that affirmative action – typically making an effort to get people of color into the candidate pool – has not reversed white advantage in employment (e.g. Reskin 1998; Harper and Reskin 2005; Pincus 2003). For all of the talk of affirmative action as reverse discrimination, whites still have advantages at every stage of the labor process.

There has certainly been progress toward greater racial equality at work. The Civil Rights Act of 1964 made it illegal to continue the race-based employment discrimination that had permeated the American labor market up to that point. People of color gained access to occupations that had been closed to them by whites, and their wages increased. The Equal Employment Opportunity Act in 1971 brought substantial gains in employment, particularly for African Americans, making it possible for them to get further along in the footrace to economic success than ever before.

Yet exemplary research studies show race-based inequities in: getting a job; the types of jobs, industries, and occupations available; income and earnings; promotion opportunities; likelihood of being fired; and quality of work life. Recent large-scale changes in the number and types of jobs available have disproportionately hurt low-income people of color. Further, laws are only effective if they are enforced, and the will to do that has waxed and waned, even over the past several decades.

This chapter is divided into two parts. The first begins with an overview of racial-ethnic patterns relating to jobs, occupations, and workplace dynamics, and then turns to some timely topics that require significant critical thinking. The second section focuses on poverty because contrary to popular depictions of lazy poor people hanging out in their neighborhoods, the majority of able poor people of working age are in the labor force. They are disproportionately from racial groups other than white.

PART 1. RACIAL-ETHNIC PATTERNS: KEY INDICATORS

Deriving the many benefits of paid work in U.S. society is impossible if you do not have a job at all. In addition to income, jobs are linked to health insurance, childcare, parental leave, and retirement accounts. Our discussion begins, then, by considering whether race matters to getting a job.

Access to Jobs

Unemployment

Unemployment statistics are often in the news because they are an important measure of a country's economic health. Race-ethnicity has long played a key role in who gets the jobs and who has to keep pounding the pavement. Because "unemployed' is defined as actively seeking work, unemployment figures typically mask the severe lack of opportunity of American Indians and young African American and Puerto Rican men, in particular (Tinker and Loring 1991; MacLeod 2009; Austin 2013a;2013b). There are untold numbers of so-called "discouraged workers" who have given up trying to meet employers in the labor market to exchange their labor power for wages and are therefore no longer counted as unemployed.

Even so, studies consistently find that African Americans, Latinos, and American Indians have higher unemployment rates than whites (e.g. Ritter and Taylor 2011; Couch and Fairlie 2010; Kim 2012;

Austin 2013b). Recent figures show an 11.5 percent rate for Latinos compared to 7.9 percent for whites (U.S. Department of Labor 2012). Starting in 1940, the unemployment rate of blacks has hovered at double the rate of whites (Fairlie and Sundstrom 1999; DeSilver 2013). Analysis of data from Current Population Surveys from 1989–2004 showed that the probability of moving from unemployment one month to employment the next was 29.4 percent for black men aged 25–55 compared to 33.6 percent for their white counterparts (Couch and Fairlie 2010). In 2011 black men *with some college or a two year college degree* were almost as likely to be unemployed (13.1%) as white men *without a high school degree (12.7%)*. (U.S. Department of Labor 2012).

Women are a major component of the unemployed in each racial-ethnic group; for example, women are 46.9 percent of the black unemployed, 43 percent of the white and 41.9 percent of the Latino unemployed (U.S. Dept. of Labor 2012). These figures go against cultural norms that continue to emphasize mothering and family as women's responsibility, particularly among some Latino groups (Browne and Misra 2003). As discussed, when men from their race and class groups cannot find "good enough" jobs, women are propelled into the labor market.

Analyses of American Community Survey data showed that between 2009 and 2011 across 34 states, there were "large, very large, or extremely large" disparities in the employment rates of American Indians compared to whites. The author showed that even when they are similar to whites in age, sex/gender, education level, and marital status, American Indian odds of being employed are 31 percent lower than the odds of whites (Austin 2013a: 13). During the recent severe economic downturn known as the Great Recession employment rates declined nationally but the decline among American Indians was *four* times greater. The author of the report concluded that American Indians *typically* live under recession economic conditions, with impacts four times as harmful as the Great Recession's overall effects on whites (Austin 2013a: 5).

A Bureau of Labor Statistics report (DeSilver 2013) has an interesting finding that is a reminder of how important it is to interpret statistics *in context*. The author notes that during the entire period for which the Bureau of Labor Statistics has collected useable data by race, the smallest discrepancies in unemployment rates between blacks and whites came in 2009, during the Great Recession. Does that mean that the country was moving away from white advantage in hiring? Were there programs to make sure that blacks did not bear a disproportionate burden? No. According to the author, this pattern reflects the fact that white unemployment rose so high so fast that it narrowed the gap slightly. More whites were joining blacks in the unemployment lines. However, it did not represent an improvement for blacks who continued to be unemployed at higher rates than whites.

The unemployed – especially those perceived to have the fewest marketable skills – accumulate economic and human capital disadvantages that often lead to chronic unemployment or underemployment. Though many unemployed workers do find new jobs, they often pay a price. Research suggests a 20 percent lifetime earnings loss for the unemployed (Davis and von Wachter 2012; Brand and von Wachter 2013). Older workers, those who have to change industries to find jobs, and those who experience several job losses will have larger or more significant earnings deficits (Brand 2015). During their longer periods of unemployment compared to whites and Latinos (U.S. Dept. of Labor 2012), African Americans are accumulating disadvantage.

Underemployment, including involuntary part-time work and jobs below one's skill level, is also faced disproportionately by African Americans, American Indians, and some Latino groups (DeAnda 2000; Slack and Jensen 2002). Studies comparing women of Mexican origin to Anglo women revealed higher rates of underemployment even when people with similar backgrounds and jobs were compared (DeAnda 2000; 2005). The disadvantages of unstable work histories cumulate as it is difficult to move from underemployment to better jobs (De Anda 2005). Unemployment reduces both psychological and practical readiness for work and diminishes human capital. This makes it unlikely that an employer would choose an unemployed over a similar employed worker (cf. Diprete and Eirich 2006: 287).

Though the economic downside of unemployment and underemployment is obvious, there are social, physical, and psychological losses as well. Researchers are still trying to pinpoint the causality, but losing or being unable to find a job is associated with high stress, depression, anxiety, low self-esteem, and more visits to the doctor (Brand 2015).

Not only is it easier for whites, as a group, to find jobs, but it is also easier for them to keep their jobs. There is strong and consistent evidence that whites are more likely than blacks to be evaluated positively by their supervisors (Roth et al. 2003, McKay and McDaniel 2006) and that Latinos and blacks are more likely than whites to be fired unfairly (Hodson 2001; Zwerling and Silver 1992). These findings emerge even though researchers control for skills and organizational position. For instance, among the possible contributing factors that Zwerling and Silver controlled were human capital, job tenure, title, disciplinary actions, and absenteeism; yet blacks were twice as likely as whites to be fired.

In 2002 the popular national salon chain Supercuts settled a $3.5 million complaint that upper level management had directed regional managers to fire (and fail to hire) black employees in order to "balance the platform." The suit was brought by a white manager who had overseen seventy-six stores in three states and Puerto Rico. He was fired when he refused to follow the directive (EEOC 2003; Fleischer 2003).

Studies of racial discrimination cases have found many instances in which people of color were fired for actions or inactions identical to those of white co-workers (Roscigno 2007; Ortiz and Roscigno 2009). Mong and Roscigno's analysis of Ohio cases identified a practice of holding blacks to more stringent performance standards and then firing them for failure to comply. They also found cases in which "on the job" training was withheld from blacks who were then fired for incompetence. One black construction worker got permission to take a day off yet was fired for doing so (2010: 11–1 2). In Fresno, California the Farmer's Insurance Exchange settled a lawsuit brought by two Hmong (southeast Asian) employees who were fired for improper coding although employees from other racial-ethnic groups who used the same coding kept their jobs.

A white employee who testified in the Farmer's Insurance case was also fired. When the suit was settled, the director of the Equal Employment Opportunity's Fresno Office made a statement praising the claimants who "had the courage to come forward," noting that often those from "Asian and Pacific Islanders communities are reluctant to complain." She also emphasized that federal law "prohibits retaliation, and EEOC takes very seriously its mission to fight it." (EEOC 2016).

Simply being black is a risk factor for getting fired or laid off even from top echelon jobs. A study of men in management and supervisory positions, or "upper-tier occupations," revealed that blacks were much more likely than whites to be terminated – particularly if they worked in the private sector. Though blacks were also more likely than whites to be fired from public sector jobs, the rates and the gap were a lot smaller (Wilson and McBrier 2005). A study of layoffs further confirmed the importance of the race hierarchy to job security. Elvira and Zatzick (2002) found that whites were less likely to be laid off than people of color. Among the groups of color studied, Asians were significantly less likely to be laid off than blacks or Latinos. The latter two groups were most negatively affected by downsizing. Blacks were twice as likely and Latinos were one and a half times as likely to be laid off as Asians.

Job Seeking Studies

Matched pairs studies have provided compelling evidence that employer preferences for whites over African Americans, Latinos, and Asians are in play when they consider (or fail to consider) job applicants (Bendick, Brown, and Wall 1999; Pager 2003; Bertrand and Mullainathan 2004; Pager and Quillian 2005; Pager, Western, and Bonikowski 2009; Kang et al. 2016).

One of the most widely cited studies sent out nearly 5,000 identical resumés for both entry level and professional jobs. The resumés carried names that would typically be associated with whites or blacks to over 1,300 employers in Chicago and Boston. Candidates with "white names" had a call-back rate twice as high as those with "black names." When the researchers improved credentials on the resumés, this gave the "whites" a better chance (by 30%), but made no change in the chances of "blacks." Nor did the patterns change when the researchers sent resumés for professional jobs. Employers whose job ad specifically noted that they were an equal opportunity employer were not more likely to call back those with the black sounding names (Bertrand and Mullainahan 2004). The last three findings are particularly noteworthy in the context of complaints of reverse discrimination. They provide concrete evidence that employers are not jumping at the chance to bring in highly qualified black candidates, no matter what signals they might send about their interest in doing so.

Another widely publicized experimental study investigated how white and black job seekers would be affected by the negative "credential" of a criminal record when they applied for 350 entry-level positions. Sociologist Devah Pager (2003) paired young black and white men who were able to make good first impressions; they presented the same educational, work experience, and other background characteristics to employers. The finding that has been repeated most often is this: the race of the applicant was equally or more important than whether he had a criminal record. While 17 percent of whites *with* criminal records received a call back, only 14 percent of blacks *without* a criminal record got to this next step in the hiring process. Their "blackness" hurt young men's prospects for jobs almost as much as having a criminal record hurt whites. It is therefore probably not surprising that when black testers were given criminal records, they were less likely than similar whites to get a call after they filled out an application. Blacks believed to be ex-offenders were called back about one third as often as blacks without a record; whites with criminal records were called back about half as often as whites without a criminal record.

Some academics take issue with how well such controlled experiments match real life, suggesting that because real people have more than just a race designation, controlling for everything else overestimates the impact of race (e.g. Heckman and Siegelman 1993). We can quibble about how much emphasis to assign to some understanding of "race" as a single variable, but the salient reality is that of the race discrimination *system* (e.g. Bonilla-Silva 2006; Feagin 2006; Reskin 2012) which stacks the deck in favor of white people.

In the Occupation and on the Job

The historical overview of Chapter 2 showed that the creation of different labor markets and wage scales by race was a major way whites gained economic advantage over people of color. Even today, the kinds of jobs which labor process analysts have critiqued as alienating for the worker are filled with people of color. Entry level jobs in labor-intensive industries are typically physically demanding, with the pace of work and the tasks closely controlled by supervisors who have a lot of discretion (Newman 1999; Roscigno et al. 2009). It is hard to see the results of one's work or find meaning in its tasks. These jobs are also more likely to involve "dirty work," including cleaning up after other people. A common thread connecting such jobs is the lack of respect and low wages accorded to the people who do them.

In contrast, visible and "important" jobs are most likely to be held by whites. Whether at the top or the bottom of the occupational hierarchy, whites have a better shot at good jobs than people of color with similar credentials. In restaurants, waiters are more likely to be white, while African Americans and Puerto Ricans are more likely to be dish washers or bus boys. High-profile class-action discrimination suits settled against companies such as Abercrombie and Fitch in 2004 reveal companies' desires to have white women or men as the "face" of the company.

These processes operate even within companies such that whites are promoted more often and more quickly. The pattern holds at all levels of occupational and organizational job ladders (e.g. Rosette, Leonardelli and Phillips 2008; Moss and Tilly 2001; Stern and

Alienated Labor: The Walmart Associate

Many young people pass through the low-level jobs that people in the lowest social class positions get stuck in. This contributes to job segregation by race and class because the workers passing through are more likely to be white and middle class. Anyone who has ever had one of these jobs might relate to journalist Barbara Ehrenreich who found herself changed by her entry level "associate" job at Walmart (Ehrenreich 2001) – even though she knew it was temporary and she had the benefit of being white.

The new Walmart associate found the lengthy set of rules off-putting and mind-numbing. One tidbit: no jeans except on Friday and you had to pay $1 to wear them. Ehrenreich or "Barb" as she would become at Walmart, was surprised at how demanding and exhausting the job of organizing clothing turned out to be, both physically and emotionally. Her first task was to memorize the layout of her department, which took up between one and two thousand feet of space. When she finally had it memorized, she arrived at work to find that it had changed. She never had the satisfaction of completing a task, because as soon as she would get items put back in the right place there would be another pile of returns or discards from the fitting room to fill up her cart. Sometimes there was so much to do that things would back up at the fitting room, where the woman in charge could make or break Barb's day by what she put in her to-do cart. In her second week Barb was moved to another shift but no one told her; it was simply on the schedule.

Barb felt oppressed not only by the way her work was organized and controlled but also by the surface acting required of her; she was expected to be "ladylike," keeping her voice down and her vocabulary clean. She started hating customers and resenting co-workers. In her words: "What I have to face is that 'Barb', the name on my ID tag, is not exactly the same person as Barbara . . . Take away the career and the higher education, and maybe what you're left with is this original Barb, the one who might have ended up working at Wal-Mart for real if her father hadn't managed to climb out of the mines. So it's interesting, and more than a little disturbing, to see how Barb turned out – that she's meaner and slyer than I am, more cherishing of grudges, and not quite as smart as I'd hoped" (2001: 169).

Westphal 2007; DiTomaso, Post, and Parks-Yancy 2007). According to Yang's (2007) analysis of the 2001–2 California Workforce Survey, Latinos were less likely to receive employer-paid job training than whites, supporting the view that Latinos were relegated to "dead-end" jobs. Two thirds of a small sample (N= 187) of African American employees from various companies never got promoted by their organizations (Khosrovani and Ward 2011). The promotion advantage of white men is more pronounced in blue-collar than white-collar occupations and Latinos often have higher promotion rates than their black counterparts (Wilson and Maume 2014).

The U.S. Secret Service recently settled a longstanding race discrimination lawsuit brought by more than one hundred black agents, arguing that less qualified white secret service agents were routinely promoted over blacks (for the period 1995–2005). According to the suit, lead plaintiff Reginald Moore's bids for more than 180 promotions at the grade level just above his had been denied. Moore was also required to train a white agent who had been given one of the promotions he was denied.

A study of science and engineering jobs showed that U.S.-born white men were in the positions most likely to lead to promotion (DiTomaso et al. 2007). Another found that Asian American men supervised fewer employees (by 14%) than their white counterparts (Takei and Sakamoto 2008). Whites are more likely than their counterparts from other racial-ethnic groups to advance into leadership roles in their work organizations (Rosette et al. 2008).

While the number of women of color in management has grown significantly, they are more often found in positions on truncated job ladders. They are also more likely to be in departments with less prestige and limited access to the jobs that are seen as pivotal to movement up the corporate ladder. Finally, women and men of color are given tasks that match stereotyped employer views of their skill and interests, rather than tasks that match their own views of what they can and want to do. Americans of African and Asian descent are placed in management roles that have been "racialized"; these positions are not directly linked to economic outcomes and therefore have less status (Woo 2000b; Wilson and McBrier 2005; Durr and Wingfield 2011; Hiramatsu 2013).

Woo's (2000) in-depth study of an aerospace company discovered that while employees of Asian descent were well represented in professional jobs, there were no Asian Americans in upper management. It was even difficult for Asian Americans to get into key mid-level managerial jobs. Respondents emphasized a double standard. White men who were incompetent would be promoted over others and if they failed it would not affect the next white man who might be considered. In contrast, women and men of color and white women were scrutinized more closely and their group would be tarnished if anyone failed. Another study showed that although African American women leaders were judged more harshly than their male and white counterparts when companies were struggling, there was no difference in how they were viewed under conditions of success (Rosette et al. 2012).

Race, Ethnicity, and Gender

As Chapter 3 noted, the success of "ethnic entrepreneurship" rests partly on the exploitation of co-ethnic and other immigrant labor. Employers use networks to draw in workers from their own ethnic group. To keep labor costs down and their products or services at an attractive price, some owners skimp quite a bit on employee pay. If you have ever been to, or walked by, a nail salon, you may have noticed that the majority of technicians were of Asian descent. But if you are like most people, you probably did not think about their work conditions. I know I did not. The jobs in what researchers call "ethnic niches" are often dead-end, low paying, and unregulated. Modern versions of bonded labor persist as "entrepreneurs" sneak human labor into the United States for hefty sums that need to be paid back by the person smuggled in. An investigation of nail salons in New York City found systematic harsh treatment of employees including fees to obtain work, subsistence wages (as low as $10 a day), and verbal and physical abuse. There was also an ethnic hierarchy in NYC nail salons, which are disproportionately owned by Koreans; employees who came from other Asian and Latin American countries received the lowest wages and the harshest treatment (Nir 2015).

Gender and race-ethnicity intersect in occupational segregation to create particular niches. Thus, those nail salon technicians are mostly Asian women and domestic service jobs are largely filled by Latinas, while engineering jobs have high proportions of Asian American men. A reprint of an article written in 1986 was titled "Why Are There No Male Asian American Anchor*men* on TV?"(Fong-Torres 1995). The author noted that there were many Asian American anchorwomen on television news programs, so it seemed odd that men could not seem to attain these "glamorous" positions.

Fong-Torres provided a number of answers to his question, foreshadowing explanations in the next chapter. One pointed to differences in how women and men of Asian descent are defined in comparison to whites. Though there are commonalities in the stereotyping of Asian Americans, there are also some important differences by gender (Espiritu 2008). For the job of TV anchor, the definition of the Asian American woman as meek and exotic, as well as her attractiveness to white men, works in her favor. She pairs well with the white male anchor. Fong-Torres interviewed Asian American men who were reporters, and found they hit up against a ceiling because, as one put it, "a strong [Asian] man with authority and conviction – I don't think people are ready for that." Have we become ready? A look at local and national news anchors would provide a preliminary answer.

A ten-year comparison of major occupations for African American women (1990–2000) showed remarkable stability. They continued to be overrepresented in industries with large proportions of public employers. Care work provided expanded job opportunities but African Americans also increased their share of this type of service work instead of moving into better paying occupations (Parks 2010).

Raises, Wages, and Income

Many studies have shown that whites tend to get larger raises and make higher wages and incomes than comparable blacks and/or Latinos (Tomaskovic-Devey and Skaggs 1999; Browne et al. 2001; Grodsky and Pager 2001; Huffman and Cohen 2004; Yang 2007). A recent study showed increasing disparities in pay between blacks and whites since the mid 1990s (Rodgers 2008). Yang's analyses uncovered a gap in pay between people who identified as white compared to Latino, which was explained by human capital and job differences between the groups. The same study found that even when blacks had the same skills and worked in the same occupations as whites, however, they were less apt to get raises. Analysts have shown that occupations with high concentrations of Latino and black workers start out with lower pay and are more susceptible to wage erosion (Catanzarite 2002; 2003).

Research that takes a longer view of the black-white wage gap suggests that even if the gap does not show up at early stages of work trajectories, it may loom large later on. One exemplary study found little evidence of a black-white wage gap among men when they were young, yet uncovered a 14 percent difference when the men got to their forties (Tomaskovic-Devey, Thomas and Johnson 2005: 76). Another body of research suggests that wage gaps are underestimated because job seekers of color are less likely to get jobs. Western and Pettit (2005) concluded that high unemployment rates overestimated comparative earnings by somewhere between 7 and 20 percent; and by as much as 58 percent for young men (cf. Pager 2007).

Race disparities in wages respond to policy and economic developments. For example, wages of black and white women were comparable in the late 1970s. Yet the gap in wages between the two groups widened in the following decade (Bound and Dresser 1999), which included a major economic downturn and cuts in domestic spending. Young black women had made large relative gains in the post-Civil

Rights era, but their wages eroded during the downturn, and those losses persisted, even during later periods of economic growth. The wage trajectories of black women were flatter than those of white women, even among the college-educated (Dozier 2012).

Gender, race-ethnicity, and immigration status intersect to create pay discrepancies. For example, according to analyses of Current Population Survey data on the largest Latino groups, Latinas have lower wages compared to both white women and men from their ethnic subgroup. The same study found variation by country of origin. Cuban women had higher hourly wage rates than women of Mexican, Puerto Rican, Central, or South American origin. Yet even more detailed analysis revealed that Cuban women who were recent immigrants had the lowest average wages of all the Latina groups studied (Browne and Askew 2006: 235).

In the Workplace

Because U.S. employees devote so much time to work, those who have positive experiences reap a major benefit. Researchers have found that race privilege plays an important role here too, yielding a higher quality of work life for whites than for people of color working in the same industries, occupations, firms, and jobs. For example, white employees are supervised less closely than African Americans whether in low-level or high-status professional jobs. Whites in professional jobs have an easier time than their African American and Latino counterparts finding mentors to promote their work or groom them for advanced positions. Legal cases reveal a pattern of whites hoarding key positions, information, and social support (Feagin, Early, and McKinney 2001; Roscingo 2007).

Even in the twenty-first century, most workplaces are "white spaces" by default, set up with white employees and managers in mind. The "white racial frames" (Feagin 2010) used to guide organizational practices and govern workplace behavior draw from (elite) white cultural scripts, without necessarily recognizing them as such. Most of us do not think of workplace rules and spaces as racialized, no matter what our race-ethnicity, because we accept unmarked white practices as normative (Feagin 2010; Chou et al. 2012). Recall that the white advantage built into the guidelines for securing a plumb assignment is mostly invisible (Dyer 1997). People of color who want good jobs find themselves in organizations in which white "tastes, perceptions, feelings, and emotions and their views on racial matters" are the norm (Bonilla-Silva 2006: 104; Chou et al. 2012).

An innovative study of 250 randomly selected racial discrimination cases filed by African Americans and verified by the Ohio Civil Rights Commission, referenced above, found a variety of covert practices in work settings that lead to unfair advantages for white employees (Roscigno 2007; Light et al. 2011: 49). For example, a black professional working in mental health had a less than stellar portfolio because, as she put it, "high profile, high priority and well-funded projects were assigned to all white employees" (Light et al. 2011: 49). Other employees reported that they were not given pertinent information, which kept them from getting a promotion.

Whites, who are "racial insiders," are more likely to have access to information that is passed on informally such as which corners can be cut, which supervisors have top management's ear, and why other employees have been promoted or fired. Having a work position or social group that connects one to information and opportunity is important. As organization theorists emphasize, newcomers need information about the workings of their organizations as well as about their jobs in order to be successful and committed to their employer (Morrison 2002). When that information is more readily available to people from some racial-ethnic groups, it helps to preserve race-based advantages.

Gendered patterns in work dynamics such as likelihood of promotion have often been established using samples that were overwhelmingly white. Yet research has uncovered variations for people of color (Smith 2002; Watkins-Hayes 2009), highlighting the importance of including race in studies of gendered work processes whenever possible. As one example, Christine Williams' (2013) classic study of men in fields dominated by women found no evidence of the glass ceiling limiting how far women in occupations dominated by men can advance. Instead, the men she studied rode a glass escalator to the top of their occupational ladders. Yet Wingfield (2009) found no such glass escalator for African American men in nursing.

Hostility, Exclusion, and Harassment

Middle-class African Americans report hostile, isolating, and psychologically damaging work environments. They are often the targets of overtly racist comments and assumptions. Their white co-workers and supervisors test and taunt them, trying to draw out their anger

(Feagin, Early, and McKinney 2001). If blacks do respond with anger, this confirms the "controlling image" that they are unable or unwilling to rein in their emotions. Working in white-dominated spaces, African American professionals report that they have to keep their anger in check at all times. Yet they observe that whites have much more leeway to express their anger without repercussions (Durr and Wingfield 2011; Wingfield 2010).

Studies find that overt harassment is a common workplace experience for people of color – especially in lower level occupations (Feagin, Vera, and Batur 2000; Bruce 2006; Dietch et al. 2003; Dipboye and Halverson 2004). The pages of local newspapers provide examples of openly hostile treatment of American Indians, African Americans, Latinos, and Asian Americans. Co-workers or supervisors threaten, mock, and demean with words or actions and engage in verbal or physical aggression because of an employee's racial group membership.

Racial slurs, humiliation, and threats are common complaints in suits brought by the EEOC on behalf of Native American, Latino, and African American employees. The suits contain evidence of "egregious race-based hostility" in the workplace, posting of "racially tinged" materials in employee break areas, and "hangman's nooses" displayed in common areas or at work stations. Often the affected employees register complaints with "higher ups" who ignore, downplay, or mock their claims. While the co-workers and supervisors accused of bullying and racial harassment are often white, that is not always the case. A recently settled case at a California airport, for example, alleged that black, Filipino, and Guatemalan employees were the targets of "a barrage of harassing comments" from a Salvadoran co-worker who was promoted after the behavior was reported. As religion becomes increasingly racialized, there may be more complaints filed on behalf of Muslims. In April 2010, a construction company in Texas resolved a lawsuit claiming that a supervisor used "racially charged language" aimed at Hispanics, African Americans, and a Muslim employee who was called "terrorist," "Taliban," "Osama," and "Al-Qaeda" (EEOC 2015).

The researchers of the Ohio racial discrimination cases also found plenty of "old-school" racist actions; 26 percent of the cases filed involved offensive lists of jokes, mocking cartoons, and pictures on display, and the use of racial slurs within earshot of people trying to do their jobs. The researchers note that acts of open racial hostility were reported by both women and men in a variety of jobs. Because only very determined individuals with clear cut cases are likely to file with a Civil Rights Commission, such studies provide us with detail about the tip of the iceberg of race-based hostility (Roscigno 2007; Mong and Roscigno 2010).

Research and lawsuits also show that disrespect and hostility toward employees of color comes from uncomfortable or hostile clients and customers, adding yet another dimension of difficulty that is not faced by white counterparts.

Racial Bias in a High-Status Occupation

We might not expect to find much racial bias in a highly specialized profession such as physicians. After all, a physician is one of the highest status occupations in the United States, open to a select number and requiring rigorous training.

Yet national studies of physicians routinely report biases that make it easier for white physicians to do their jobs (Coombs and King 2005; Nunez-Smith et al. 2009). Recent data from a national survey of physicians showed that physicians of African descent were significantly more likely than whites to agree (or strongly agree) that "they feel they are under more scrutiny than colleagues" and also that they are asked to take on particular responsibilities because of their race-ethnicity. More than any other group, black physicians reported that patients have refused their care (Nunez-Smith et al. 2009). This takes a toll. In the words of one, "over the years, the inability of patients and others to believe that I am a doctor has left me utterly demoralized" (Lumumba-Kasongo 2006).

It is interesting that in the Nunez-Smith study, whites were far less likely than physicians from other racial-ethnic groups to agree that race influences their relationships with colleagues and yet more apt to say they are comfortable talking about race-ethnicity at work. If you think about the different experiences of the top and bottom positions on the race hierarchy, it makes sense that whites are less likely to see that race matters in all of their work relationships. Though it is common these days to hear whites say they are uncomfortable talking about race, there is clearly another dynamic at play in this case. Further investigation is needed to establish how occupations and workplaces shape whether people feel free to talk about race.

As the authors of the national study argue, the results are a reminder of the broad-based and longstanding legacy of racism in the United States.

Researchers note that women of color experience a unique form of hostility which they call *racialized sexual harassment*. This is a corrective to the substantial literature on sexual harassment at work, which has typically assumed a generic process based on samples of white women. Women of color experience harassment from men because of their sex/gender and from whites because of their race-ethnicity. A study of both racial and sexual harassment in five organizations from metropolitan areas found that women of color reported significantly more harassment than either men of color or white women (Berdahl and Moore 2006). Though some research studies using mixed race samples find similarities in sexual harassment across race groups, there is more research evidence that women of color have different and more frequent experiences of sexual harassment than do white women (Bruce 2006).

Sexual harassment studies (using white respondents) have shown that women are more likely to be harassed by men who have more workplace power over them. Yet women of color in positions of authority are also harassed by subordinates. For instance, black women in positions of power have reported significantly more harassment from subordinates than black men or white women (Rospenda, Richman, and Nawyn 1998). A group of black professional women from a variety of occupations reported being sexualized in the workplace by white women as well as men (Buchanan 2004).

Stereotypes about particular racial-ethnic groups affect the content of race-based sexual harassment. For example, the African American professionals were expected to play "the role of servant and seductress, regardless of their organizational rank." Their co-workers "believed they had the right to impose their ideas, beliefs, and curiosities on black women" in the workplace (Buchanan 2004: 304–5).

Woo's study of the aerospace company revealed a backlash from whites against those of Asian descent who made it into managerial positions. As one manager recounted:

> There was a young Asian female who was selected for [a certain managerial level] position. She got great pressure . . . from other applicants who were white males, who said "You just got it because of Affirmative Action. And you didn't get it because you could do the job . . . [but] because of some quota. . . . She called me and, you know, I was livid . . . This person had great experience, or else she never would have been selected. . . . I had to tell her . . . 'You had the credentials, you had the capability, you had the qualifying merit.'" (2000: 172)

Exclusion, degradation, and harassment of women of color has been found in studies across a range of jobs – from low-level female-typed jobs such as domestic and caretaking work (Hondagneu-Sotelo 2001; Duffy 2007) to male-dominated blue-collar professions such as policing (Texeira 2002) and firefighting (Yoder and Aniakudo 1997) to high-level, high-status professional occupations (Bell and Nkomo 2003; Hyun 2005).

Workplace incivility and harassment produce negative consequences for both the targets and the organization. It is not surprising
that those who experience racial-ethnic harassment have lower levels
of job satisfaction and report more job-related stress (Dietch et al.
2003). Research reviewed by Cortina (2008: 56-7) reports that companies suffer because targeted employees also report less commitment
to their work organization and greater intent to quit. Further, even
employees who observe incivility that is not directed at them report
more job burnout, lower organizational commitment, and a stronger
intent to quit. This holds whether they tend to see the world through
more positive or negative lenses, so the results cannot be attributed
to temperament.

There are a number of variables affecting whether there will be
discrimination against people of color in particular workplaces and
also whether employees perceive race-based discrimination. The
attitudes of supervisors, the company culture, the racial and ethnic
make-up of the people with whom one works most closely, and
the types of policies and procedures in place are all variables that
can enhance or diminish racial bias in the workplace (Hirsch and
Kornrich 2008).

PART 2. COMPLICATING THE STORY

Remember that our focus has been on general patterns. We all know
of or have heard of examples that do not fit even the most robust
social science findings (although sometimes we have heard from
someone else, so we don't know for sure about accuracy). Still, this is
a good time to repeat that not all people of color fare worse in labor
markets and work experiences than all whites of similar background
and experience. Whiteness does not make one immune from layoffs
or guarantee a well-paying job. Poor whites work in jobs that do
not pay enough to provide for their families. It is also important to
acknowledge that sometimes the biased beliefs or actions holding
back a particular person of color in the workplace are coming from a
person who is not white, but of a different racial-ethnic group from
the target. Recall, also, that everyone in U.S. society – no matter what
their racial ethnic group – learns what Feagin called white racial
frames. Even *within* a particular racial-ethnic group, there is often
a color hierarchy; those who appear closest to white European are
positioned at the top and accorded greater social status. This, too, has
consequences for work lives.

Colorism

People with widely different countries of origin and physical appearance are lumped together in the broad socially constructed race groups of "black" (African descent) or "Latino/a." Increasingly, researchers are investigating the effect of skin tone and phenotype within broad race designations.

Studies consistently show that employees who are closer to white in appearance (e.g. lighter skin) receive higher pay and have higher annual family incomes (e.g. Hersch 2008; Hochschild and Weaver 2007). Fine-grained analyses suggest the possibility that for blacks "lightness" confers a version of white privilege. Researchers showed that when they controlled for background characteristics such as human capital and neighborhood, the gap in pay between whites and light-skinned blacks was no longer significant. However, the wage gaps between whites and blacks with medium or dark complexions remained even when the other characteristics were similar (Goldsmith, Hamilton and Darity 2007: 707).

Using data from the New Immigrant Study of 2003, Hersch (2008) found that immigrants with the lightest skin color earn on average 17 percent more than immigrants with the darkest skin color, even after controlling for education, English language proficiency, occupation in source country, family background, ethnicity, race, and country of birth.

In-depth studies of a particular racial-ethnic group remind us that (1) race and ethnicity are not the same, (2) the race hierarchy is powerful, and (3) gender and race-ethnicity combine to create different outcomes. One study showed that Mexican Americans who were more assimilated to the dominant culture had higher earnings; however, this pattern only held for those with light complexions and European phenotypes (Mason 2004). Another found that Latina/os with lighter skin color were more likely to have jobs in higher-paying, racially integrated job sites, while those with darker skin were concentrated in lower paying jobs filled by other Latina/os (Morales 2008).

Legal scholars note that inter-ethnic discrimination has not been prosecuted because of the misguided belief that racially diverse workplaces are harmonious ones. Instead, there are many ways that subgroups of Latinos, for example, are complicit in social closure, participating in decision-making that excludes other Latinos or African Americans, while protecting whites and some Latinos from their own ethnic group (Hernandez 2010).

The experience of working in a co-ethnic workplace varies by perceived race in combination with gender and immigration status. Analyses of data from the Los Angeles Study of Urban Inequality showed that even when Central American and Mexican Latino immigrants are employed in co-ethnic work sites, those with lighter skin have higher earnings than those with darker skin. The wage deficit that comes with darker skin is even larger among immigrants, and women immigrants make less than native-born Latinas do (Morales 2009).

As stated in Chapter 3, some employers exploit their co-ethnic employees. Employment in a co-ethnic work site has been shown to depress wages and offer little upward mobility (e.g. Hum 2000). Yet one study uncovered an interesting exception. Morales (2009) found a gender gap in pay among the Latina/o employees in Latino co-ethnic job sites but having a lighter complexion translated into a wage *advantage* for women. This makes sense, given that women's appearance is so often considered to be important to their work. Though individual Latinas benefit, the emphasis on women's bodies rather than their skills, and the preference for light skin tones, perpetuates gendered racial bias.

Asian Privilege?

In 2014, TV commentator Bill O'Reilly made internet waves when he claimed that there was no such thing as white privilege, arguing that we should be talking about Asian privilege instead. His reasoning was that Asian Americans have higher incomes and are more affluent than whites. O'Reilly made the common mistake of using an outcome (overall income) as an explanation; evidence of higher incomes among Asians meant to him that they have an advantage over other racial-ethnic groups, including whites. He did not examine national income statistics critically, missing important counter-evidence. He also used the notion of race privilege incorrectly.

To make his argument that Asian privilege exists, O'Reilly would need to show that Asians dominate in corporate America, claiming top occupations by keeping whites and other racial-ethnic groups out. He would also need to show that when Asians and whites have the same credentials, Asians are more likely to get the job or the promotion. O'Reilly did not understand that a key component of race privilege is being considered on one's individual merits rather than being seen first and foremost in terms of race-ethnicity. Nor did he seem to comprehend that even the most accomplished person of Asian descent is not seen as fully American (Woo 2000b; Wu 2002; Thrupkaew 2002; Chou and Feagin 2008).

The empirical evidence does not support the notion that Asians have race privilege, as earlier sections indicated. It is certainly true that native-born Asian Americans have largely achieved economic parity with whites. The myth that Asian achievement somehow signals the demise of white privilege results from the omission of some key facts. First, Asian immigrants (largely from China and India) who arrived in the United States after the 1965 Immigration and Naturalization Act tended to be highly educated. The legislation listed priorities; after re-uniting families, the next priority was to bring in professionals and scientists of "exceptional ability."

The belief in Asian superiority (and the corollary that other race groups are inferior) is also perpetuated by the way statistics on income are typically presented. Average income masks variation in income among the many ethnicities lumped together in the Asian category. Political refugees who came from countries such as Cambodia and Vietnam brought fewer skills and resources, and thus were concentrated at the bottom of the occupational hierarchy. Even median household income is misleading, because Asian Americans often have more working adults under one roof than is true for other race and ethnic groups (Thrupkaew 2002; Woo 2000a; Wu 2002; Chou and Feagin 2008). Finally, national figures do not take into account that people of Asian descent cluster in some of the most expensive regions in the country; when region is taken into account, median incomes for Asians fall below those of non-Hispanic whites (Ong and Hee 1994).

Asian Americans appear to have socioeconomic parity with whites because they have *more* education, live in expensive places, and are more likely to be in STEM fields than the average white. Results of a carefully constructed study showed white men with an 8 percent earnings advantage over native-born Asian American men with similar credentials. The researchers explained that earnings of the 1.5 generation (who immigrated to the U.S. as older children) are comparable to white men with similar credentials largely because those of Asian descent enter lucrative fields. Asian American men who were not educated in the United States experienced a higher earnings disadvantage compared to whites (Kim and Sakamoto 2010).

The myth of Asian privilege assumes, further, that employees of Asian descent do not face hiring or workplace bias. However, this supposition is contradicted by research and first-hand accounts. Employees of Asian descent seek jobs and promotions in white spaces where their "otherness" stands out (Chou et al. 2012). There is an invisible "bamboo curtain" in many companies, keeping Asian Americans from getting to the top or being considered for certain kinds of occupations, as we have seen (Woo 2000a; Hyun 2005;

Kim and Mar 2007). Asian Americans are pre-judged as different from whites, as culturally Asian, and therefore as forever foreign – no matter how long their families have been in the United States or how much they assimilate (Kim 1999; Tuan 1998). They face the constraints of such views from potential employers, mentors, and co-workers, and if they internalize the stereotypes, from themselves as well (Chou and Feagin 2008). Asians, too, are more likely to get call-backs when they "whiten" their resumés; this holds true even when applications are sent to companies that claim to value racial and ethnic diversity (Kang et al. 2016). Though the negative bias faced by other racial-ethnic groups appears to be stronger, it is incorrect to assume that Asians carry an invisible knapsack of race privilege to the workplace. That is still reserved for whites.

The concept of the model minority introduced in the discussion of entrepreneurship plays out in employment as well. Though they started out as "near black" Asians ultimately became "near white," their intermediate position on the race hierarchy helping to preserve the boundaries around whiteness and keeping blacks anchored at the lowest rung (Okihiro 1994). The media holds them up as evidence that it is indeed possible for anyone to succeed in America (Osajima 1999). Despite their success, they are unable to pierce the boundary into whiteness, and thus share the designation of "racial other" with African Americans, American Indians, and many Latinos. As Chapter 2 showed, Asian Americans' intermediate position on the race hier-archy helped preserve white economic dominance throughout U.S. history. The mechanisms sometimes change, but their role has been remarkably consistent (Kim 1999).

The Upside of Bureaucracy

Bureaucracies often evoke negative feelings; trying to get through the rules and regulations – the proverbial red tape – can be annoying at best and crazy-making in an urgent situation. So it may come as a surprise that Max Weber, one of the major founding figures in sociol-ogy, argued for the superiority of bureaucratic work organizations. He extolled principles such as choosing officials on the basis of tech-nical qualifications, having chains of command and job requirements clearly spelled out, establishing stable rules that can be learned by and applied to everyone, and keeping written records.

The military is one of the best examples of a bureaucratically run work organization and studies show that African Americans and Latinos have achieved more work success in the military than in private companies (e.g. Moskos and Butler 1997). Lundquist's (2008) analysis of the Pentagon's Survey of Active Duty Personnel revealed that black men in the military had better occupational standing than whites (except in the position of officer). The military is certainly not a place we would expect people who are not qualified to be promoted, so it is unlikely to be the result of some reverse discrimination against whites.

Instead, the answer lies in the bureaucratic procedures Weber described; formalized procedures leave less room for the kind of race-based favoritism that allows whites to sail past equally or better qualified men and women of color. Of course seemingly race-neutral rules sometimes mask race advantage and procedures are only effective if people are willing to follow them. Furthermore, as an environment in which men and masculinity dominate, the military is also a place where women face racialized sexual harassment and violence. This is an extremely important caveat to the view of the military as a site of considerable racial equality.

Still, the military has come a long way from its days of race segregation. The U.S. army, in particular, made a comprehensive effort to rid its employment system of race discrimination, perhaps fueled by the need for qualified personnel when the armed services became all-volunteer (Reskin 2012). It made great strides fairly quickly (Moskos and Butler 1997; Moskos 1986). Dempsey and Shapiro's (2009) analysis of a 2004 survey of army personnel yielded no significant differences among whites, Latinos, and blacks in the enlisted ranks in: reports of racial discrimination, assessment of mentoring, perceptions of opportunity or faith in army leaders. The military also provides ample opportunity for its personnel to enhance their educational credentials, and Lundquist (2008) found that African American and Latino men and women were more likely to take advantage of this than white men.

As an institution that relies on authority and strict adherence to procedure, with tremendous control over its employees, the military system could be adapted relatively easily to new policies about race (Reskin 2012). When he studied the military in the late 1980s, Moskos contended there was a degree of racial equality that was rarely encountered in the larger society, though he acknowledged that racism had not been eliminated. Dempsey and Shapiro found a major stumbling block at the officer level, consistent with Lundquist's findings. Over one quarter of the Latino and African American officers they studied reported race discrimination. And, as Moskos acknowledged in reporting tank mechanic Specialist Williams Jones' words, "You can still bump into an invisible shield of racism, but you have to ignore it" (1986: 12).

These findings show that when systems are more equitable, more blacks and Latinos achieve. Bureaucratic procedures likely accomplish less in civilian workplaces because there (unlike in the military) much day-to-day interaction is outside the purview of formal rules (Vallas 2012). Still, public employment, known for its bureaucratic structures, has traditionally provided better work opportunities for those at the bottom of the race hierarchy than has private employment. This continues to be the case today (Parks 2010; Wilson and Maume 2014).

Reverse Racism

As noted at the outset of this chapter, it is common to hear whites complain about people of color taking their jobs. But the research evidence does not support that view. For example, Stainback and Tomaskovic-Devey (2009) show that in 1966 white men held almost all of the managerial jobs in the private sector – a whopping 91 percent – even though the 1964 Civil Rights Act called for an end to white men's monopoly on the best work opportunities. Their sophisticated analyses showed that black women and men gained greater access to managerial positions during the 1970s. Even though the trend toward greater black managerial representation stalled during the 1980s, it improved slowly in the 1990s. By 2000, the representation of women and men of color in managerial jobs showed a notable increase.

However, white men were still over-represented in managerial jobs. The researchers also found significant race/gender differences in *who* these managers had in their units. Black men were most likely to manage other black men and least likely to manage white men or women. Black women were most likely to manage other black women and least likely to manage black men (p. 812). How can these results be explained? The researchers conclude that the gains made by blacks who had formerly been kept out of managerial jobs came from an expansion of the service sector, not from wresting jobs away from whites.

Poverty, Unemployment, and Underemployment

Poverty is a major race/work issue. A substantial proportion of poor adults are working, and whites are less likely to be poor than all but a few (Asian) groups. Over the past twenty-five years, the racial gaps in poverty have diminished somewhat but the overall patterns remain remarkably the same. American Indians, African Americans, and several Latino groups (e.g. Mexicans, Guatemalans, Puerto Ricans, and Dominicans) have poverty rates more than twice the size of the poverty rate for whites. The groups at the bottom of the race and class hierarchies were affected most by economic downturns in 1979 and 1982 which led to the permanent loss of many manufacturing jobs. During the 1990s black and Latina women who worked and headed families were twice as likely to be poor as their white counterparts, and those with young children were three times as likely to be poor (Newman 1999: 42–3). These groups were also particularly hard hit by the Great Recession (Mather and Jarosz 2014).

The limits of Asian cultural "superiority" over other racial-ethnic groups are revealed by statistics showing high poverty rates for those of Cambodian, Laotian, Hmong, and Vietnamese descent. The poverty rates for Chinese and Korean groups are also higher than the rates for whites (Macartney, Bishaw, and Fontenot 2013). Poverty is also gendered; women are more likely to be poor than men within every racial/ethnic group (see Table 4.1). Single mothers are disproportionately poor because the jobs they can get do not pay enough. Unlike their white and middle-class counterparts, they cannot rely on the men in their lives to provide for them. The fathers of their children are often among the ranks of the unemployed (Edin and Kefalas 2011; Franklin 1997).

As noted earlier, the poor are often portrayed as lazy or irresponsible people who avoid hard work. Yet the facts paint a different picture. The majority of able poor adults are working and many more would work if they could find jobs. Poor job seekers often have to settle for "last resort" jobs; the ones that people with any other option reject. The low wage service sector in which

Table 4.1 Percentage of U.S. Adult Women and Men in Poverty by Race-ethnicity, 2014

	Women	Men
White (non-Hispanic)	10.8	8.1
African American	25.0	18.7
Hispanic	22.8	16.4
Asian American	12.2	10.7
Native American	25	20.3
Total	14.7	10.9

Source: U.S. Census Bureau. 2014 Current Population Survey. Annual Social and Economic Supplement

low-income workers cluster is characterized by strong managerial control and little investment in workers; policies and practices ensure that workers are easily replaceable. Low wages, "dead-end jobs," part-time hours, reduced fringe benefits, and frequent firing make it extremely difficult for many workers in such sectors to keep out of poverty. This is compounded by a feature of the United States that is rather unique. Benefits of citizenship in western European countries, for instance, such as health care, childcare, and parental leave have been largely managed by employers in the United States. The best paying jobs are also rewarded with the best benefit packages while those with the lowest paying jobs – the people who need the benefits the most – receive the worst benefits packages (Kalleberg et al. 2000). This privatization of social welfare benefits has become even more pronounced in recent decades, starting in the 1990s (Oliver and Shapiro 2007).

Researchers also point to an increase in what they call economic insecurity – a precarious position resulting from job loss, underemployment, and the risk of economic loss that accompanies unpredictable events (Western et al. 2012; Brand 2015). Those who have the most difficult time finding good jobs are also those who are hardest hit by adverse life events. It is considerably easier for whites than for some groups of color to move out of poverty. Sharkey's (2008) analyses of national data revealed that over 70 percent of African American children who grew up in the poorest quarter of neighborhoods studied were living in that same quarter as adults, compared to 40 percent of whites. The study also revealed that since the 1970s more than 50 percent of black families, compared to 7 percent of white families, have lived in the poorest quarter of neighborhoods for more than one generation.

There is a connection between poverty and incarceration, and there is overwhelming evidence of racial bias in the criminal justice system (e.g. Pettit and Western 2004; Blair, Judd, and Chapleau 2004; Alexander 2012). Incarceration is a main reason that it is particularly difficult for poor African Americans and Latinos to move into the working class. Research shows the negative impact of incarceration in the work lives of men, and increasingly women, from poor communities of color (Western and Pettit 2005; Heimer et al. 2012; Johnson and Johnson 2012; Western et al. 2015). Recall that having a criminal record made a bigger impact on the chances of black testers to get a job interview. The vicious cycle among poverty, a criminal justice system that targets poor people of color, and lack of good jobs is an important focus of the study of race and work.

The Intersection of Race and Poverty

In the 1980s Jay MacLeod (2009) did a small but exceedingly thorough participant observation study of the work aspirations of two groups of poor teen boys living in the same housing project. One group had given up on the American dream – in fact one of the boys called it a hallucination. These teens believed the economic system was stacked against them, so they focused instead on the values of their subculture which included hostility toward schooling, the importance of violence, theft, drugs, and the like. The other group of boys believed in the American dream. Raised in poverty, they were not quite sure how to achieve their dreams of good jobs and the happy families, nice cars, and homes in leafy suburbs that would ensue. However they were doing everything they could to achieve it, including trying to do well in school, developing good work ethics, and staying out of trouble.

The first group, who MacLeod called the Hallway Hangers, was made up of mostly white teens while mostly black teens were in the second group, nicknamed the Brothers. The white families had been in the projects a lot longer; they had little to offer the Hallway Hangers in the way of a roadmap to "mainstream" success. The study demonstrated how poverty can lead to prison time being more of a marker of manhood than a good job. It may be much easier to "go directly to jail" than it is to try to make it in labor markets that seem set up to exclude you from good jobs.

The study also showed that class is never the full explanation for poverty among people of color. At the end of the first phase of his study MacLeod wrote, "with a high school diploma, a positive attitude, and a disciplined readiness for the rigors of the workplace, the Brothers should be capable of landing steady jobs" (p. 198). MacLeod was surprised when he followed up with these young men seven years later. He found that the black teens' education, work experience, and positive work ethic had not yielded good jobs.

When some groups can more easily maximize their work potential than others, it affects not only their own lives, but those of their families and future generations. Because whites typically get higher paying jobs and because their parents and grandparents did also, they have greater wealth than African Americans, Native Americans, and some Latino groups, in particular (Hacker 2003; Hamilton 2006; Stainback and Tomaskovic-Devey 2009; Oliver and Shapiro 2006). Whites disproportionately pass on financial safety nets to their children. It might be in the form of a down payment on a house or car, help with rent or student loans, or money to tide their kids over between jobs. Oliver notes that in contrast, the overwhelming majority of black kids start their adult lives with no assets (Estrada 2007). In contrast, a disproportion of African Americans and American Indians in particular – but also some Latino and Asian groups – pass on poverty and the social ills that accompany it to their children.

The next chapter delves further into the social processes that explain major racial disparities in work opportunities and experiences.

5
Explaining Race Differences in Work Outcomes

People often try to explain the racial disparities just discussed by blaming the race groups who have been stuck at the bottom of job queues. Recently, a group of students reviewed data on race-based gaps in wages and promotions. Then a Chinese-American student asked, "doesn't everybody have a responsibility to try hard?," as classmates of various racial-ethnic backgrounds nodded in agreement. Many pundits and politicians also place the responsibility squarely on individuals, as any internet search of the topic shows. These are common reactions in a society that prides itself on the notion that everyone has the same chance to get ahead. People typically do not know the full context in which race-based patterns were created and in which work inequities continue. Many want to believe in the power of individual initiative and so, perhaps, they fail to ask the questions or consider the evidence that demonstrates the strength of social forces. They are sure that most people do not seek to cause harm to those in different racial or ethnic groups, and so declare no harm done.

In the social science version of this type of thinking, scholars explain racial income disparities in terms of the skills and abilities people bring to the labor market or learn on the job; what economists call "human capital." Economist Gary Becker is well known for his assumption that individuals get from work what they put in. This explanation has been criticized by economists and sociologists who contend that it "assumes away" the reality that gender, race, and class affect not only chances to develop human capital but also the value given to one's human capital as well as the chance to develop more human capital at work. Social scientists typically include human capital variables like education and work experience in their models of income and wealth. This results partly from the tendency to look for the most immediate, tangible causes of racial disparities in employment. Individual characteristics are also easier to measure than are structures of racism.

Still there is a long tradition in sociology, beginning perhaps with W. E. B. DuBois, of seeking answers in the structures of racism. In fact, some argue (e.g. Wilson 2009) that contemporary social scientists are so concerned about not blaming people for their economic circumstances that they fail to consider the role that individual action and attitudes play. Even Becker acknowledged that if employers exercise what he called "tastes for discrimination" women and men of color will not get fair wages – because they are "discriminated out" of good jobs, and channeled into lower paid work. Though such an argument shifts some of the blame away from those oppressed by the system, it is couched as a rational and unproblematic response on the part of employers. Further, it fails to consider the workings of racist policies and practices, which are exogenous to, or beyond, the explanatory model.

By their own accounts, researchers who study structures of inequality have done a better job of documenting than explaining race-based inequalities in work and employment (Reskin 2003; Avent-Holt and Tomaskovic-Devey 2010). Moreover, though critical race theorists emphasize covert and overt discrimination, in the post Civil Rights era sociologists have taken "scrupulous efforts" to avoid attributing race disparities in work outcomes to discrimination. With structured racism unacknowledged in models of racial disparities, researchers are unable to explain its impact or how it operated (Reskin 2012: 27). As Reskin (2003) urged, we need to zero in on the *mechanisms* through which white advantage is perpetuated in labor markets and workplaces. Drawing from both structural and social psychological perspectives, we will get closer to answering *why* and *how* racial inequities persist into the twenty-first century, even as the doors to ever more prestigious jobs have opened to women and men from all racial-ethnic groups.

Individuals and Structures

Why is it, then, that jobs in which women and men of color predominate pay less? Why is it easiest for whites to keep their jobs and get promotions? Why do many employees of color experience exclusion or hostility at work? Why is it *particularly* difficult for poor Native American, African American, and Puerto Rican men to find jobs? Or, as the question is often posed: "Why don't those people go to work and get their families out of poverty?"

This last question is often at the center of debate about how much of the answer to these queries lies in the skills and attitudes of *individuals* versus how much has to do with *structures* that are largely beyond an employee's control: social hierarchies, organizational practices, and the actions of employers and co-workers. Let's begin there.

Human Capital and Soft Skills

Skills, which are important human capital, certainly matter. But the quality of one's human capital is part of a "web of discrimination" that may be invisible to those who do not study or live it. As earlier chapters showed, racial disparities in work are only one part of a multifaceted race-discrimination system; they link to other systems of white advantage, such as housing, education, and family – and in the process they reinforce society-wide racism (Reskin 2012).

One structural reason for the high unemployment and underemployment rates among men and women of color from poor communities is that there are fewer and fewer jobs matching their skill levels (Wilson 1997, 2009; Kalleberg 2007). Jobs for which they would be qualified are often located too far away from where unemployed workers live. There are not enough jobs on or near American Indian lands. Further, many of the well-paying factory jobs that men of color without high school or college degrees secured in the past have been shipped overseas or upgraded to require more specialized or different kinds of skills.

Poor men of color have been hit hardest by deindustrialization; they are least likely to have the skill presumed necessary for available jobs. An individual (or cultural) argument for their lower skill set focuses on the worldviews and habits of their neighborhoods, emphasizing that these differ from "appropriate" beliefs and practices. A more contextual view is that the racism structured into the institution of work also led to the creation of separate living spaces for the "racial other" – especially for American Indians and African Americans. The poor from these racial-ethnic groups have been cordoned off from whites and left largely to fend for themselves through race-based housing segregation – even today. In fact, there is deeper poverty in the twenty-first century than there was in prior decades (Schaefer and Edin 2013).

When poor and poorly educated people have children of their own, they have limited economic and educational resources to pass on to them. These children typically enter grossly under-resourced schools, getting a late start in developing some of the skills already available to their middle-class peers – unless they get into an intervention program, such as Head Start. When children of color are poor, they are more likely to be deemed uneducable, even at young ages. School is a place of alienation and marginalization for many. There is more emphasis on disciplining than teaching them, in comparison to their white classmates and peers (E. Morris 2005; M. Morris 2016). White students get a better education than black students *even when they are in the same schools* (Anyon 1997; Ferguson 2001).

Thus it is true that American Indians, African Americans, and Latinos have a difficult time finding jobs partly because they are more likely to be poor and have skill deficits or less human capital. But that does not mean that they are inherently less capable or motivated. This point is as obvious to some as it is resisted by others; resistors include people who shape public opinion, such as "talking heads," journalists, politicians, and scholars. As systematic studies have shown, the lower skill levels of poor men and women from all racial-ethnic groups emanate from their economic circumstances (Myrdal 1944; MacLeod 2009) and not from unchangeable aspects of their culture or temperament. The impact of being born into poverty is so multifaceted, and makes an impact so early in life, that it is easy to mistakenly associate outcomes such as lower reading scores with lower intelligence rather than with inadequate instruction and less exposure to books.

Those last few sentences bear re-reading because in the United States there is a long tradition of justifying inequality by pointing to the lesser abilities of people on the bottom rungs of the racial hierarchy. Today fewer people believe that African Americans are less intelligent than whites than ever before, yet there is also a new kind of pseudo-scientific racism purporting to show that African Americans, in particular, are not as smart as whites and Asians. The major study in this regard, The Bell Curve, has been widely discredited for failing to take into account the many ways in which its measures of intelligence are flawed. It also failed to acknowledge the quality gap in poor and affluent schools and the racial disparities *within* a given school just noted. Meanwhile, sophisticated comparative studies, such as that conducted by economists Ritter and Taylor (2011) demonstrate that higher rates of unemployment among black men are not attributable to differences in cognitive skills.

Employers are partly correct when they contend that poor men of color are less likely to have "soft skills," which are newly prized aspects of human capital in today's economy (Moss and Tilly 2003; Ritter and Taylor 2011). Soft skills include attitudes and competence such as a desire to please customers, ease of communication, and the ability to work in groups and manage emotions. These skills are at odds with what is valued in the subcultures some poor men share with peer groups and communities. Exercising agency, there are poor men from all racial-ethnic groups, including white, who create alternative value systems to withstand the deprivations imposed by the dominant value system (Schwalbe et al. 2000), as a variety of in-depth studies have documented (Willis 1977; Harvey 1993; Anderson 2000; MacLeod 2009). Soft skills also conflict with self-definitions for some poor men, as they try to shore up their masculinity in a society that deprives them of the typical markers, such as good jobs. Alternative subcultures are a rational, protective response to deprivation, allowing people to feel okay about themselves even when they cannot get decent work. At the same time, the adaptive views, values, and habits they develop "virtually ensure" that they will not make it out of poverty (Schwalbe et al. 2000: 428).

Remember, though, that many research studies control for differences in human capital and *still* find a wage gap between whites and African Americans, Native Americans, and some Latino and Asian groups. That means that a white and an American Indian who have the *same skill set* (or lack thereof) *do not* have the same chance of getting the job. As described in more detail below, African Americans, American Indians, and some Latino groups are pre-judged as lacking soft skills, even if they actually have them. Soft skills may also be serving as a proxy for compliance.

Employer Preferences and Biases

The economists who rejected the cognitive deficit explanation for high black unemployment rates offered a different explanation: employer preferences (Ritter and Taylor 2011). Those with the power to choose who gets hired and at what pay level use what they know (or think they know) about particular racial-ethnic groups. Recall that race and gender are among our most visible characteristics, consistently used to define and sort us. It is not surprising that those who do the hiring, set the pay scales and decide who gets promoted draw from broader race and ethnic social constructions that are in the scripts everyone uses. Thus the precarious employment situations of poor African American, Native American, and Latino youth result partly from hiring officials across the nation using the stereotypes that have been used to justify oppressing the "racial other" since the concept of race was created.

When decision-makers apply what they think they know from their own experience or media depictions of an entire group of people, they may be engaging in *statistical discrimination;* applying actual or perceived average characteristics of a group to every individual from that group. They may be acting on exaggerated or misleading information and fail to find out about or notice the ways that individuals do not fit the group stereotype. As statistical discrimination theory highlights, labor market transactions are often conducted with limited information about potential employees (Charles and Guryan 2011).

A Latina branch manager of a temp agency claimed that "in the Spanish population, it's common for temp workers to show up late or not at all on the first day of work . . . They'll have plenty of lies about why they couldn't make it" (Sweeney 2011: 88). She is drawing from her experience; yet this is *only* her experience. Studies show that stereotypes, even about one's own group, are more easily confirmed than disconfirmed so the manager might not notice the "Spanish" person who comes on time. There may be class-based reasons that these particular Latino temps or employees are habitually late, such as lack of transportation and heavy family responsibilities. But any Latino or Latina who comes in the door is assumed to share a propensity for lateness. In interviews, a sample of white employers in Atlanta drew from the stereotypic image of the black single mother to explain why they believe that black women are unmotivated, unreliable, ill prepared employees (Kennelly 1999). Statistical discrimination based on race works in favor of whites, as the field experiments using paired testers introduced in the previous chapter show.

Though there have been relatively few direct studies of employers' attitudes about people from various racial-ethnic groups, the data is consistent, showing that many employers do use "racial lenses" to evaluate employees. Most such studies arose as an attempt to explain why poor African American and Latino youth of color could not find jobs (Wilson 1997; Moss and Tilly 1996; Waldinger 1997). All revealed racial biases on the part of employers. For example, 74 percent of the employers interviewed for Wilson's Chicago study had negative perceptions of blacks. Across the four different regions Moss and Tilly studied, employers depicted young blacks, in particular, as lacking the motivation, work habits, honesty, and skill for entry level jobs. One third of the employers interviewed for the Moss and Tilly study "denigrated the motivation of black workers" (2003: 143). Some employers put Latinos in the same category, emphasizing cultural differences. For example, a factory manager in the Boston area described Latinos as "more slow paced because of their background and the countries they come from don't have the hustle and bustle of the United States" (Moss and Tilly 2003: 115–16).

The Wilson study showed that employers judged whites to be more dependable and motivated to do good work. The employers likened some groups of Latinos to blacks, but they did make ethnic and social class distinctions in their attitudes toward Latinos and African Americans. One employer emphasized that Mexicans were a lot more cooperative and reliable than Puerto Ricans or Cubans, for instance. Employers were *particularly* reluctant to hire blacks from poor neighborhoods, steering clear of anyone with an address from "the projects" (Kirschenman and Neckerman 1991). MacLeod (2009) found similar "address discrimination" in his study of youth from the Boston housing project.

Moss and Tilly's (1996) notion of soft skills, described above, was developed to help explain the judgments of black men by employers. These qualities and abilities stemming from attitudes and behavior rather than from formal training, education, or technical knowledge (1996: 253) have become particularly important at the bottom rungs of the occupational hierarchy where manufacturing jobs have been replaced by service jobs. Employers tend to *perceive* black or Latino men to be particularly weak on soft skills (Bourgois 1996; Moss and Tilly 1996; Wilson 1997), making it less likely that these men will get a job.

Yet as analysts of the history of labor relations (and Chapter 3) suggest, even what might appear to most people to be a poor work ethic or a "bad attitude" could be a rational reaction to a hostile environment (e.g. DuBois [1935]1998; Edwards 1980). Journalist turned Walmart worker Barbara Ehrenreich found her negative attitude stemming from the job itself, and she was only "passing through." Classic longitudinal research suggests that Ehrenreich is not unusual; most people are affected by the nature of their work (Kohn and Schooler1983). In addition, employer biases may keep them from seeing the soft skills that men of color possess. A small study found that black men in nursing drew upon soft skills, forging relationships with patients, unlike what has been reported about their white counterparts. These black men saw caring and nurturing as an important part of their jobs (Wingfield 2009).

Furthermore, employer views on various racial-ethnic groups sometimes mask their drive for profit. For entry level jobs, in particular, control may be more important to profit than skill. There is evidence that the emphasis on soft skills stems from the desire for a quality that is unrelated to skill: subservience. It is much easier to extract surplus value, or profit, from labor when those who perform it are compliant. Thus employers in labor intensive industries prize employees willing to take orders, accept long hours or difficult working conditions, and work hard without complaint (Harrison and Lloyd 2013). Recent immigrants of Asian and Mexican ancestry, for example, are seen as ideal workers who will be docile and hard-working (Moss and Tilly 2003; Nir 2015; Maldonado 2009). That is why they predominate in certain kinds of entry level jobs. Economists Bowles and Gintis have long argued that education is important for its role in transmitting attitudes and habits useful to employers seeking control. They cite research showing that cognitive abilities, education level, and experience are less important to employers than attitude and other soft skills that signal how easy it will be to control their labor (2001: 10).

Finally, ethnographic research has uncovered strong motivation and work ethics among poor young men and women of color, even in the face of tremendous difficulty. For example, Newman's in-depth (1999) study of places like the fast food restaurant she called "Burger Barn" highlighted the diligence required by poor people to get and keep their jobs. "Carmen," who emigrated from the Dominican Republic at the age of 14, began working during high school. Carmen would be in school from 8: 30 in the morning to 3: 30 in the afternoon. She worked a full shift at Burger Barn from 4: 00 pm to 2: 00 the next morning. Then she would go home and study for an hour or so before falling asleep over her books (p. 17). Jamal, a young man with a child to support – and no financial or emotional support from his parents – would wake up at 4:30 am to meet the bus by 5:00, which he rode for *an hour* to get to Burger Barn. He was making very little money even when he worked the full eight hours, but he could easily be sent home early if the place was not too busy. His total wages were so low that a lot of people around him thought it was not worth the effort he had to put in just to get to and from the job. Jamal had been pounding the pavement looking for something else, a job "where I can really be somebody who has something" because he hated the job at the burger joint. He had searched "all over Manhattan, Queens, and the Bronx" for more than three years (p. 5). Jamal is swimming against a tide of assumptions that he is not suitable for jobs beyond minimum-wage fast food service.

Jamal and Carmen are real people whose exceptional motivation is lost in statistics showing the large gaps in income between poor people of color and everyone else. Their strong work ethics and determination to improve their lives are also invisible to those who judge them solely on the basis of what kind of job they have, what their income is, or the fact that they live in poor neighborhoods. Surely there are others in their circumstances who have given up, joining the ranks of discouraged or underground economy workers. But if it takes that kind of effort to secure paltry wages, how many of us would stick it out the way Jamal and Carmen did?

MacLeod's study, introduced in Chapter 4, showed that social class alone did not explain the employment outcomes of the teens from Clarendon Heights. The labor market was hostile to the Brothers not only because they came from low-income neighborhoods, but also because they occupied a particularly precarious position at the intersection of class and race. "Because they do not immediately convey a mastery of middle-class culture, they bear the public taint of the 'underclass', with all the racially coded characteristics that term has come to imply." The Brothers, says MacLeod, have become "symbols of danger and degeneracy" in the public mind; they are not to be trusted. This is *completely* at-odds with the qualities that Macleod found in the youth he spent so much time observing and interviewing. With only one exception, MacLeod described them as "veritable puritans. They have a strong work ethic. They are sexually responsible. They don't smoke. They don't use drugs. They drink only in moderation. They respect adult authority. The Brothers are not angels, but they sometimes seem to be, even in comparison to the well-heeled but hard-partying university students up the street who steer safely clear of the Brothers and their ilk" (p. 228).

Given the frequency with which people of color are accused of "playing the race card" it is noteworthy that the Brothers did not use racism to explain their employment difficulties. They believed in the American dream, so they blamed "anything but racism" (Bonilla-Silva and Baiocchi 2008), including themselves. In counterpoint, the Hallway Hangers used racial slurs and accepted the popular notion of reverse racism, assuming that the Brothers were able to parlay their race into better jobs.

Noted sociologist C. Wright Mills argued that it would be difficult for those in poverty to change their circumstances without deep and lasting changes in the institutions which channel them into such positions. MacLeod is certain that the structure is stacked against the Hallway Hangers, the Brothers, and all the poor youth growing up in the United States. Although every one of the young men he followed felt he was responsible for his own job history, MacLeod (pp. 252–69) argues forcefully for the primacy of structure over agency, rejecting the all-too pervasive view that those in poverty create their situation. Instead, he says, it is inequalities in labor markets, housing, and educational systems that *cause* poverty. When poor kids make bad choices they do so as individuals, of course. Yet those choices and their consequences are also structured by abiding systems of race, class, and gender disadvantage, just as the choices of white middle-class professionals' sons are structured by systems of advantage. The latter group carries a knapsack full of white privileges which are enhanced by their gender and class position.

Occupational Stratification

Scholars have consistently explained the sometimes wide economic gulf between whites and other racial-ethnic groups on the basis of occupational stratification, or the sorting of people into different kinds of jobs. Differences in the types of industries, occupations, firms, and jobs available to whites compared to people of color account for much of the racial-ethnic gap in income and promotion rates. When researchers control for the type of work that different racial-ethnic groups do, a portion of the income discrepancy among the groups disappears. Since industrialization, the gender stratification of jobs has been particularly pronounced, and it has combined with race sorting to catapult white men to the top of the occupational hierarchy. The growth in female-typed occupations at the expense of blue-collar jobs typically reserved for men has fueled unemployment and underemployment among men of color, widening the racial wage gap.

There is ample evidence that many people of color have lower incomes than whites because their jobs are not as good. But explanations rooted in job quality beg the question of *how* people are sorted into different occupations and industries, and even different assignments when they have the same job titles. In the post Civil Rights era with its anti-discrimination laws and strong social support for equality of opportunity, how do we explain the continued race and gender segregation of jobs and industries?

The answers are found in a set of processes. The explanation begins at the societal level, with the social construction of both jobs and types of workers. Remember, the race hierarchy was reproduced in a hierarchy of jobs. The best jobs are seen as the purview of whites and the groups at the bottom of the race hierarchy are channeled into low-paying, menial jobs. Employers order race and gender groups in labor queues from most to least preferred (Lieberson 1980; Reskin and Roos 1990). White men at the top of the labor queue get the first choice of jobs. They have status simply from being white and male, particularly if they are from the middle or upper social classes. In addition to their cultural capital, they carry the invisible and unmeasurable advantage that they are seen as good matches for the best-paying, most prestigious jobs in every field. White women have higher social status than women of color so within female-typed jobs and industries that men avoid, white women get the best jobs.

Job queues are the rankings of potential employees as they scan the labor market. Not surprisingly, those who have first choice typically choose the best jobs. On the dimension of race, that means that whites have "first dibs" on jobs with good incomes and chances for promotion. These are socially constructed processes and job preferences are changeable, leading to fluid rather than fixed job queues. When pay and conditions in a particular field improve, higher ranked race-gender groups will choose that field. When choices are constricted because of technological change, or economic crises, higher status workers will enter jobs they had previously eschewed, bumping others further down in the jobs hierarchy.

Changes in pay rates and work tasks, as well as cultural or legal thinking about who belongs in particular jobs sometimes alter job queues (Reskin and Roos 1990). For example, auto manufacturers in search of greater profit moved from what used to be called the industrial heartland in the north and midwest to the southeastern United States where labor unions were not as strong. Technological developments made it even easier for companies to shift more of their operations to countries in which labor costs are much lower. The auto companies, like so many other manufacturers, began shipping jobs overseas as a way to increase profit. Service industries filled the jobs gap left by the manufacturers, making a substantial change in the composition of job queues. The manufacturing jobs had been a source of a good family wage and fringe benefits for white men and eventually for black men, although not as much in non-unionized plants. The service jobs were in far less lucrative industries, such as retail, fast food, and personal services, disproportionately paying minimum wage. Even today most service jobs are "women-typed," and entry level service jobs are characterized by wages that cannot support a family and offer few or no fringe benefits. Many of the jobs are part time.

However, labor queues have changed only a little. The relative ranking of the race and gender groups has remained mostly constant throughout U.S. history. The top and bottom positions on the race hierarchy of status and power have been impervious to socioeconomic change. Even today, whites hold the top spot on the race hierarchy while African Americans and American Indians continue to anchor the bottom.

Assumptions and Expectations

When we are not looking at the full picture or video clip, it is easy to make assumptions that justify occupational patterns. If men of Asian ancestry are overrepresented in engineering or computer science jobs, we reason that they must be especially good at that kind of work – and, by extension, not especially good at other kinds of work, such as managing large companies, or delivering news on TV. Asian women are seen as more desirable for certain kinds of jobs than African Americans or even whites, but not for the jobs that require skills that run counter to stereotype, such as managerial positions requiring self-promotion or a "killer instinct" (Woo 2000a). The latter types of jobs bring more prestige and money. Thus cultural stereotypes limit the options even of racial-ethnic groups about whom there are many positive attitudes (Okihiro 2000; Wu 2002; Sue 2006). Employers and co-workers also lose out if the best person for the job is passed over.

When it comes to jobs that require face-to-face interactions with customers, employers use the race, gender, and class markers of their employees to send a message to customers about what type of service they can expect (Macdonald and Merrill 2009). This highlights the role that *social expectations* play in matching people to jobs. Managers cater to customers' desires – real or imagined – as they choose what types of people to put into which jobs. Because of its high visibility, race is a major consideration as applicants and employees are sorted into jobs. Even an employer who is comfortable having a Latino immigrant greeting customers may put him in the backroom job in anticipation of customers' desires. Research evidence supports the view that some white customers have racial biases. As a white personnel manager of a retail store in LA told interviewers, their primarily white clientele were unhappy with the fact that the employees were black. ". . . we were always getting complaints that there were all black employees and it's because they were black. That would be the first thing the customer would bring up was 'black.' It was because they were black that they didn't do their job right." The manager of a home health care agency said there were always some, though not a lot, of patients who would say 'I don't want Hispanics. I don't want blacks. So we deal with that. And that's tough because you could have the most compassionate home health aide and here she is black . . .'" (Moss and Tilly 2003: 106).

As we have seen, racial-ethnic stereotypes intersect with gender, in particular – and there are other factors that may come into play too, such as sexuality, age, and religion; the person deemed most appropriate for a given job is not always the white middle or upper-class man. But jobs associated with those on the lower rungs of race, gender, and social class hierarchies typically have less prestige and pay associated with them. Members of the dominant group assign high value to their own characteristics and in tandem downgrade attitudes and behaviors associated with other groups. This is a major, though hidden, mechanism through which the "racial other" is closed out of good jobs.

One reason occupations typically filled by women and men of color pay less is precisely *because* those jobs are filled by women and men of color (Tomaskovic-Devey 1993). Catanzarite's (2003) longitudinal study was able to establish causal ordering; as occupations fill with those at the bottom of labor queues, the wages go down (cf. Reskin and Roos 1990). The low social status of people of color results in less value being accorded to their skill set and the work they perform (Catanzarite 2003: 16). The occupation itself is "tainted," affecting everyone in it. Thus in the two decades Catanzarite studied, the median wages of white men in occupations with large concentrations of black men decreased as well. But how, exactly, does that happen? The author suggests one way: the jobs in which women and men of color are concentrated are more likely to be de-skilled because of the belief that the people doing the work are not as competent.

Job Choices

An individual explanation for why white men are overrepresented in the best jobs is that people sort themselves into particular jobs by where they look, and what they want to do and how much money they expect to make. In comparison to recent immigrants, for example, black men may pass over available jobs as they seek higher wages (Wilson 2009). Yet even job choice is affected by social forces.

Cultural ideas about the types of people who belong in particular jobs get planted not only in the minds of employers but also in the minds of job seekers. People can more easily imagine themselves in jobs where they see a lot of people who "look like" them. They may expect less hostility and a better chance for promotion if they choose a job populated by people with the same group characteristics. This explains why a gay man of color might be more apt to seek work as a florist or designer than as a truck driver or financial analyst – though of course there are gay men of color in those latter occupations too.

When they have choices, job-seekers are also more likely to choose jobs which they know about and to which they have access. They avoid or leave jobs in which they face hostility or cannot excel. When individuals leave jobs or firms to avoid the stereotypes that hinder them they may end up with less satisfying, lower paying work (Hiramatsu 2013). All of these individual decisions contribute to broader patterns of race-based job sorting or the racial stratification of occupations.

Though we choose freely, our job choices are constrained by what is or seems possible given our race, gender, and class positions. There was a time when common academic wisdom was that highly paid blue-collar workers had an instrumental orientation to work – valuing money more than intrinsic rewards such as autonomy or the chance to find meaning in their work. Yet data from surveys and interviews with blue-collar workers showed that most were very much interested in intrinsic job rewards. They had to make trade-offs between money and meaning in their jobs that people in more prestigious jobs do not face (Loscocco 1989). Blue-collar workers do not wish they had white-collar jobs (Torlina 2011); they just want their jobs to provide both intrinsic and extrinsic rewards (and the skilled trades often do). The take-away is that one cannot calculate what people want from their jobs by knowing what work they are doing. Work choices are shaped by preexisting definitions of jobs, occupations, and industries as particularly suited to people from specific gender and race groups.

Thus, the racial division of labor is reproduced through the beliefs and actions of constrained job seekers and employers who rely on anecdotal evidence and cultural messages about who belongs in what kinds of jobs. Yet owners of the means of production and their representatives have tremendous power to choose. Their decision-making is a chief mechanism through which race-based advantage and disadvantage in every aspect of paid work are reproduced.

Social Closure

One major process that contributes to occupational segregation by race is what theorist Max Weber called *social closure*, presented back in Chapter 1. This highlights agency on the part of dominants as they hoard resources and rewards by keeping others out of the best lanes of the footrace. It is a reminder that group interests are often at the heart of race-based exclusion. Social closure is a mechanism used not only by supervisors and employers, but also by other employees. Chapter 2 showed that employers' motives are to maximize profit but they do so partly by colluding with white workers to preserve white privilege for people of all socioeconomic classes. Co-workers trying to protect their careers and work spaces are often responsible for exclusion, as the discussions of labor unions and workplace harassment indicated.

Researchers have found evidence of social closure within local labor markets as well as companies, and in top management as well as lower-level positions (Tomaskovic-Devey 1993; Elliott and Smith 2001; Roscigno, Garcia, and Bobbitt-Zeher 2007). Whites at the top of the labor queue try to keep others out, hoarding not only material resources but also authority and control (Kanter [1977] 1993; Elliott and Smith 2001). People from dominant or privileged groups (or sometimes people of color representing the dominant group) make key hiring and promotion decisions that keep people like them in plum positions, channeling racial-ethnic and gender "others" into less desirable jobs. Managers have tremendous leeway, whether it is in writing up a performance evaluation or deciding on raises (Ritter and Taylor 2011; Wilson and McBrier 2005). Some white ethnic groups have been able to control who gets into local jobs such as sanitation, construction and policing, and firefighting. They too choose "their own," closing out people of color (Waldinger 1996).

Note that what appears to be social closure may result from risk aversion rather than resource hoarding. A white personnel manager may simply be trying to reduce uncertainty when he or she chooses a person of the same racial-ethnic group. He or she feels the white person is more of a "known commodity." Sometimes employees close ranks to preserve occupational or workplace culture. Many white men rely on their jobs as places to display and claim their masculinity as well as their race privilege. If they welcome women and men of color, it may undermine the camaraderie and trust that comes from being with other white men. This has been documented as particularly salient in jobs such as firefighting and mining, where a worker's life may depend on co-workers (Yount 2004; Baigent 2005). In all types of workplaces, a white man or woman who expresses no ill-will toward people of color may practice exclusion because of a desire to be among people with whom they are comfortable. This is aversive or color-blind racism playing out. I can tell myself: "I'm not a racist; I just prefer to be with people I know well." Whatever the reasons, which we will explore further, the actions of managers and co-workers contribute to racial-ethnic work inequities.

Employees from dominant groups may try harder to close out people of color in organizations that use *or are perceived to use* some type of affirmative action initiative to increase representation of racial-ethnic groups who had been locked out of particular jobs. Co-workers can blame affirmative action or other initiatives, convincing themselves that people of color are not qualified, as we saw in Woo's study of an aerospace organization. Leading organizational theorists Baron and Pfeffer (1994) suggest that whites tighten boundaries to protect their status and privilege within work organizations. When privilege feels threatened, there will be more vigilance about those boundaries.

Sometimes employees from marginalized racial-ethnic groups will appear to prefer to "keep to themselves" (Vallas 2003; Yoder and Aniakudo 1997). However this is different from social closure or overt racism; they are not trying to hoard resources for themselves, close out whites from good jobs, or keep whites from doing their jobs. It means something *different* to surround oneself with people from your group when you are a "racial other," particularly if there are very few of you. The need to feel understood, in control, and even safe, may necessitate closing oneself off from co-workers. Faced with a hostile environment created by members of the numerical majority (usually whites, but not necessarily so), it may feel all but impossible for some people of color to do their jobs well. In that case, isolating oneself is a strategy for work survival (e.g. Yoder and Aniakudo 1997). An unfortunate vicious cycle may ensue, because such choices keep people of color from key networks of information and influence in work settings. They reinforce whites' perception that people of color prefer to keep to themselves, making racial segregation at work seem natural (cf. Vallas 2003).

Social Networks

Another key mechanism fueling racial disparities at work can be difficult to pinpoint. You have probably heard that most jobs are not advertised and that "it's not what you know, but who you know" when it comes to getting a position or promotion. Researchers show that the networks so vital to getting a good job are organized in ways that provide systematic advantage to whites. This is because those who are doing the hiring are most likely connected to other whites, and most jobs are found informally (Royster 2003; DiTomaso 2012). Royster (2003) studied two groups of young working-class men as they made the transition from school to full time work in Baltimore, Maryland. She created matched samples, so that the youth in each group had similar education and work experiences before trying to find a full time job. Yet the networks of the white youth were far more useful for getting good blue-collar jobs. DiTomaso (2012) asked hundreds of white people from the working, middle, and upper classes about a total of 1,463 jobs and found that 70 percent of those jobs had been located or obtained on an inside track, through personal connections.

Most network research has compared whites and blacks, establishing that blacks have less access to so-called "high quality" contacts across a variety of occupations (McGuire 2002; Royster 2003; McDonald 2011). In fact, women and men of color have worse employment outcomes when they rely on social networks to find jobs (Trimble and Kmec 2011). Royster showed that a key reason for occupational segregation is that white men do not bring young black men into their networks.

Race and class intersect such that personal networks are least useful for blacks who live in areas of intense poverty. Their connections to people with similar backgrounds yield few and low-quality job leads (Gowan 2011). Furthermore, blacks from low-income neighborhoods are reluctant to connect friends and family to jobs because of the risk they incur if the referral does not succeed (Newman 1999; Smith 2005). Their own positions are too precarious. As the concept of the "racial other" instructs, blacks are often judged by the actions of other blacks because their race is seen as their most salient characteristic. Because they are members of the dominant (mostly invisible) racial group, whites are rarely held back by what other whites do or say.

Social networks are vitally important avenues for hiring (and reinforce racial-ethnic occupational sorting) when employers rely on their current employees to bring in more people like themselves. This is a common strategy of employers who seek the inexpensive labor of undocumented immigrants, making it more likely that Latino and Asian newcomers will be hired over African Americans (Waldinger 1997; Maldonado 2009). When employers advertise jobs informally, whites have an advantage over job seekers from other racial-ethnic groups (Peterson, Saporta, and Seidel 2000; Parks-Yancy 2006). One researcher compared the chances for whites and blacks to get a job when employers placed ads in newspapers compared to when they used referrals – in Atlanta, Boston, Los Angeles, and Detroit. The results showed that when employers from predominately white firms used referrals, it reduced the chance of a black worker getting a job by close to 75 percent (Mouw 2002: 527).

The networks *within* work organizations also contribute to white advantage in mentorship, support, sponsorship, and inside information (Pager and Shepherd 2008). A major explanation for why whites get promoted more quickly and more often is because of the quality of their connections within occupations and work organizations. It is more difficult for people of color to make the ties that will be most useful for career success. Because whites are most often in positions of influence, men of color have to cross race lines and women of color have to cross both race and gender lines, to develop networks. While whites often get social as well as practical support from their contacts, people of color are typically unable to get social support from the people in their workplace networks (Ibarra 1995; Forret 2006).

Cultural Schema

As discussed back in Chapter 1, early racial inequality in work created by power and resource imbalances was consistently reinforced by culture. Recall that racist ideologies justified unfair advantages by crediting white achievements to superior abilities and effort. Judging groups of color by dominant white standards led to their denigration and devaluation. The "lazy" Mexican or African, the "ignorant" American Indian, the "alien" and "sneaky" Asian – were stereotypes used to justify keeping the best jobs for whites, relegating people of color to the jobs that whites did not want. These stereotypes, drawing on characteristics of culture, still apply today when employers criticize Latinos for their "*mañana, mañana*" attitude toward life or claim that African Americans and Native Americans do not have strong work ethics. When employers pass over Asians for prestigious jobs because of the belief that Asians are too meek, they are also drawing on age-old stereotypes.

Stereotypes are ubiquitous and it is hard to imagine how we would navigate our way through social life without them. Our pre-conceived notions about professors and students help us figure out what to expect when we enter a classroom, for example. There are four major ways that racial and ethnic stereotypes (in combination with gender) reinforce structured work inequality. First, racial-ethnic stereotypes are not evaluated against reality; the "idea" is much stronger than the evidence (Shelby 2003). Second, deep-seated emotion is attached to how people think about and react to racial-ethnic groups. Third, even the seemingly personal thoughts and hunches employers use in making decisions are influenced by the stereotypes that are in our cultural scripts. Fourth, the first three processes can easily happen without awareness (Schwalbe et al. 2000; Massey 2007).

Deeply embedded and ever-present racial-ethnic stereotypes enter not only into employment decisions, but also those about promotions, raises, layoffs, and firing (e.g. Sue 2006). Ideas about leadership qualities are racialized, with whites viewed as the most natural leaders. White men are consistently perceived as being competent until they prove otherwise. This is why white men predominate in positions that put them in line for promotion, whether in science and engineering (DiTomaso et al. 2007) or nursing (Williams 1989). Although the woman quoted in Chapter 4 had to persuade people that she was actually a physician, her white male colleagues were immediately presumed to be physicians; as one commented, "I can walk in wearing a T shirt and jeans and I'll always be seen as a doctor, even without an introduction" (Lumumba-Kasongo 2006).

Variations in stereotypes – rooted in specific labor histories as well as cultures of origin – lead to different work opportunities for various groups of color. Against the white idealized image of a top manager or leader, African American women managers are judged as "too direct" (Livers 2006) while Asian Americans are not aggressive enough (Woo 2000). Perceptions of white men's abilities, skills, and "place" propel them onto glass escalators that take them to the top of female-dominated occupations (Maume 1999; Williams 2013). In contrast, African American men carry the burden of negative stereotypes including assumptions that they are less competent. Though white men in fields dominated by women are often promoted with women's support (Williams 2013), the black men in nursing studied by Wingfield found that white women had an aversive reaction to them.

In discussing their finding that blacks are more likely than whites or Asians to be let go when employers reduce labor costs, Elvira and Zatzick (2002) suggest: "Asians may benefit from perceptions that they are hardworking, highly educated, and committed to the firm" (p. 353). While stereotyped behavior is fixed as a cultural trait in many people's minds, it may result from attempts to overcome structural circumstances. Kim (1999) suggests that Asians may work really hard *as a reaction* to their treatment as "forever foreign."

Some analysts point to American corporate culture as the major impediment to the movement of men and women of color into top management positions (e.g. Cabezas et al. 1989). It is an intensely competitive culture with what sometimes appears to be a single-minded pursuit of profit. At the historical junctures and in the work organizations for which this characterization holds true, boundaries tighten and racial and gender "others" are closed out.

There is also a lingering sense that whites should dominate people of color, emanating from the construction of race hierarchy. This explains why black managers are targeted with harassment, hostility, and subterfuge (Livers 2006). Black women and men who are managers upset the racial hierarchy which has always given even whites on the lowest occupational rung the "psychological wages of whiteness" identified by DuBois so long ago. Thus some white subordinates resent or are uncomfortable having to take instruction or orders from a black boss. Among the many advantages of whiteness is the likelihood of having a supervisor of the same race; to be under the authority or control of a person of color is at odds with the typical white experience. Blacks most often get jobs supervising other blacks (Elliott and Smith 2001), keeping the racial "pecking order" intact. Thus the best managerial jobs go to whites and the longstanding racist taboo against people of color having control over whites is upheld.

> We've had to be very creative to come through some situations. Imagine if we could use our creativity, adaptability, and flexibility at work. Imagine how competitive it would make you.
> (Black woman manager interviewed by Livers 2006)

Equal opportunity legislation was passed decades ago. In 2008 and again in 2012, U.S. citizens chose a black man to lead the country. There are more people from all racial-ethnic groups in top economic and political positions than ever before. Surveys show that people do not harbor as much racial animosity as they once did. Why do whites still exclude people of color from networks and leadership positions? Why do decision-makers pre-judge people of color? Why do co-workers avoid or reject others who have a different phenotype or country of ancestry? Unless you have studied implicit bias, you may feel confident that you would not do such a thing. Keep reading.

Unconscious or Implicit Bias

There are surely some human resource managers and employers who harbor outright hostility toward particular racial groups. Yet much of the race-based job sorting that occurs comes from more subtle decision-making processes. Work life seems easier if there is no need to adapt to people who are "different." As Kanter ([1977] 1993) showed in her path-breaking work on occupational ladders in a corporation, owners and managers seek to reduce uncertainty. Particularly among the ranks of top management, where there is more discretion and the work is deemed highly important, keeping "outsiders" at bay seems like a good strategy. That is why top managers (who are still most likely to be white men) are inclined to hire and promote people like themselves. This leads to what Kanter called *homosocial reproduction*; the same kinds of people continue to fill the same top positions.

Though most employers would likely say they have a rational process for ranking candidates for jobs and promotions, many would also acknowledge that they use hunches or feelings about how well a person would "fit." Because they are members of the default and dominant racial group, many whites do not readily see what they have in common with people from other racial/ethnic groups, making it less likely for whites to imagine them in top positions. DiTomaso argues that whites do not fill their networks with other whites in an active attempt to keep people of color from getting jobs; instead, they are turning to the people with whom they are connected (2012). This is extremely easy to do without a second thought, because even today there is considerable racial segregation in neighborhoods, community organizations, houses of worship, and schools and colleges (Feagin 2010; Chou et al. 2012).

With increasing public pressure to be free of racial bias, stereotypic attitudes about people of color are more likely to be hidden – perhaps even from those who hold them. What used to be explicit bias has morphed into implicit or unconscious bias (Dovidio et al. 2002). Research psychologists have demonstrated that everyone has biases in reaction to another's perceived race-ethnicity; they are called implicit or unconscious biases because they happen without awareness or intent, below the level of conscious thought (Sue 2003; 2006; Banaji and Greenwald 2013). Having been taught to treat others without prejudice or make friends across the color line does not inoculate you against this cognitive process. In a society built on racism, everyone is primed to view one another through racial lenses. Our vision is clouded by the stereotypes embedded in the cultural scripts from which we learned our lines.

Using the Implicit Association Test, researchers have found that members of all racial ethnic groups have more positive attitudes toward whites, which is one reason people of color in a position to help promote others from their group do not necessarily do so (the scrutiny they are under in white-dominated institutions is another). Implicit biases also help to explain the better employment outcomes of Latinos who look white, even in labor markets in which co-ethnics are doing the hiring. The preference for "near white" is deeply ingrained in our society and our psyches. We all bring race-based (and many other) biases to our workplaces, activating them through day-to-day interaction and decision-making. That can happen even if no one in the workplace is overtly racist. Acting without awareness co-workers, colleagues, supervisors, managers, and owners contribute to white advantage. The result is that people of color have a lower quality of work life than whites. (You can take The Implicit Association Test (IAT) at: https: //implicit.harvard.edu/implicit/takeatest.html.)

A fascinating example of unconscious bias was revealed when the way people were chosen for orchestras changed. In 1970, women made up only 5 percent of the musicians in the top U.S. orchestras. When orchestras began to have musicians audition behind curtains, women's chances of being hired went up 50 percent (Goldin and Rouse 2000). Had all of the prior decision-makers been actively trying to avoid hiring women? That was surely not the case. But they filtered how they heard women's performance through brains that perceived men to be better musicians.

Seemingly insignificant comments or actions (to the speaker or actor) that make a person feel unwelcome or de-valued because of their race are common in work environments. These are what scholars label "microaggressions" and they are often unintentional. A typical experience for women of color is that their idea is ignored until proposed by a man. Often the process goes unremarked, especially by those at the top of the race and gender hierarchies. When people discredit a colleague's opinion or work, they are often completely unaware of the deeply entrenched biases behind their action. The person who is the microaggressor may think he or she just said something complimentary (you are so articulate; I'm surprised at how good your report is; I don't think of you as Asian) or pleasant (I love black music; what do people like you do on the weekend; my favorite food is Mexican).

Even when well-intentioned, comments that treat a person as a race group member rather than an individual create an unwelcoming or hostile work environment. This in turn can affect performance. When managers apply the same kind of thinking to decisions about assignments, pay, and promotion – seeing people of color as members of racial-ethnic groups rather than the individuals they are – they inadvertently reinforce racial disparities in job opportunities.

There is ample research evidence of hostile and biased work environments for African American employees at all rungs of the occupational ladder, partly because of the extreme "othering" of blacks. There is also tension and mistrust among the "in-between" racial-ethnic groups and the whites and blacks above and below them on the race hierarchy. Note also that there are many people who acknowledge their racial biases and attempt to monitor their decisions, actions, and attitudes.

Whites lead "race traitor" and "ally" movements to encourage others to recognize white privilege as the first step toward making it less powerful. Of course true allies take action (Bonilla-Silva 2006) as the whites described in Chapter 3 did. There are Latinos, Asian Americans, and African Americans who work to understand the commonalities and differences of their experiences as the "racial other." As has been true throughout U.S. history, there are people who "get" racial bias in work settings across the country. The black woman physician mentioned earlier described a white man in his eighties for whom she was setting up an IV: "I noticed that he was staring at me. Finally he said, 'It must have been very hard for you to make it.' After a pause, he added, 'A woman – and black.' We both laughed. Someone understood" (Lumumba-Kasongo 2006).

Internalized Stereotypes

The stereotypes supporting the race hierarchy also affect the self-perceptions of people classified as the "racial other." As noted earlier, while whites are buoyed by knapsacks of race privilege, their co-workers of color are weighed down by knapsacks full of concrete blocks of exclusion. Psychologist Claude Steele and colleagues identified one such concrete stumbling block and labeled it "stereotype threat": a concern about being judged by negative stereotypes about one's race group. The weight of knowing that people do not expect you to be qualified can lead to actions and inactions that keep one from doing one's best. A wide range of well-designed social experiments show that simply reminding people of their race or gender status creates anxiety which takes over parts of the brain needed to do the task at hand, or, presumably, even perform well in a meeting (Steele, 2010). The negative impact of having to haul to work the possibility that you will confirm people's negative ideas about your ability probably cannot be overestimated. Keep in mind that this is mostly happening at a subconscious level.

Intentional Racism

In the Post-Civil Rights era, scholars have increasingly focused attention on the subtle dimensions of race-based work inequality. The attitudes of whites toward blacks continue to change for the better and many people assume that means there is no longer any discrimination against blacks; and if blacks are not discriminated against, then no other race group is either. Yet long after racial discrimination became illegal, it has continued to haunt people who are just trying to do their jobs. As you know from the previous chapter, sometimes outwardly hostile practices keep a person of color from getting the pay and promotions they deserve. Intentional discrimination also poisons the work environment, placing undue stress on its targets and other employees.

With the various explanations provided here as a backdrop, the next chapter explores race and work issues that are currently in the headlines.

6
Trending Race and Work Issues

The work landscape is ever changing. With the increase in 24/7 work cycles and the blurring of boundaries between work and personal lives, work has a bigger impact on people than ever before (Vallas 2012). This section examines some trends that are pertinent to the study of race-ethnicity and work. The focus is whether such developments increase or decrease racial-ethnic disparities in work and employment.

American Capitalism and Increasing Inequality

Capitalists have always used geographical mobility to increase profits. Yet recent technological and political developments have made it even easier for American companies to move some or all of their operations to countries in which standards of living, and therefore labor and operating costs, are much lower. The manufacturers were the first to go, but many other industries have followed. In the 1980s it would have been hard to imagine that so much customer service work would be outsourced to India and Mexico, but American consumers have come to expect it. While global labor markets are a boon to corporations, they put a large swath of American workers at a decided disadvantage. Eight million U.S. factory workers lost their jobs from 1979–2009. Between 1998 and 2008, 12.5 percent of U.S. manufacturing plants were shut down, hurting entire working-class communities (Lach 2012). According to a recent analysis by the Wall Street Journal "Thirty-five big U.S.-based multinational companies added jobs much faster than other U.S. employers in the past two years, but nearly three-fourths of those jobs were overseas" (Thurm 2012).

Starting in the 1980s, the country entered a period of greater unchecked capitalism and increasing corporate power. A sociopolitical climate affirming the superiority of capitalism and of quintessentially American values – competition, privacy, individual autonomy, and personal freedom – has contributed to greater inequality (Bonilla-Silva 2001). Historian John Hope Franklin showed that the anti-government platform on which Ronald Reagan was elected President in 1981 "encouraged policies and measures that denied equal opportunity and equal treatment" (1993: 11). Franklin wondered "what would have happened, what might have happened, had not the Republican party sensed that it could capitalize on the prevailing climate by appealing to and welcoming into its folds the opponents of racial equality and justice (1993: 41)."

Some political observers argued that Donald Trump's campaign for the presidency in 2016 followed an even more extreme path, openly encouraging whites to take out their anger on immigrants, blacks, and Muslims. Hochschild's (2016a) study of Tea Party (and Trump) supporters in Louisiana suggests that Trump did indeed tap into struggling whites' belief that they were losing *because* other racial-ethnic groups were gaining. They believe that the Obama administration gave the other groups an edge, helping people of color to overtake whites like themselves in the footrace (marathon?) to the American dream. The whites Hochschild interviewed are far less likely to blame corrupt politicians or the kinds of policies supported by environmental conservatives, though both can be tied directly to the economic and health problems of respondents' communities (Hochschild 2016b; Rich 2016).

Labor unions have been in an extended period of weakness vis-à-vis employers. Organized labor may not have been able to adapt quickly enough to a web of changes (Hirsch 2008) that have fueled its decline since the mid 1970s. These include job loss in unionized industries, anti-union legislation and sentiment, computerization, and the ease with which owners can move their operations. The success of major corporations, such as Walmart and Starbucks, at staving off unionization stems from some of these changes and further weakens organized labor. So too, the number of "right to work" states, which weaken union power, has been increasing. Under right-to-work law, employees of a unionized firm do not have to join or pay union dues, although the union is required to provide every employee the same protections and benefits. Those in favor of right to work laws claim that they make it easier to attract businesses. Those against the laws argue that they make it much easier for capitalists to do as they please; wage gains from new employers may be temporary or inadequate, and working conditions non-negotiable.

Unionization reached a 97-year low in 2013; only 11.3 percent of employees were members of labor unions. In 1983, 20.1 percent of the workforce was unionized while unionization was at 35 percent during its peak in the post-WWII 1950s (U.S. Bureau of Labor Statistics 2015; Greenhouse 2013). Even as job growth surged in recent years, the rate of union membership continued to fall. Unions have consistently brought higher wages and more benefits to members. Yet the benefits of unionization extend even further. Strong organized labor has provided a major constraint on capitalism, establishing norms of wage equity in unionized and non-unionized firms alike. The decline of unionization has contributed directly to the trend toward greater economic inequality in the United States (Western and Rosenfeld 2011).

Indeed, the past few decades have wrought increasing class inequality, growing poverty, and a struggling middle class. Many middle-class and working-class families have been unable to reconcile reports of a booming economy with how hard they have to work just to stay in the same economic place. Former routes to upward mobility for poor and working-class families disappeared (Mouw and Kalleberg 2010; Putnam 2015). The level of inequality – in wages, earnings, and total family incomes – is higher today than at any point in the past forty plus years (McCall and Percheski 2010). Though poverty declined during the late 1990s when the economy was strong, it began growing in 2000. By 2012, there was more poverty than there had been in 1996 (Reich 2015) when social welfare was curtailed or ended (depending on one's perspective) under Democratic President Bill Clinton.

The middle, working, and impoverished classes were hit hard by the Great Recession in 2007 and the economic blow was worst for American Indians (Austin 2013b), blacks, and Latinos. For example, Latino wealth (the household median, adjusted for inflation) in 2009 was 66 percent lower than it had been in 2005 and black wealth fell by 53 percent. During the same period white wealth fell by 16 percent. Latinos were affected the most by the bubble that burst in the housing market (Kocchar, Fry, and Taylor 2011).

Racial-ethnic disparities in the impact of the economic crisis were also evident during the economy recovery. Between 2010 and 2013 the median wealth of white households crept up by 2.4 percent, but among Latinos wealth was 14.3 percent lower. Black households saw a steep decline in median wealth over the three year period; it was 33.7 percent less in 2013 than in 2010 (Kocchar and Fry 2014). (As is often the case, comparable numbers were not compiled for American Indians).

The "one percent" – who became a focus of the Occupy Wall Street movement begun in the fall of 2011 – received a disproportionate share of income in the years following the Great Recession. In 2010, wealthy "one percenters" received 17 percent of the total U.S. income. The top 10 percent of households accounted for 44 percent of all the income paid that year (Keister 2014).

Wealth (which includes homes, cars, stocks, and the like) has become even more concentrated at the top – 10 times more than income (Saez and Zucman 2016). The Allianz Global Health Report of 2014 showed that the United States had the largest wealth inequality gap of fifty-five countries studied, leading the writers of the report to re-name it "The Unequal States of America" (Sherman 2014). Changes to tax codes have fueled unprecedented growth for the wealthiest families and their heirs. According to former Secretary of Labor Robert Reich (2015), "the nation is on the cusp of the largest inter-generational transfer of wealth in history. A study from the Boston College Center on Wealth and Philanthropy projects a total of $59 trillion passed down to heirs between 2007 and 2061." A smaller and smaller number of people are getting richer and richer. Wealth is skyrocketing among those at the very top – the 0.1% (Saez and Zucman 2016).

CEO pay and benefits have been increasing over the past several decades. In 1965, the average CEO earned 24 times more than the average worker; by 2000, that figure was up to 300 (Mishel 2006). Another set of analyses averaging firm-specific ratios showed CEO to worker compensation was 20 times higher in 1965, but had risen to 383.4 times higher in 2000. The ratio dipped to 193.23 as a result of the Great Recession, but the average CEO made 295.9 times the average employee in 2013 (Davis and Mishel 2014).

A recent study concluded that the United States is unique in compensating its CEOs so well. Researchers found that the median CEO pay in the United States was 23 percent higher than in the United Kingdom and 55 percent higher than the rest of Europe (Conyon et al. 2009). Though U.S. trends toward higher compensation are clear (not only among CEOs but also among Hollywood stars and professional athletes), the reasons for the trends are murkier (Kaplan and Rauh 2010). The answer is likely found, at least partly, in the cultural values of the United States, which discourage putting brakes on income attainment. If some people can command salaries in the stratosphere, many Americans see no reason why they should not do so.

All of these trends contribute to racial disparities in work and wealth because they play out in a society that began with white capitalists and workers hoarding economic opportunities while closing out people of color. The white advantage embedded in U.S. systems and policies, and the resulting spoils, accumulated from one generation to the next. Though some overt discrimination was eliminated through the laws and consciousness raising of the 1960s' Civil Rights Movement, there were not major alterations in the structures of "economic resources and business inheritances that have favored whites for centuries and still persist today" (Feagin 2014: 173). Thus white men continue to be overrepresented among the ranks of both CEOs and the "one percent." Further, recent increases in wealth inequality are racialized. A rigorous study of the same families showed that between 1985 and 2009 the difference in wealth between white and black families tripled: increasing from $85,000 to $236,500 (Shapiro, Meschede, and Osoro 2013). During economic downturns, the least skilled workers, disproportionately poor people of color, lose job opportunities to people higher up in the labor queue. There are variations between and within particular racial-ethnic groups of course. One study discovered that Latino immigrants, especially women and those with low skills, were hurt more by the Great Recession than immigrants from Asian countries (Li and Edwards 2012).

The 1990s witnessed the most robust labor market in decades, but some groups were left behind, and this trend has shown little sign of changing. In the middle and at the end of that decade the unemployment rate for blacks was almost double that of whites (Marable 2015: 279). Table 6.1 shows that unemployment rates are affected by education for black Americans, in particular. While almost 16 percent of black high school dropouts cannot find work, only 3.9 percent of

Table 6.1   Unemployment Rate by Highest Level of Educational Attainment and Race-Ethnicity, 2015

	Less than a high school diploma	High school diploma only	Bachelor's degree only
Black	15.9	9.7	3.9
Latino	6.6	5.9	3.7
White	6.8	4.6	2.6
Asian	5.4	4.1	3.2

Source: Bureau of Labor Statistics, 2015 Current Population Survey data, "Employment Status of the Civilian Noninstitutional Population 25 Years and over ..." http://www.bls.gov/cps/aa2015/cpsaat07.pdf.

college graduates face that situation. In 2015, blacks with or without a high school diploma were about twice as likely as comparable whites, Latinos, or Asians to be unemployed.

Black women continue to have higher employment rates than black men with comparable education largely because they fill lower level jobs in female-dominated industries. As discussed earlier, young men of color have been particularly affected by the trend that new jobs for those without higher education have been increasingly concentrated in female-dominated occupations. Employers seek skill sets they do not believe African American and Latino men possess. Some of the jobs go to recent immigrants.

Lower income Latina and African American women are propelled into the labor force by the high rates of incarceration, unemployment, and underemployment of the men from their racial-ethnic groups. Rates of employment for poor women of color also increased in the 1990s because of changes in social policy; young mothers on social welfare had to get paying jobs. The combination of changes in the economy and social welfare policies have been particularly devastating for single mothers, increasing numbers of whom find themselves with neither a job nor aid for months at a time (Turner et al. 2006). The major overhaul of welfare in the mid 1990s got a lot more poor mothers into the labor force, but the jobs they are able to secure do not necessarily lift them out of poverty (e.g. Hofferth 2002).

Shaefer and Edin's ambitious multi method study found a notable rise in *extreme poverty* which started at the end of the 1990s and continued into the twenty-first century, ahead of the Great Recession. From 1996 to 2013 (well into the economic recovery), there was a 311 percent increase in the number of families receiving SNAP benefits (food stamps) who had *no other income* (Shaefer and Edin 2013). They also discovered that the poorest families with children fueled a rise in spells of very low income because this has become a chronic rather than an episodic experience (Shaefer, Edin, and Talbert 2015). It appears that welfare reform has both decreased child poverty rates and sunk the poor who do not have jobs into deep poverty, though analysts debate the overall impact.

Incarceration Nation

The incarceration trends touched on earlier have reached epidemic proportions; if you do a google search for the term "incarceration nation" you will find it referenced in numerous books, articles, and

Table 6.2   Comparison of General and Prison Populations for Four Racial-Ethnic Groups, 2010

Racial-ethnic Group	Percentage of General Population	Percentage of Prison Population
(non-Hispanic) White	64	39
American Indian	0.9	1
Hispanic	16	19
Black	13	40

Source: Calculated by the Prison Pipeline Initiative from U.S. Census Summary File 1, 2010 http: //www.prisonpolicy.org/profiles/US.html

interviews. The incarceration rates of young black men increased considerably during the 1990s and continued to rise in the twenty-first century. Recent figures presented in a National Research Council report (2014) show that the U.S. incarceration rate is 5 to 10 times higher than in western European and other democratic countries. In 2014, 707 out of every 100,000 U.S. citizens were incarcerated, compared to 474 per 100,000 in Russia, 284 in Iran, 111 in Greece, and 77 in Germany (Collier 2014). The tremendous increase in incarceration has altered work trajectories among African Americans, in particular. Recent data (Table 6.2) reveal that whites are underrepresented in prison but three other racial ethnic groups are overrepresented. There is a large disproportion of African Americans in prison. Of all those incarcerated, 40 percent were African American, yet African Americans made up a little more than 13 percent of the U.S. population. A report by the Lakota People's Law Project in 2015 tells a similar story. American Indians are put behind bars at much higher rates than their white counterparts: four times higher among men and six times higher among women. The total number of American Indians (per capita) incarcerated in state and federal prisons was estimated at 38 percent above the national average.

Those who are poor and poorly educated are most likely to end up in the criminal justice system. Young African American men (under thirty-five) without a high school degree were *more likely to be in prison than to have a job* (Western 2007). There is a vicious cycle such that poor youth – failed by failing schools and with no prospects for decent jobs – turn to illegal or harmful ways to get money and status. However we also know that poor youth of color are far more likely than their white and middle-class counterparts to go to jail for minor offenses. There is also a preponderance of evidence showing racism at *every step* of the criminal justice process.

Western notes that "[b]y the early 2000s, the chances of imprison-ment were more closely linked to race and school failure than at any time in the previous twenty years." As a lack of jobs and low wages became permanent features of life in the inner city, an increasingly "punitive criminal justice system" removed large numbers of inner-city youth from the scene, locking them up for minor infractions and making it hard for them to get out (Western 2007: 79). Some analysts contend that incarceration is a modern day version of slavery, with the goal of exploiting, controlling, and excluding blacks (Marable 2015; Alexander 2012). While they are in prison inmates are removed from labor markets and their labor is exploited, and useable job skills are eroded. When they are released they have little power to bargain over the terms of their employment in some of the worst jobs avail-able (Western 2007). Recall the studies showing that employers are especially reluctant to hire young blacks and Latinos they believe to have been convicted of a crime. The economic consequences of a con-viction vary by race.

Immigration

The United States is considered a nation of immigrants. However we have seen that only immigrant groups who are able to claim whiteness gain the full benefits of being American. The last major wave of immigrants in the early 1900s came from Europe while the majority of today's immigrants come from Latin American and Asian countries and they are defined as non-white. There has been consid-erable backlash. Some whites in the working and middle classes are concerned that immigrants are taking jobs away from them. During and after the 2016 Presidential campaign Donald Trump's promise to deport more undocumented immigrants and build a massive wall on the Mexico border held considerable appeal.

Are immigrant workers taking good jobs away from the native-born? A recent report from the U.S. Bureau of Labor Statistics (2015) shows that workers born outside the United States are concentrated in low wage occupational sectors, while native-born workers claim managerial and professional jobs. The pattern is more pronounced among women: 32.4 percent of foreign-born women had service sector jobs compared to 19.5 percent of native-born workers while 31.5 percent of native-born workers were in sales and office jobs compared to 22.2 percent of foreign-born women.

As told in the preceding chapter, capitalists in labor intensive industries actively recruit Mexican and Asian immigrants who will do the jobs that no one else wants. Industries seeking immigrants to perform dirty, difficult, or low status work for very low wages include: agriculture, low-end manufacturing, building, cleaning, maintenance and construction, and hospitality. Employers can justify the subsistence wages they pay immigrants by pointing to the even lower wages those workers would make in their home countries (Maldonado 2009). The subservience of immigrant workers offers an advantage in the competitive search for profit.

Unauthorized immigrants are disproportionately found in the most menial, lowest-paying jobs. Construction is one new (male-dominated) industry in which the share of undocumented immigrants has grown considerably since the turn of this century. Perhaps these industries are trying to cut labor costs; alternatively the people who used to fill these jobs may be doing other work. Immigrants who are in the country without permission also fill certain kinds of service jobs in numbers that far exceed their percentage of the labor force. They are 28 percent of dishwashers, 21 percent of parking lot attendants and 27 percent of maids and housekeepers. Yet these immigrants make up 5.4 percent of the civilian labor force (Passel and Cohn 2009: 15).

Undocumented immigrants have no recourse and few alternatives when faced with harsh working conditions, long hours, unreasonable supervisors, or really low wages. Workers who have been smuggled into the country are particularly vulnerable because they have big debts to pay off. Another advantage of undocumented immigrants for employers is that they tend to arrive during economic upturns (Hanson 2009).

These immigrants are not taking good working and middle-class jobs as many fear. Because undocumented immigrants are typically low skilled workers, their presence puts downward pressure on the wages of low skilled jobs (Hanson 2009). When they compete with native workers for the same jobs, they are preferred because employers believe they will work harder and be easier to control (Maldonaldo 2009). A study of the hotel industry discovered that employers preferred Latinos and Latinas who could not speak English over African Americans, who have a "bad attitude" label attached to them (Zamudio and Lichter 2008).

Immigrants are also a common source for the reproductive labor that used to be done by housewives. The steady flow of women into full time positions as well as their greater presence in professional jobs has fueled a demand for immigrants who will provide personal services at low cost. Latino and Asian women are sought for the low-level service work that abounds in jobs in large retail stores, hotels, restaurants, and hospitals. They are also recruited for so-called "downgraded manufacturing" jobs with pay levels too low to attract U.S.-born workers (Hondagneu-Sotelo 2002).

Thus immigrants are favored for jobs that might have gone to low-skilled U.S. workers most in need of jobs; they are disproportionately American Indians, African Americans, and Puerto Ricans but include poor whites. In economic terms, immigration "redistributes income from low-skilled native workers to employers and it creates a net gain in national income by allowing employers to use their land, capital and technology more productively" (Hanson 2009: 9). As has been true throughout labor history, immigrants bear the brunt of the average American's frustration with economic insecurity, while the capitalists who make money from immigrant labor stay under the radar.

Worker–Job Mismatches and Work–Family Conflict

The mismatching of people and jobs is considerably worse today than in earlier historical periods and is likely to increase in the future (Kalleberg 2007). As Chapter 4 reported, spatial mismatches (when the jobs are not where the people are) are common among the racial-ethnic groups who are disproportionately poor – American Indians, African Americans, and Latinos (such as Puerto Ricans and Dominicans in New York City and Mexicans in the west). Meanwhile working and middle-class whites enjoy access to jobs with good incomes in areas "protected" from the urban poor (Kalleberg 2007: 143).

Trends in job growth suggest that the lack of appropriate jobs for men from poor communities of color will continue. Employment projections prepared by the U.S. Bureau of Labor Statistics (2015) show that most of the occupations expected to grow substantially between 2014 and 2024 are those considered to be women's work.

Though 36.5 percent of jobs available today require post high school education or training (U.S. Bureau of Labor Statistics 2014a), analysts predict that a higher percentage of jobs will require these advanced credentials in the future (Carnevale et al. 2014). While skill and education requirements are being inflated at all levels of employment, more low skill jobs are being added to the labor market (U.S. Bureau of Labor Statistics 2014b). Still, many people who used to have positions that accorded middle-class lifestyles have been pushed into the lower level jobs that poor people of color might have had (Autor 2015).

Unless there are major policy changes, companies will continue to seek (especially women) immigrants to perform the plentiful menial jobs, leaving poorly educated U.S.-born workers as Marx's proverbial reserve army of the unemployed. Career paths are nonexistent for the majority of low wage workers. Much has been written about invisible "glass ceilings" that represent the exclusion of women from the top tiers of powerful organizations. Now analysts use the concept of "revolving doors" to capture the experience of precarious employees who shift from one low wage job to another, and "glass boxes" to depict the reality that many workers in entry level positions will not move up during their entire work lives (e.g. Williams 2013).

Another consequential trend is the mismatching of people and hours of work; those who most need work cannot find enough of it, while others have too much work (Schor 1991; Kalleberg 2007). The Families and Work Institute found that well over half of wage and salaried employees would prefer to work *fewer* hours. Working too much contributes to feelings of "time famine" and the sense that work intrudes on personal life. Seventy-five percent of employees reported feeling deprived of time with children. Why do people work more than they want to? They say it is because they need the money (Tang and Wadsworth 2008: 9).

Mismatches in hours put undue stress on employees and families burdened by work overload while they wreak havoc on those without enough work to make ends meet. Sometimes the latter groups are already working long hours, but the pay is not sufficient to support their families. Employers also use part-time work to bypass paying out fringe benefits or they cut people's hours when things get slow. Many workers have to piece together several part-time jobs, which can be a scheduling nightmare for those raising children. Because people lower down the race and gender hierarchies have less market power, they are more likely to experience a mismatch between their desires or qualifications and the kinds of jobs they can get (Kalleberg 2007). One study found that whites were less likely than blacks to be working in jobs below their skill set (Vaisey 2006).

Women of all ages and all stages of life continue to be major participants in the labor force, leading to work–family conflict for most. Some families can make the choice to cut back on work or have one person withdraw from the labor force, but the majority of families do not have such options. Many families send more and more of the tasks – and pleasures – of day-to-day life into the marketplace. Their lives feel sped up and they report a state of constant exhaustion as they try to juggle increasingly demanding jobs with their personal lives (Schulte 2014). The demand for quality, affordable childcare is far greater than the supply. All of these pressures are intensified for those who have the fewest economic resources.

Among racial-ethnic groups with high unemployment rates for men, women are propelled into the labor force even when they have very young children. These single mothers do not reject the economic stability and social status associated with marriage; on the contrary, they value it so much that they are delaying marriage until they find a spouse who can help offer "the whole package" (Edin and Kefalas 2011). Their options for childcare are severely limited. They may have to settle for substandard childcare if they are unable to rely on family members – who are also likely to be struggling to make ends meet.

Moreover, these are the workers who are most likely to strain to get to jobs on time because they rely on public transportation (think of Jamal from Chapter 5). The kinds of jobs they have can quickly be put in jeopardy when such employees are late or absent because of childcare issues. Women and men at the bottom of the occupational hierarchy have jobs that are also notoriously inflexible, so low-income parents are far less likely to be able to participate as fully as their middle-class counterparts in their children's schools. This is how webs of disadvantage work, keeping class inequalities created by the race hierarchy intact.

Interactive Service Work

Work that requires interaction with customers or clients has grown tremendously and is expected to continue to do so. It is a unique form of labor because it is simultaneously produced and consumed, requiring capitalists to create new methods to maximize the value of labor power they have purchased. Now management seeks to control not only work tasks and pace of work, but also employee displays of emotion. Those who do interactive service work (disproportionately African American and Latina women), must adhere to specific proto-cols when helping customers, who are additional "bosses" they are expected to please (Macdonald and Sirianni 1996). Management tries to "squeeze out" the human element from this service work, "leaving only automatons, whose actions and interactions with customers are controlled and decided in advance by the corporation" (Ritzer 2010: 37).

Appearance also becomes more salient, as employers know that how employees look affects the customer's experience. As one group of authors put it, "employee heads, hearts and now bodies feature in the wage-effort bargain" (Warhurst, Thompson, and Nickson 2009). Bodies have always been important to owners for what they could *do* but for interactive service work, bodies matter because of what they represent. Given their continued higher social status, white bodies carry a greater exchange value in the labor market (Witz 2003: 41). Those "bodies" are accorded more deference and respect, especially from other whites (Williams 2006).

Work that requires display of "appropriate" emotion no matter what one is feeling has been critiqued as particularly alienating (Hochschild 2003); it may be especially so for employees of color who typically face customer antagonism and lack of respect, especially if they are women. In fact studies show that women are expected to be "nicer than natural" as they serve customers (Forseth 2005: 44). Gender and racial-ethnic identity combine to affect how much emotional labor is required to do what management requires, and how much of an affront it is to the employee's sense of self-worth (MacDonald and Merrill 2009: 114–2 7). Thus young black men in the fast food industry prefer working with food rather than people because the cashier jobs require "swallowing one's pride and accepting abuse calmly" (Leidner 1991: 163).

One of the most difficult aspects of interactive service work is dealing with irate customers. When sociologist Christine Williams worked in toy stores, she discovered that corporations create rules about this with particular customers in mind. At a major toy chain where she worked it was okay to veer from customer service rules when the offending customers were black men (by calling the police) whereas when white women acted out, they got what they wanted. Williams concludes that "white women were immediately seen as potential spenders; black men, as potential thieves" (Williams 2006: 131). The company norms have statistical discrimination built in.

Careers in the New Economy

Chapter 1 described work careers as sets of jobs that form a progression, typically involving increases in responsibility, authority, and pay. Careers used to unfold within the same company, and the same location. But technological change, company restructuring, and global markets have altered the nature of careers. Organizational careers have been replaced by "boundary-less careers" which are more entrepreneurial and occupation-based. They span locations, companies, and industries (Arthur and Rousseau 2001). Increasingly, work is done in teams composed of people with diverse skills. Employees are judged more on results than commitment or "face time." They are also increasingly evaluated by peers, as the once-ubiquitous organizational pyramid has been flattened considerably; there are fewer layers of management. A typical career of the future will have even more rungs than in the past, involving lateral as well as upward mobility (Williams, Muller, and Kilanski 2012), and, if the Great Recession that began in 2008 is an indication, of downward mobility too. Given that African Americans and Latino immigrants are particularly vulnerable to firing or demotion, they are likely to be most affected by such trends.

The shift to a global economy and an increasingly multicultural U.S. workforce calls for cultural competence: the ability to think critically about one's own culture as well as to understand and appreciate cultural differences. To be successful, careerists need to work well with people from racial-ethnic groups and cultures different from their own.

This may be a particular issue in the United States. The predominant mode of sociopolitical thought in the twenty-first century United States downplays the validity of culture differences and assumes the superiority of American values (Bonilla-Silva 2001). While people from any country probably have a tendency to think their ways of doing things are best, Americans have a reputation for being particularly ethnocentric. This comes from a history of global cultural dominance, the relative isolation of the United States from other nations and the emphasis on American exceptionalism. Whites raised and educated in predominantly white spaces may find themselves particularly ill equipped for the work and organizations of the future requiring appreciation of non-dominant viewpoints and practices.

This historical period has witnessed tremendous progress for some people of color; work barriers have yielded to their tenacity, education, motivation, and really hard work. At the same time this overview has revealed an intensification of practices and policies that lead to greater income inequality, and therefore continued race-based inequality. Race discrimination continues. As discussion shifts to ways of reducing work-related race disparities, you might think about the activism and resistance described in Chapter 3. There is always something that can be done.

7
Reducing Race-Based Inequities at Work

The way people explain racial-ethnic patterns in work opportunities and experiences affects what kinds of solutions they propose to change them. U.S. culture encourages us to explain white advantage in employment, pay, and promotion rates by emphasizing individual initiative and skill, emanating from "appropriate" cultural practices. It follows, if one accepts this view, that racial disparities will be eliminated when all racial-ethnic groups accumulate the requisite human capital and soft skills, the social networks, and the drive to succeed.

Yet work lives play out in a larger, dynamic web of discrimination that shapes U.S. society. The various components of that web exert multifaceted influences on the chances for people to get good jobs and have successful careers – or to get any job at all. Thus without eliminating neighborhood poverty, for example, it is difficult to ensure that the next generation of poor youth will present the skills employers seek. Even William Julius Wilson, who has emphasized cultural factors in accounting for race patterns in poverty and unemployment, concluded that "structure trumps culture." In Wilson's words: "[C]ulture matters, but I would have to say it does not matter nearly as much as structure ... it is hard to overstate the importance of racialist structural factors" (Wilson 2009: 152). He makes an additional important point. While many pundits and policy-makers zero in on what they see as cultural dysfunction among poor people of color, the *dominant* culture, having been birthed with racism, plays a larger role in perpetuating race inequities in economic success. This is because racist cultural attitudes became embedded in work (and all of the other) institutions. As the theorists introduced at the beginning of the book emphasize, structured or systematic racism is propped up by cultural messages and symbols.

Thus there is no quick fix for the racial inequality at the heart of the U.S. economic system. The disparities have been accumulating for so long and are so firmly entrenched that it would take a concerted effort at all levels of society to knock the race hierarchy out from under the nation (Marable 2015; Hacker 2003; Reskin 2012). Large scale social change is the surest route to eliminating racial disparities in work opportunities and experiences. A crucial step is to chip away at stereotypic cultural schema, so that the images lodged in the unconscious shift. Educational, media, and work organizations are already doing that; more and better campaigns to help re-mix the cultural recordings that play in our heads will elevate us to the next level. The "democratization" of messages made possible by internet access and the huge audiences that can be reached via social media and video channels is a double edged sword. Media can be harnessed to promote racial equality but are just as easily used to promote fear and division along racial, ethnic, and religious lines.

The economic realm offers an especially important site to create change. Because it is such a central and vital social institution, a major blow to racism in work would crack the racist foundations of linked institutions. Changing demographics and global marketplaces are already pushing organizational leaders to eliminate racism. Further, the workplace is the single most common location where adults from different racial-ethnic groups have close and continuing interaction (Estlund 2003; Hyun 2005).

Organizational Change

As research reviewed earlier indicated, work organizations can be set up to minimize racial bias and maximize positive cross-race and ethnic interaction. It is a choice.

Formalized Procedures

The example of the military shows, for instance, that race disparities in work outcomes can be shrunk by changing systems, irrespective of the attitudes held by personnel. Policies and practices that everyone simply takes for granted are a good starting place. Employees and leaders can collect data on how promotions and raises are allocated rather than assuming that the process is neutral (Acker 2006). In their case study of careers of geoscientists in oil and gas companies, Williams and her colleagues (2012) found that a lack of common job descriptions and career ladders left a lot of room for supervisor discretion. Research has consistently shown that discretion invites race and gender bias, even if it is at a subconscious level. When there are systematic procedures in place, there is less racial bias in personnel decisions including hiring, firing, and performance evaluations (Reskin 2003; Elvira and Zatzick 2002). In general, highly formalized and rational systems lead to greater racial-ethnic diversity in hiring, fuller representation of people of color in positions of authority, and smaller wage disparities (Pager and Shepherd 2008).

Organizational policies and practices can mitigate the tendency for racial bias in hiring, firing, wages, and promotions (Tilly 1998; Petersen and Saporta 2004). Sometimes this requires revamping practices that have been explicitly designed to reduce racial bias. For example, one firm assigned newly hired people of color to supervisors who were also people of color. Because the supervisors were in less powerful positions than their white counterparts, it was the white newcomers who benefitted from this decision (Lefkowitz 1994). Human resource departments could copy best practices from marketing and finance, using hard data to make a range of personnel decisions ("people analytics") rather than relying on informal networks, gut feelings, and guesses about work ethic (Bohnet 2016: 15).

Accountability is vital. When managers and supervisors know they are going to be held accountable for the personnel decisions they make, they are more likely to make them fairly (e.g. Kalev, Dobbin and Kelly 2006; Castilla 2008). Research also suggests that oversight reduces race-based work inequalities. In Thomas' L.A. study, the employers subject to affirmative action law demonstrated less racial bias than those who were not (2003). Sweeney's (2011) in-depth study of hiring and branch managers in temporary hiring agencies also showed this clearly. Other scholars had suggested that temp agencies would be less inclined to use race-based stereotypes to discriminate because they would likely gather a lot more data on potential employees than is typical. Instead, Sweeney discovered that most of the managers interviewed relied on their images of "race" (along with class and gender) in "describing, analyzing, and matching job applicants with job openings." There was one manager, however, who would remind employers of the law when they made race-coded or overt requests for whites. The employers would quickly back off from the request and the manager was free to send the most qualified candidates.

Although American companies are spending small fortunes on diversity initiatives to provide racial-ethnic equity for women and men the desired results are fairly elusive (Castilla 2008). As one pair of researchers put it, "we are surprised at the difficulty that some organizations continue to have with diversity management, and their inability to resolve and prevent discrimination lawsuits (Wooten and James 2004: 24)." Perhaps there is a false sense that a company is immune to racial bias if its leaders are spending a lot of money on diversity initiatives.

Reducing Bias

Instead, organizations must make creating and managing diversity a central *strategic* goal in order to inoculate themselves against race (and gender) discrimination lawsuits (Wooten and James 2004).

One interesting strategy comes from the study of financial markets. After the Great Recession, financial regulators required major banks to conduct "stress tests" to diagnose hidden weaknesses. Many of the same invisible mechanisms that such tests reveal – "faulty assumptions, a lack of internal safeguards and unrecognized biases" contribute to racial-ethnic inequality in workplaces. Thus, organizations could be required or encouraged to conduct periodic racial inequality stress tests (Harris and Lieberman 2015: 10–11.)

Researchers typically conclude that diversity initiatives have to be thorough, ongoing, and built into performance evaluations to be successful. Though people on diverse work teams are often uncomfortable or hostile, this is less common when they believe their company values diversity (Bohnet 2016). If an organization attaches negative sanctions for overt or covert bias against women and men of color, employees and managers are more apt to align their behavior. Attitude changes may follow or not, but the atmosphere will change. Workplaces free of expressed racial bias would have eliminated a layer of racism, making it easier for people from all racial-ethnic groups to do their best work, and for organizations to attract topnotch employees.

In the age of social media and 24/7 news cycles, swift and harsh punishments are sometimes meted out to those who make racially offensive comments. Executives and supervisors may feel pressure to exact harsh penalties to send a strong signal to customers and competitors. This climate leads some whites, in particular, to avoid people of color out of fear of saying or doing the wrong thing, which diminishes everyone's productivity. Employers who give employees the chance to learn what constitutes inappropriate behavior (and why) stand to reap the rewards of greater productivity and satisfaction – and fewer embarrassing moments in the public spotlight.

Given that most workplaces have been framed as "white spaces," it is particularly important for whites, including those at the very top, to learn what it is like for people of color to work in such places. As recounted earlier, even professional employees of color find their talent underestimated. Across the occupational spectrum, employees of color are often viewed first and foremost in terms of race stereotypes. They experience small and large acts of rudeness and exclusion on a day-to-day basis from peers, superiors, and subordinates. There are rich and varied research reports and first-person narratives available to provide an inside view for whites who do not understand this reality.

Researchers can help by analyzing white work spaces, exposing the unmarked racial practices that continue to advantage whites under the guise of equal opportunity for all (Feagin 2010; Bonilla-Silva 2006). In an illustrative letter, a high-level black manager asks the white boss to be seen, truly seen, as an invested and involved partner whose work environment is muddied or fogged up by a "miasma" of practices that mark them as the racial other. The writer notes that "you probably can't see [this] but I can tell you about it . . . And maybe in the future you'll see it for yourself" (Caver and Livers 2002: 12).

Of course people of color sometimes exhibit racial bias as well – toward members of other racial-ethnic groups, and even toward members of their own group. Sometimes, say experts on black and white leadership development, black professionals have had so many difficult experiences with whites that they do not trust even those whites who might be good allies (Caver and Livers 2002). Some diversity consultants suggest tailoring educational programs to people from particular racial-ethnic groups (e.g. Crowfoot and Chesler 1996) to allow for the different social realities of diverse groups.

Another promising idea is to create racially diverse "learning circles." These small groups are tasked with studying issues of diversity and inclusion in the workplace. They meet from time to time to talk about what they have found out, and discuss how that might apply in their work setting (Livers and Caver 2002). Ethnocentric or cultural blind spots can be reduced when employees are encouraged to question their assumptions and to recognize that what we call "American" ways of working and managing use elite white men as the standard.

Anything that gets people listening to one another talk about their experiences in the racial structures of workplaces is a step in the right direction. Shining a light on what is so often unseen – especially by people at the top of the race hierarchy – is essential. Once employees' awareness of their learned racial-ethnic biases is raised, employers need to provide them with specific tools researchers have developed to help make better decisions (Bohnet 2015: 58).

IAT researchers provide some good news about how even deep-seated racial-ethnic biases can be reduced. Teaching people about stereotypes and biases reduces their tendency to think in those terms, as measured by the Implicit Association Test. Repeated exposure to counter-stereotypic examples, images, and experiences makes a difference as well (Dasgupta and Greenwald 2001; Dasgupta 2004). Of course it remains to be seen whether such changes "stick" and how well the experimental setting translates to the real world. Still, experiments beyond the laboratory suggest that it is possible to change deep-seated biases and the actions that might stem from them. Employers, supervisors, and co-workers can control implicit race and gender biases, though it takes motivation, introspection, and training to do so (Quillian 2006).

Unfortunately, some whites point to universal bias as a way to dodge their own responsibility for improving their understanding of how race operates in labor markets and work settings. The argument goes something like this: "If everyone is biased, then I'm not to blame and there's nothing we can do about it." Companies will make greater progress toward racial equality when managers, supervisors, and employees from all racial-ethnic groups see how their actions and seemingly race-neutral workplace practices and policies give unfair advantage to whites – and then set about changing that. Recall that work organizations and employees of all race-ethnicities benefit from fair processes and inclusive work environments (Feagin et al. 2001; Cortina 2008).

Employee Strategies

The jobs of people of color have typically included having to disprove the pre-judgments that weigh down the heavy invisible knapsacks they haul to the workplace. No matter what the other work tasks, the planning, self-control, and emotional labor required to prove bosses and co-workers wrong makes any job harder. Preparation to handle difficult questions and situations is crucial (Hyun 2006). Employees who are informed about potential workplace obstacles will deal with them most effectively. Internal and external mentorship also buffers the stresses of working in an unwelcoming or hostile environment (Livers and Caver 2002). When people of color actively seek jobs that require co-ordination with other units, they put themselves in the position to make visible contributions, break down stereotypes, and make themselves more promotable. White employees who monitor their work spaces for racial harassment or unfair treatment and support their co-workers of color make tangible contributions to their organizations. If undoing racial discrimination in workplaces becomes part of more job descriptions, social change is more likely to ensue.

The more frequent career moves of the new economy make networks even more imperative for success. In fact, strong networks will be increasingly important to making it through the periodic downsizing expected to characterize careers in the new economy (Williams et al. 2012: 568). We know that people of color do not have access to as many useful network ties as their white counterparts. Thus it will be more crucial than ever for them to focus on building networks full of useful contacts.

Studies have shown that people of color improve their chances for career success when they take an active role in developing social networks at work and look outside their company for social support. For example, African American men in male-dominated professions gain from cultivating relationships with influential white men (Wingfield 2012). Women cannot use male camaraderie so they have to be even more creative, resourceful and expansive in networking (Smith 2006; Wingfield 2012). Within work organizations whites can make a point to mentor, sponsor, and even just share information across racial lines. They can also help break down the visible and invisible fences that keep people from different racial groups apart.

Chapter 5 showed that people of color in low-income communities have a strong need for better networks. Community members, aided by business and college volunteers, can use their own ties and resources to help entry level job seekers strengthen their networks and build up their human capital, including soft skills.

Further research on the impact of workplace culture and subcultures, as well as the organizational environments in which companies operate is important (Reskin 2003). The studies of the military suggest the tremendous significance of such social contexts. We also need more studies about what causes people to reject negative stereotypes about people from racial-ethnic groups different from their own. As researchers pinpoint when and why implicit bias is activated – in hiring and promotion decisions as well as workplace interactions among peers and supervisors – further solutions for changing that behavior will be available.

It can seem daunting to challenge the structures that produce work inequality, but "the little things are linked to the big things" so even small changes matter (Schwalbe 2007: 269). Because work inequality is created partly through social interaction, one individual's actions can help to undo it. Employees can write new rules, create cultures of solidarity, and challenge seemingly race-neutral everyday behaviors that legitimate inequality. As workplaces fill with whites and people of color willing to speak out about racial harassment, micro aggression, and other forms of racial bias in workplaces as well as to fix weaknesses in practices (perhaps revealed by racial inequality stress tests), the quality of work and work lives will improve for everyone. Recall that even employees who witness hostility are negatively affected and that top orchestras did not have the best performers until their audition practices changed.

Social Policy and Social Movements

In the past decade or so, there have been renewed protests against the tremendous economic inequality in the United States and the cultural values that reinforce it. During the 2016 presidential primary, candidate Bernie Sanders' call for greater economic equality resonated with young people, suggesting the possibility that change may be ahead. Racial and economic inequalities have always been linked, so to the extent that progressives are able to reign in capital's "werewolf hunger for profit" they contribute to a more level playing field for all racial–ethnic groups.

In recent years, labor organizers, and low-wage workers have been visibly fighting for higher pay. In November of 2012, there were a series of strikes of fast food establishments in New York City. By 2014 fast food workers had been joined by retail workers (especially Walmart employees), home health care aides, airport workers, and adjunct professors in multicity walkouts, protests, and marches. Organized labor kept up the pressure for a $15 an hour minimum and they have gained some traction. Several cities have implemented the $15 minimum wage and several more are in the process of doing so. The first two states to adopt this increase to the minimum age were California and New York, where the cost of living is very high.

In November of 2016 voters in four additional states passed minimum wage increases. There were also nationwide marches for the right to unionize as well as the $15 minimum wage – organized by coalitions of service workers in several industries, with the addition of Uber drivers. The group Fight for $15, organized by NYC fast food workers, was out in the streets carrying signs that said "Not One Step Back." Protesters voiced concern that the incoming presidential administration would not be receptive to their proposals or, worse, roll back gains that have been made. Donald Trump campaigned as an advocate for working people; perhaps that *will* extend to low-paid service workers, though his Labor Secretary has been strongly against the idea of a minimum wage hike.

Proponents of increasing the minimum wage argue that it would lift millions out of poverty and stimulate the economy. Opponents argue that the most vulnerable workers will be pushed out of jobs by the increase, as employers would likely respond by cutting or moving jobs to maintain profit margins.

Working to improve wages and working conditions could unify the many different ethnicities that make up the "in between" racial groups of Latino and Asian (e.g. Trumpbour and Bernard 2002). As the demographic composition and the industrial distribution of jobs have changed, labor unions have become more inclusive. Though men are still somewhat more likely to be union members than women, the growth in unionization has come from industries where women predominate, such as health care and social assistance.

The racial composition of labor unions has changed markedly. Today workers of African descent have higher rates of union membership than Asians and most Latino groups (Bureau of Labor Statistics 2015). Public sector employment is highly unionized and has high proportions of African Americans, which partly explains this trend. Workers born in Puerto Rico (who are U.S. citizens) have high unionization rates as well. While recent immigrants have very low rates of union membership, immigrants who came to the country before 1980 have higher unionization rates than workers born in the United States (Milkman and Luce 2015). These trends suggest that one way forward for unions will be to continue to reach out to newer immigrants and to make sure the leadership and the agenda is aligned with the needs of its members from all racial-ethnic groups.

Surely unions would benefit from the same formalization, racial inequality stress tests, and diversity programming recommended for companies. Though rife with its own race-based hoarding and exclusion, organized labor has a long and important history of improving the work and family lives of average U.S. workers. According to labor relations experts and union leaders alike, it is important that labor unions visibly and vigorously re-assert themselves in the fight to get workers a fairer sized slice of the economic pie. If the full "power of the people" is harnessed across racial-ethnic lines, it can play a far bigger role in reversing some of the recent trends toward greater race *and class* inequality in work and employment. The benefits would accrue to the much-discussed white working-class men whose anger at being pushed out of their lanes to the American dream yielded a voting bloc for Donald Trump.

Many current labor leaders recognize that the chance to have a good job is a social justice issue. According to Gary Chaison of Clark University, U.S. labor unions have been helping the most exploited workers, who are not likely to be their members. He said "it's not about union members protecting themselves. It's about moving other people up. This is the whole civil rights movement all over again" (Greenhouse and Kasperkevic 2015). Initiatives such as Janitors for Justice combine community organizing with labor organizing. This is particularly consonant with the experiences of people of color, who have often relied on community in the fight for better wages and working conditions (Takaki 2008; Marable 2015; Glenn 2002; Trumpbour and Bernard 2002). During the Civil Rights Movement, the Southern Christian leadership conference provided crucial support for strikes and unionization. Reverend Martin Luther King Jr. was deeply concerned about economic issues. The title of his most famous protest was "The March on Washington for Jobs and Freedom." His goal was to draw attention to the "twin evils of discrimination and economic deprivation" (Engler 2010).

In the 1990s Dennis Rivera, who was educated in Puerto Rico, became the leader of New York City Local 1199 of the Service Employees Industrial Union. This local had a history of mobilizing its increasingly Puerto Rican and African American base. Under Rivera membership more than doubled and the local also became a "leader in arts and cultural programs for the labor movement." The union created its own childcare programs and summer camps. Rivera was known for speaking up about broader issues. He was an outspoken critic of Starbucks for eliminating unions, for instance (Trumpbour and Bernard 2002: 139). George Gresham took over in 2007. He has been at the forefront of national growth in union membership among healthcare workers. According to the Local 1199 SEIU website, Gresham has been "a leader for social justice, including advocating for quality healthcare, living wage (including the Fight for $15), supporting antipolice protests, environmental protection, and equal rights for women, immigrants, the LGBT community, and people of color." In his own words:

Ordinary people are under attack on so many different fronts in the current economic climate – from the skyrocketing cost of housing to out-of-reach college tuition – that we must take a holistic approach to advocating for them writ large, not only through collective bargaining. It is also becoming clear that – with the increasing attacks on the rights of women, communities of color and immigrants – social and economic justice are inextricably linked. In order for the labor movement to remain relevant, we must truly transform ourselves into facilitators of progressive coalitions. We must engage deeply with community allies, share resources, march side-by-side and support common policy goals. We should seek to understand, learn from and be guided by young activists who are bringing new energy and ideas to a wide range of causes such as gay, lesbian and transgender rights, immigration reform, climate change and Black Lives Matter.

(Gresham 2015)

State and federal policies, and therefore politics, also matter. Today the government makes it difficult for American Indian nations to develop their valuable energy resources. "As energy production in the United States reaches record levels, tribes find themselves missing out on a revolution that is bringing economic opportunities" to many other communities. Complicated bureaucratic procedures and government oversight interfere. Impoverished communities are sitting atop resources that amount to "dead capital." They continue to push for more control over their land (Regan 2014). It is ironic that the casinos which breathed economic life into many American Indian communities are now being legalized in many more states, creating greater competition and threating their gains.

Martin Luther King Jr. argued that job creation could not be left to capitalists. "Call it democracy, or call it democratic socialism, but there must be a better distribution of wealth within this country for all God's children." He proposed that government create new jobs "that enhance the social good" for those denied jobs from traditional labor markets (Engler 2010). This is exactly what the federal government did in 1935 when it instituted the Works Progress Administration which created jobs for the unemployed. As Ronald Reagan put it, the WPA was productive because "it gave men and women a chance to make some money along with the satisfaction of knowing they earned it" (Reagan 1990: 69).

Arguments in favor of creating a modern day version of the WPA include the idea that there is much useful work even those without a lot of human capital could do; there are bridges, roads, and other building projects desperately needed, as President Trump pointed out in his inaugural address. A federal works program could provide workers with new skills to take to other jobs, a benefit to private businesses. The major arguments against a WPA-type program are that it would be too expensive and that government should leave job creation to the more efficient private sector.

Given that the private sector does not seem to be creating enough well-paying work for those with the fewest formal skills, politicians might be wise to carefully consider government subsidized employment programs. A recent analysis of four decades of such programs concluded that this is a robust overall strategy for raising incomes and wellbeing (Dutta-Gupta et al. 2016).

Programs at the local level can facilitate better matching of the poor to available jobs by determining the needs of employers, identifying areas of local job growth, and providing training in soft and hard skills. To give one example, a report from the United Way of Los Angeles (2009) touts collaborative programs that provide people from poor communities with the skills needed to work in industries, such as oil, where there are a lot of employees slated to retire soon, or in growth industries, such as "green" construction or "green" energy. Initiatives like this one show that strategic partnerships can undo some of the economic damage that has been done during preceding decades.

The story of U.S. history has always been about a struggle to move the nation toward greater conformity with its founding principles of equality and justice (Massey 2007). As the campaign for the successor to President Obama showed, poor, middle, and working-class people in the second decade of the twenty-first century are frustrated, fearful, and fed up. As they lose their numerical dominance, some whites from every social class (including those at the top) seem to be looking for assurances that they will not lose their white privilege. Trump's popularity showed, among many other things, that using social division by race, ethnicity, and immigration status is still an effective way to keep the spotlight off elites, who benefit while so many others struggle.

Of course racial inequality contributes to class inequality *among whites*. The whites at the top benefit while the working and middle-class people to whom they appeal remain in subordinate positions, with little economic or political power. The challenge for the future is to turn that spotlight around and clarify for struggling families of all racial groups the real sources of their predicaments. As discussed, the major culprit is a largely unchecked capitalist system facilitated by a cultural emphasis on individualism over collectivity. Though part of the critique of capitalism has always been that it requires inequality, a capitalist economic system does not dictate that resources be allocated by race-ethnicity or that a lot of class inequality is optimal for the economy (cf. Bowles and Gintis 2001; Massey 2007).

The study of race and work is the first step toward getting rid of persistent inequality. The next step is to make changes wherever and whenever possible (cf. Schwalbe 2008). Will there be widespread activism to press for further race, class, and gender work equality? Will millennials energized by progressives' condemnation of present-day American capitalism mobilize to curb the quest for ever-increasing profit? How committed are people to eliminating racism at work?

It remains to be seen to what extent the employment systems and workplaces awaiting today's young people will be free of racial inequities. And it all depends . . . on all of us.

References

Acker, Joan. 2006. *Class Questions, Feminist Answers*. Lanham, MD: Rowman & Littlefield.

Alba, Richard D. 1985. *Italian Americans: Into the Twilight of Ethnicity*. Upper Saddle River, N.J.: Prentice Hall.

Albers, Patricia C. 1996. "From Legend to Land to Labor: Changing Perspectives on Native American Work." pp. 245–73 in Alice Littlefield and Martha C. Kanck, eds. Native Americans and Wage Labor: Ethnohistorical Perspectives. Norman and London: University of Oklahoma Press.

Aledo, Milagros "Mimi" and Maria C. Alvarado. 2006. "Dolores Huerta at Seventy-Five: Still Empowering Communities." *Harvard Journal of Hispanic Policy* 18: 13–18.

Alexander, Michele. 2012. *The New Jim Crow: Mass Incarceration in the Age of Colorblindness*. New York: The New Press.

Allen, Theodore. 1976. *Class Struggle and the Origin of Racial Slavery*. Somerville, M.A.: New England Free Press.

Aptheker, Herbert. 1983. *American Negro Slave Revolts*. International Publishers.

——1993. *Anti-Racism in U.S. History: The First 200 Years*. Westport, CT: Praeger.

Austin, Algernon. 2013a. "Native Americans and Jobs: The Challenge and the Promise." *Economic Policy Institute*. Briefing Paper #370. Washington, D.C.: EPI.

——2013b. "High Unemployment Means Native Americans are Still Waiting for an Economic Recovery." *Economic Policy Institute*. Briefing Paper #372. Washington, D.C.: EPI.

American Indian Relief Council. 2016. "History and Culture: Boarding Schools." http: //www.nrcprograms.org/site/PageServer?pagename=airc_hist_boarding schools.

Amott, Teresa L. and Julie A. Matthaei. 1991. *Race, Gender and Work: A Multicultural Economic History of Women in the United States*. Boston: South End Press.

Anderson, Elijah. 2000. *Code of the Street: Decency, Violence, and the Moral Life of the Inner City*. New York: W.W. Norton.

Anyon, Jean. 1997. *Ghetto Schooling: A Political Economy of Urban Educational Reform*. New York: Teachers College Press.

Arthur, Michael B. and Denise M. Rousseau. 2001. *The Boundaryless Career: A New Employment Principle for a New Organizational Era*. New York: Oxford University Press.

Arvin, Maile, Eve Tuck, and Angie Morrill. 2013. "Decolonizing Feminism: Challenging Connections between Settler Colonialism and Heteropatriarchy." *Feminist Formations* 25(1): 8–34.

Autor, David H. 2015. "Why Are There Still So Many Jobs?: The History and Future of Workplace Automation." *Journal of Economic Perspectives* 29: 3–30.

Avent-Holt, Dustin and Donald Tomaskovic-Devey. 2010. "The Relational Basis of Inequality: Generic and Contingent Wage Distribution Processes." *Work and Occupations* 37: 162–93.

Baigent, Dave. 2005. "Fitting In: The Conflation of Firefighting, Male Domination, and Harassment." pp. 45–64 in *In the Company of Men: Male Dominance and Sexual Harassment*, ed. by James E. Gruber and Phoebe Morgan. Boston: Northeastern University Press.

Banaji, Mahzarin R. and Anthony G. Greenwald. 2013. *Blind Spot: Hidden Biases of Good People*. New York: Delacorte Press.

Baron, James N. and Jeffrey Pfeffer. 1994. "The Social Psychology of Organizations and Inequality." *Social Psychology Quarterly* 57: 190–200.

Barrera, Mario. 1979. *Race and Class in the Southwest*. South Bend, IN: University of Notre Dame Press.

Barrett, James E. and David Roediger. 1996. "How White People Became White." pp. 402–6 in *Critical White Studies: Looking Beyond the Mirror*, ed. by Richard Delgado and Jean Stefancic. Philadelphia: Temple University Press.

Belkhir, Jean Ait. 2001. "Marxism Without Apologies: Integrating Race, Gender, and Class: A Working Class Approach." *Race, Gender, and Class* 8(2): 142–71.

Bell, Derrick. 1992. *Faces at the Bottom of the Well: The Permanence of Racism*. New York: Basic Books.

Bell, Ella L. J. Edmondson, and Stella M. Nkomo. 2003. *Our Separate Ways: Black and White Women and the Struggle for Professional Identity*. Cambridge, M.A.: Harvard Business Review Press.

Bendick, Marc Jr., Lauren Brown, and Kennington Wall. 1999. "No Foot in the Door: An Experimental Study of Employment Discrimination." *Journal of Aging and Social Policy* 10(4): 5–23.

Bennett, Lerone Jr. 1975. *The Shaping of Black America*. Chicago: Johnson Publishing Company.

Berdahl, Jennifer L. and Celia Moore. 2006. "Workplace Harassment: Double Jeopardy for Minority Women." *Journal of Applied Psychology* 91(2): 426–36.

Bertrand, Marianne and Sendhil Mullainathan. 2004. "Are Emily and Brendon More Employable than Lakisha and Jamal?: A Field Experiment on Labor Market Discrimination." *American Economic Review* 94: 991–1013.

Blair, Irene, Charles Judd, and Kristine Chapleau. 2004. "The Influence of Afrocentric Facial Features in Criminal Sentencing." *Psychological Science* 15: 674–79.

Blasdell, Bob. 2000. *Great Speeches by Native Americans*. Mineola, N.Y.: Dover Publications.

Blauner, Bob. 1972. *Racial Oppression in America*. N.Y.: Harper & Row.

——2001. *Still the Big News: Racial Oppression in America*. Philadelphia: Temple University Press.

Bobo, Lawrence, J. Kluegel, and R. Smith. 1997. "Laissez-faire Racism: The Crystallization of a 'Kinder, Gentler' Anti-Black Ideology." pp. 15–42 in *Racial Attitudes in the 1990s: Continuity and Change*, ed. by S. A. Tuch and J. K. Martin. Westport, CT: Praeger.

Bohnet, Iris. 2016. *What Works: Gender Equality by Design*. Cambridge, M.A.: Harvard University Press.

Bonacich, Edna. 1972. "A Theory of Ethnic Antagonism: The Split Labor Market." *American Sociological Review* 37: 547–59.

——1973. "A Theory of Middleman Minorities." *American Sociological Review* 38: 583–94.

——1975. "Abolition, the Extension of Slavery, and the Position of Free Blacks: A Study of Split Labor Markets in the United States, 1830–1863." *American Journal of Sociology* 81: 601–28.

Bonacich, Edna and John Modell. 1980. *The Economic Basis of Ethnic Solidarity: Small Business in the Japanese American Community*. Berkeley: University of California Press.

Bonilla-Silva, Eduardo. 1997. "Re-Thinking Racism: Toward a Structural Interpretation." *American Sociological Review* 62: 465–80.

——2001. *White Supremacy and Racism in the Post-Civil Rights Era*. Boulder, CO: Lynne Rienner Publishers.

——2006. *Racism without Racists: Color-Blind Racism and the Persistence of Racial Inequality in the United States*. 2nd edn. Lanham, MD: Rowman & Littlefield.

——2015. "More than Prejudice: Restatement, Reflections, and New Directions in Critical Race Theory." *Sociology of Race and Ethnicity* 1(1): 73–87.

Bonilla-Silva, Eduardo and Gianpaolo Baiocchi. 2008. "Anything but Racism: How Sociologists Limit the Significance of Racism." pp. 137–51 in *White Logic, White Methods: Racism and Methodology*, ed. by Tukufu Zuberi and Eduardo Bonilla-Silva. Lanham, MD: Rowman & Littlefield.

Bonilla-Silva, Eduardo, Tyrone A. Forman, Amanda E. Lewis, and David G. Embrick. 2003. "'It Wasn't Me!' How Will Race and Racism Work in the 21st Century America?" *Research in Political Sociology* 12: 111–34.

Bound, John and Laura Dresser. 1999. "Losing Ground: The Erosion of the Relative Earnings of African American Women During the 1980s." pp. 61–104 in *Latinas and African American Women at Work: Race, Gender and Economic Inequality*, ed. by Irene Brown. New York: Russell Sage.

Bourgois, Philipp. 1996. *In Search of Respect: Selling Crack in El Barrio*. Cambridge: Cambridge University Press.

Bowles, Samuel and Herbert Gintis. 2001. "*Schooling in Capitalist America* Revisited." *Sociology of Education* 75(1): 1–18.

——2002. "The Inheritance of Inequality." *Journal of Economic Perspectives* 16(3): 3–30.

Branch, Enobong Hannah. 2011. *Opportunity Denied: Limiting Black Women to Devalued Work*. New Brunswick, N.J.: Rutgers University Press.

Branch, Enobong Hannah and Caroline Hanley. 2014. "Upgraded to Bad Jobs: Low-wage Black Women's Relative Status Since 1970." *The Sociological Quarterly* 55(2): 366–95.

Brand, Jennie E. 2015. "The Far-reaching Impact of Job Loss and Unemployment." *Annual Review of Sociology* 41: 359–75.

Brand, Jennie and Till von Wachter. 2013. "The Economic and Social Consequences of Job Loss and Unemployment." *Population Reference Bureau Webinar*. http: //www.prb.org/Multimedia/Video/2013/job-loss-webinar.aspx on.

Braverman, Harry. 1998. *Labor and Monopoly Capital*. New York: Monthly Review Press.

Brennan, George. 2016. "Casino Competitor Backs Legal Challenge to Mashpee Tribe's Reservation." *Cape Cod Times* http: //www.capecodtimes.com/article/20160205/NEWS/160209650.

Brodkin, Karen. 1994. "How Did Jews Become White Folks?" pp. 78–102 in *Race*, ed. by Steven Gregory and Roger Sanjek. New Brunswick, N.J.: Rutgers University Press.

Brody, David. 1987. *Labor in Crisis: The Steel Strike of 1919*. Champaign: University of Illinois Press.

Browne, Irene and Rachel Askew. 2006. "Latinas at Work: Issues of Gender, Ethnicity and Class." pp. 223–51 in *Gender, Race and Ethnicity in the Workplace: Issues and Challenges for Today's Organizations*, ed. by Margaret Foegen Karsten. Westport, CT: Praeger.

Browne, Irene, C. Hewitt, L. Tigges, and G. Green. 2001. "Why Does Job Segregation Lead to Wage Inequality among African Americans: Person, Place, Sector or Skills?" *Social Science Research* 30(3): 473–95.

Browne, Irene and Joya Misra. 2003. "The Intersection of Gender and Race in the Labor Market." *Annual Review of Sociology* 29: 487–513.

Bruce, Tamara A. 2006. "Racial and Ethnic Harassment in the Workplace." pp. 25–49 in *Gender, Race and Ethnicity in the Workplace: Issues and Challenges for Today's Organizations*, ed. by Margaret Foegan Karsten. Volume 2. Westport, CT: Praeger.

Buchanan, Nicole T. 2004. "The Nexus of Race and Gender Domination: The Racialized Sexual Harassment of African American Women." pp. 294–320 in *In the Company of Men: Re-Discovering the Links between Sexual Harassment and Male Domination*, ed. by P. Morgan and J. Gruber. Boston: Northeastern University Press.

Butler, John Sibley. 2005. *Entrepreneurship and Self-Help among Black Americans*. 2nd edn. Albany, New York: State University of New York Press.

Cabezas, Amado, Tse Ming Tam, Brenda M. Lowe, Anna Wong, and Kathy Owyang Turner. 1989. "Empirical Study of the Barriers to Upward Mobility of Asian Americans in the San Francisco Bay Area." In *Frontiers of Asian American Studies: Writing, Research and Commentary*, ed. by Gail M. Nomura, Russell Endo, Stephen H. Sumida, and Russell C. Leong. Pullman: Washington State University Press.

Cable, Sherry and Tamara L. Mix. 2003. "Economic Imperatives and Race Relations: The Rise and Fall of the American Apartheid Systems." *Journal of Black Studies* 34: 183–203.

Carnevale, Anthony P., Nicole Smith, and Jeff Strohl. 2014. *Recovery: Job Growth and Education Requirements Through 2020*. Georgetown Public Policy Institute. https://cew.georgetown.edu/wp-content/uploads/2014/11/Recovery2020.ES_.Web_.pdf.

Castilla, Emilio J. 2008. "Gender, Race and Meritocracy in Organizational Careers." *American Journal of Sociology* 113: 1479–1526.

Catanzarite, Lisa. 2002. "Dynamics of Occupational Segregation and Earnings in Brown-Collar Occupations." *Work and Occupations* 29: 300–45.

——2003. "Race-Gender Composition and Occupational Pay Degradation." *Social Problems* 50: 14–37.

Caver, Keith A. and Ancella B. Livers. 2002. "Dear White Boss . . ." *Harvard Business Review* 80(11): 76–81.

Champagne, Duane. 2004. "Tribal Capitalism and Native Capitalism." pp. 308–29 in *Native Pathways: American Indian Culture and Economic Development in the Twentieth Century*, ed. by Brian Hosmer and Colleen O'Neill. Boulder: University Press of Colorado.

Chang, Gordon H. 2010. "Eternally Foreign: Asian Americans, History, and Race." pp. 216–33 in *Doing Race: 21 Essays for the 21st Century*, ed. by Hazel Rose Markus and Paula M. L. Moya. New York: W.W. Norton.

Charles, Kerwin Kofi and Jonathan Guryan. 2011. "Studying Discrimination: Fundamental Challenges and Recent Progress." *Annual Review of Economics* 3: 479–511.

Chou, Rosalind S. 2012. *Asian American Sexual Politics: The Construction of Race, Gender, and Sexuality*. Lanham, MD: Rowman & Littlefield.

Chou, Rosalind S. and Joe R. Feagin. 2008. *The Myth of the Model Minority: Asian Americans Facing Racisms*. Boulder, CO: Paradigm Publishers.

Chou, Rosalind S., Kristen Lee, and Simon Ho. 2012. "The White Habitus and Hegemonic Masculinity at the Elite Southern University: Asian Americans and the Need for Intersectional Analysis." *Sociation Today* 10. http: //ncsociology. org/sociationtoday/v102/asian.htm.

Collier, Lorna. 2014. "Incarceration Nation." *APA Monitor on Psychology* 45(9): 56. http: //www.apa.org/monitor/2014/10/incarceration.aspx.

Collins, Patricia Hill. 1993. "Toward a New Vision: Race, Class and Gender as Categories of Analysis and Connection." *Race, Sex and Class* 1: 25–45.

——2000. *Black Feminist Thought: Knowledge, Consciousness, and the Politics of Empowerment*. Revised 10th Anniversary 2nd edn. New York: Routledge.

Conyon, Martin J., John E. Core, and Wayne R. Guay. 2009. "Are U.S. CEOs Paid More than UK CEOs? Inferences from Risk-Adjusted Pay (CRI 2009–003)." Cornell University, ILR School, Compensation Research Initiative.

Coombs, A. A. and R. K. King. 2005. "Workplace Discrimination: Experiences of Practicing Physicians." *Journal of the National Medical Association* 97: 467–77.

Corbas, Jose A., Jorge Duany, and Joe Faegin. 2009. *How the U.S. Racializes Latinos: White Hegemony and Its Consequences*. New York: Routledge.

Cortina, Lilia M. 2008. "Unseen Injustice: Incivility as Modern Discrimination in Organizations." *Academy of Management Review* 33: 55–75.

Couch, Kenneth A. and Robert Fairlie. 2010. "Last Hired, First Fired?: Black-White Unemployment and the Business Cycle." *Demography* 47: 227–47.

Courtwright, David T. 1996. *Violent Land: Single Men and Social Disorder from the Frontier to the Inner City*. Cambridge: Harvard University Press.

Crenshaw, Kimberle. 1993. "Demarginalizing the Intersection of Race and Sex: A Black Feminist Critique of Antidiscrimination Doctrine, Feminist Theory and Antiracist Politics." *University of Chicago Legal Forum* 1(8): 139–67.

Crowfoot, James E. and Mark A. Chesler. 1996. "White Men's Roles in Multicultural Coalitions." pp. 216–29 in *Impacts of Racism on White Americans*, ed. by Benjamin P. Bowser and Raymond G. Hunt. Thousand Oaks, C.A.: Sage.

Dalton, Harlon L. 1995. *Racial Healing: Confronting the Fear between Blacks and Whites*. New York: Doubleday.

Dasgupta, Nilanjana. 2004. "Implicit Group Favoritism, Outgroup Favoritism, and Their Behavioral Manifestations." *Social Justice Research* 17: 143–69.

Dasgupta, Nilanjana and Anthony G. Greenwald. 2001. "Exposure to Admired Group Members Reduces Automatic Intergroup Bias." *Journal of Personality and Social Psychology* 81: 800–14.

Davis, Alyssa and Lawrence Mishel. 2014. "CEO Pay Continues to Rise as Typical Workers are Paid Less." *Economic Policy Institute*. Briefing Paper #380. http://www.epi.org/publication/ceo-pay-continues-to-rise/.

Davis, S. and Till von Wachter. 2012. "Recessions and the Cost of Job Loss." *Brookings Papers on Economic Activity* 43: 1–72.

DeAnda, Roberto M. 2000. "Mexican-Origin Women's Employment Instability." *Sociological Perspectives* 43(3): 421–37.

——2005. "Employment Hardship among Mexican Women." *Hispanic Journal of Behavioral Sciences* 27: 43–59.

Deitch, Elizabeth A., Adam Barsky, Rebecca M. Butz, Suzanne Chan, Arthur P. Brief, and Jill C. Bradley. 2003. "Subtle yet Significant: The Existence and Impact of Everyday Racial Discrimination in the Workplace." *Human Relations* 56: 1299–1324.

Delgado, R. and J. Stefancic. 1999. *Critical Race Theory: The Cutting Edge*. Philadelphia: Temple University Press.

Deloria, Vine, Jr. 1988. *Custer Died for Your Sins: An Indian Manifesto*. 2nd edn. Norman: University of Oklahoma Press.

Dempsey, Jason and Robert Shapiro. 2009. "The Army's Hispanic Future." *Armed Forces and Society* 35(3): 526–61.

DeSilver, Drew. 2013. "Black Unemployment Rate is Consistently Twice that of Whites." Pew Research Center Fact Tank. http://www.pewresearch.org/fact-tank/2013/08/21/through-good-times-and-bad-black-unemployment-is-consistently-double-that-of-whites.

DiMaggio, Paul and Walter W. Powell. 1991. "Introduction." pp. 1–40 in *The New Institutionalism in Organizational Analysis*, ed. by Paul DiMaggio and Walter W. Powell. Chicago: University of Chicago Press.

Dipboye, Robert L. and Stefanie K. Halverson 2004. "Subtle (and Not So Subtle) Discrimination in Organizations." pp. 131–58 in *The Dark Side of Organizational Behavior*, ed. by Ricky W. Griffin and Anne M. O'Leary-Kelly. San Francisco: Jossey-Bass.

DiPrete, Thomas A. and G. M. Eirich. 2006. "Cumulative Advantage as a Mechanism for Inequality: A Review of Theoretical and Empirical Developments." *Annual Review of Sociology* 32: 271–94.

DiTomaso, Nancy. 2012. *The American Non-Dilemma: Racial Inequality without Racism*. New York: Russell Sage Foundation.

DiTomaso, Nancy, Corinne Post, and Rochelle Parks-Yancy. 2007. "Workforce Diversity and Inequality: Power, Status, Numbers." *Annual Review of Sociology* 33: 473–501.

DiTomaso, Nancy, Corinne Post, R. D. Smith, G. F. Farris, and R. Cordero. 2007. "Effects of Structural Position on Allocation and Evaluation Decisions for Scientists and Engineers in Industrial R&D." *Administrative Science Quarterly* 52: 175–207.

Douglas, Karen Manges and Rogelio Saenz. 2008. "Middlemen Minorities." pp. 1448–1471 in W.A. Darity (ed.), *International Encyclopedia of the Social Sciences*. 2nd edn. Vol.5. Detroit: Macmillan Reference U.S.A.

Douglass, Frederick. 1845. *Narrative of the Life of Frederick Douglass: An American Slave*. Boston: Anti-Slavery Office.

——1857. *My Bondage and My Freedom*. Champaign: University of Illinois Press.

Dovidio, John F., Samuel L. Gaertner, K. Kawakami, and G. Hodson. 2002. "Why Can't We All Just Get Along?: Interpersonal Biases and Interracial Distrust." *Cultural Diversity and Ethnic Minority Psychology* 8(2): 88–102.

Dovidio, John F. and Samuel L. Gaertner. 2004. "Aversive Racism." pp. 1–51 in *Advances in Experimental Social Psychology*, ed. by M. P. Zanna. Volume 36. San Diego: Academic Press.

Dozier, Raine. 2012. "Young, Jobless and Black: Young Black Women and Economic Downturns." *Journal of Sociology and Social Welfare* 39: 45–67.

DuBois, William E. B. 1986. "The Souls of Black Folk" in *DuBois Writings*, compiled by Nathan Huggins. The Library of America, distributed by Viking Press.

——[1935] 1998. *Black Reconstruction in America, 1860–1880*. New York: The Free Press.

——[1924] 2009. *The Gift of Black Folk*. Garden City Park, N.J.: Square One Publishers.

Duffy, Mignon. 2007. "Doing the Dirty Work: Gender, Race and Reproductive Labor in Historical Perspective." *Gender and Society* 21: 313–36.

Dunbar-Ortiz, Roxanne. 2014. *An Indigenous Peoples' History of the United States*. Boston: Beacon Press.

Durr, Marlese and Adia M. Harvey Wingfield. 2011. "Keep your 'N' in Check: African American Women and the Interactive Effects of Etiquette and Emotional Labor." *Critical Sociology* 37: 557–71.

Dutta-Gupta, Indivar, Kali Grant, Matthew Eckel, and Peter Edelman. 2016. *Lessons Learned from 40 Years of Subsidized Employment Programs*. Washington, D.C.: The Georgetown Center on Poverty and Inequality.

Dyer, Richard. 1997. *White: Essays on Race and Culture*. New York: Routledge.

Edin, Kathryn and Maria Kefalas. 2011. *Promises I Can Keep: Why Poor Women Put Motherhood Before Marriage*. 2nd edn. Berkeley: University of California Press.

Edwards, Richard C. 1979. *Contested Terrain: The Transformation of the Workplace in the Twentieth Century*. New York: Basic Books.

Edwards, Richard. 1980. *Contested Terrain*. New York: Basic Books.

EEOC, 2003. "Supercuts to Pay $3.5 Million for Race Bias and Train Hundreds of Managers, in EEOC Settlement." https://www.eeoc.gov/eeoc/newsroom/release/archive/8-13-03.html.

——2015. "Significant EEOC Race/Color Cases" https://www1.eeoc.gov//eeoc/initiatives/e-race/caselist.cfm?renderforprint=1.

Ehrenreich, Barbara. 2001. *Nickel and Dimed: On (Not) Getting By in America*. New York: Henry Holt and Company.

Elliott, James R. and Ryan A. Smith. 2001. "Ethnic Matching of Supervisors to Subordinate Work Groups: Findings on 'Bottom up' Ascription and Social Closure." *Social Problems* 48: 258–76.

Ellsworth, Scott. 1982. *Death in a Promised Land: The Tulsa Race Riot of 1921*. Baton Rouge and London: Louisiana State University Press.

Elvira, Marta M. and Christopher D. Zatzick. 2002. "Who's Displaced First?: The Role of Race in Layoff Decisions." *Industrial Relations* 41: 329–61.

Engler, Mark. 2010. "Dr. Martin Luther King's Economics: Through Jobs, Freedom." *The Nation.* http: //www.thenation.com/article/dr-martin-luther-kings-economics-through-jobs-freedom/.

Espiritu, Yen Le. 2008. *Asian American Women and Men: Labor, Laws and Love.* 2nd edn. Lanham, MD: Rowman & Littlefield.

Estlund, Cynthia. 2003. *Working Together: How Workplace Bonds Strengthen a Diverse Democracy.* New York: Oxford University Press.

Estrada, Andrea 2007. "Wealth Gap Between Blacks and Whites Has Grown Larger, Scholars Find." *The UC Santa Barbara Current.* http://www.news.ucsb.edu/2007/012218/wealth-gap-between-blacks-and-whites-has-grown-larger-scholars-find

Fairlie, Robert W. and William A. Sundstrom. 1999. "The Emergence, Persistence, and Recent Widening of the Racial Employment Gap." *Industrial and Labor Relations Review* 52(2): 252–70.

Feagin, Joe R. 2004. "Toward an Integrated Theory of Systemic Racism." In *The Changing Terrain of Race and Ethnicity*, ed. by Maria Krysan and Amanda E. Lewis. New York: Russell Sage Foundation.

——2006. *Systemic Racism: A Theory of Oppression.* 1st edn. New York and London: Routledge.

——2010. *The White Racial Frame: Centuries of Racial Framing and Counter-Framing.* 1st edn. New York: Routledge.

——2013. *Racist America: Roots, Current Realities and Future Reparations.* 3rd edn. New York and London: Routledge.

Feagin, Joe R., Kevin E. Early, and Karyn D. McKinney. 2001. "The Many Costs of Discrimination: The Case of Middle-Class African Americans." *Indiana Law Review* 34: 1313–60.

Feagin, Joe R. and Clairece Booher Feagin. 2011. *Racial and Ethnic Relations.* 9th edn. London: Pearson.

Feagin, Joe R. and Hernan Vera. 1995. *White Racism: The Basics.* New York: Routledge.

Feagin, Joe R., Hernan Vera, and Pinar Batur. 2000. *White Racism: The Basics.* 2nd edn. New York: Routledge.

Ferguson, Ann Arnett. 2001. *Bad Boys: Public Schools in the Making of Black Masculinities.* Ann Arbor: University of Michigan Press.

Fields, Barbara J. 1982. "Ideology and Race in American History." pp. 143–77 in *Region, Race and Representation: Essays in Honor of C. Van Woodward*, ed. by J. Morgan Kousser and James M. MacPherson. New York: Oxford University Press.

Fixico, Donald. 2006. *Daily Life of Native Americans in the Twentieth Century.* Westport, CT: Greenwood Press.

Fleischer, Joan. 2003. "Supercuts Settles Racial Bias Suit for $3.5 Million" *Sun Sentinel.* August 14. http: //articles.sun-sentinel.com/2003-08-14/business/0308130966_1_supercuts-eeoc-racial-discrimination.

Fletcher, William G. and Peter Agard. 1987. *The Indispensable Ally: Black Workers and the Formation of the C.I.O., 1934–1941.* Boston: Trotter Institute.

Flexner, Eleanor. 1959. *Century of Struggle: The Woman's Rights Movement in the United States.* Cambridge, Mass.: The Belknap Press.

Foley, Neil. 2008. "Becoming Hispanic: Mexican Americans and Whiteness." pp. 55–65 in *White Privilege: Essential Readings from the Other Side of Racism*, ed. by Paula S. Rothenberg. 3rd edn. New York: Worth Publishers.

Foner, Eric. 2000. "Review of *Forced into Glory: Abraham Lincoln's White Dream.*" *Los Angeles Times Book Review.* April 9. http: //www.ericfoner. com/reviews/040900latimes.html.

Foner, Philip S. 1974. *Organized Labor and the Black Worker, 1619–1973.* New York: Praeger.

Fong-Torres, Ben. 1995. "Why Are There No Asian American Anchor*men* on TV?" In *Men's Lives,* ed. by Michael A. Kimmel and Michael A. Messner. New York: Pearson Press.

Forret, Monica L. 2006. "Impact of Social Networks on the Advancement of Women and Racial/Ethnic Minority Groups." pp. 150–66 in *Gender, Race and Ethnicity in the Workplace: Issues and Challenges for Today's Organization,* ed. by Margaret Foegen Karsten. Volume 3. Westport, CN and London: Praeger.

Forseth, Ulla. 2005. "Gender Matters? Exploring How Gender is Negotiated in Service Encounters." *Gender, Work and Organization* 12: 441–59.

Frank, Reanne, Ilana Redstone Akresh, and Bo Lu. 2010. "Latino Immigrants and the U.S. Racial Order: How and Where Do They Fit In?" *American Sociological Review* 75: 378–401.

Franklin, Donna L. 1997. *Ensuring Inequality: The Structural Transformation of the African-American Family.* New York: Oxford University Press.

Franklin, John Hope. 1993. *The Color Line: Legacy for the 21st Century.* Columbia: University of Missouri Press.

Frederickson, George M. 2002. *Racism: A Short History.* Princeton, N.J.: Princeton University Press.

Frye, Marilyn. 1983. *The Politics of Reality.* Trumansburg, N.Y.: Crossing Press.

Gates, Henry Louis Jr. 2013. "The Truth Behind '40 Acres and a Mule.'" *The Root.* January 7. http: //www.theroot.com/the-truth-behind-40-acres-and-a-mule-1790894780.

Giddings, Paula. 1985. *When and Where I Enter: The Impact of Black Women on Race and Sex in America.* New York: Bantam.

Glenn, Evelyn Nakano. 1991. "Cleaning Up/Kept Down: A Historical Perspective on Racial Inequality in Women's Work." *Stanford Law Review* 43(6): 1333–56.

——1992. "From Servitude to Service Work: Historical Continuities in the Racial Division of Paid Reproductive Labor." *Signs* 18: 1–43.

——2002. *Unequal Freedom: How Race and Gender Shaped American Citizenship and Labor.* Cambridge, M.A. and London: Harvard University Press.

——2015. "Settler Colonialism as Structure: A Framework for Comparative Studies of U.S. Race and Gender Formation." *Sociology of Race and Ethnicity* 1: 54–74.

Global Nonviolent Action Database. 2016. "U.S. Farmworkers in California Campaign for Economic Justice (Grape Strike), 1965-70." http: //nvda tabase.swarthmore.edu/content/us-farmworkers-california-campaign-econ omic-justice-grape-strike-1965-70.

Golash-Boza, Tanya and William Darity. 2008. "Latino Racial Choices: The Effects of Skin Colour and Discrimination on Latinos' and Latinas' Racial Self-Identifications." *Ethnic and Racial Studies* 31: 899–934.

Goldin, Claudia and Cecilia Rouse. 2000. "Orchestrating Inequality: The Impact of 'Blind' Auditions on Female Musicians." *American Economic Review* 90: 715–41.

Goldsmith, Arthur. H., Darrick Hamilton, and William Darity Jr. 2007. "From Dark to Light: Skin Color and Wages among African-Americans." *Journal of Human Resources* 42: 701–38.

Gonzalez, Juan. 2001. *Harvest of Empire: A History of Latinos in America*. 2nd edn. New York: Penguin Books.

Goodwin, Joanne. 1995. "'Employable Mothers' and 'Suitable Work': A Re-evaluation of Welfare and Wage-earning for Women in the Twentieth Century United States." *Journal of Social History* 29(2): 257–58.

Gosselin, Kenneth R. 2016. "Schaghticokes And MGM Unite To Fight Casino Law." *The Hartford Courant*. March 7. http: //www.courant.com/business/ hc-mgm- schaghticoke-casino-20160307- story.html.

Gowan, Teresa. 2011. "What's Social Capital Got to Do with It?: The Ambiguous (and Overstated) Relationship between Social Capital and Ghetto Underemployment." *Critical Sociology* 37: 47–66.

Greenhouse, Steven. 2013. "Share of the Work Force in a Union Falls to a 97-Year Low, 11.3%." *New York Times*. January 23. http: //www.nytimes. com/2013/01/24/business/union-membership-drops-despite-job-growth.html.

Greenhouse, Steven and Jana Kasperkevic. 2015. "Fight for $15 Swells into Largest Protest by Low-wage Workers in U.S. History." *Guardian*. April 15. https: //www.theguardian.com/us-news/2015/apr/15/fight-for-15-minimum-wage-protests-new-york-los-angeles-atlanta-boston.

Grenier, John. 2005. The First Way of War: American War Making on the Frontier, 1607–1814. New York: Cambridge University Press.

Gresham, George. 2015. "A Broader, Bolder Union Movement: Time to Get More Political." *The Daily News*. September 7. http: //www.nydailynews.com/ opinion/george- gresham-broader-bolder-union-movement-article-1.2349322.

Grodsky E. and Devah Pager. 2001. "The Structure of Disadvantage: Individual and Occupational Determinants of Black-White Wage Gap." *American Sociological Review* 66: 542–67.

Gutierrez, David G. 1995. *Walls and Mirrors: Mexican Americans, Mexican Immigrants, and the Politics of Ethnicity*. Berkeley: University of California Press.

Hacker, Andrew. 2003. *Two Nations: Black and White, Separate, Hostile, Unequal*. New York: Scribner.

Hall, Richard H. 1994. *Sociology of Work: Perspectives, Analyses, and Issues*. Thousand Oaks and London: Pine Forge Press.

Hamilton, Darrick. 2006. "The Racial Composition of American Jobs." In *The State of Black America*, ed. by G. Curry. New York: The National Urban League.

Hanson, Gordon H. 2009. *The Economics and Policy of Illegal Immigration in the United States*. Washington, D.C.: Migration Policy Institute.

Harding, Vincent. 2010. "Introduction" pp. xi-xxii in *Where Do We Go from Here?: Chaos or Community?*, by Martin Luther King Jr. Boston: Beacon Press.

Harlow, Roxanne. 2003. "Race Doesn't Matter, but ... The Effect of Race on Professors' Experiences and Emotion Management." *Social Psychology Quarterly* 6: 348–63.

Harper, Shannon and Barbara Reskin. 2005. "Affirmative Action at School and on the Job." *Annual Review of Sociology* 31: 357–79.

Harris, Fredrick C. and Robert C. Lieberman. 2015. "Racial Inequality after Racism: How Institutions Hold Back African Americans." *Foreign Affairs*. March/

April. https: //www.foreignaffairs.com/articles/united-states/2015-03-01/ racial-inequality-after-racism.

Harrison, Jill Lindsey and Sarah E. Lloyd. 2013. "New Jobs, New Workers, and New Inequalities: Explaining Employers' Roles in Occupational Segregation by Nativity and Race." *Social Problems* 60: 281–301.

Harvey, David. 1993. *Potter Addition: Poverty, Family, and Kinship in a Heartland Community.* New York: Aldine de Gruyter.

Heckman, James, and Peter Siegelman. 1993. "The Urban Institute Audit Studies: Their Methods and Findings." pp. 187–258 in *Clear and Convincing Evidence: Measurement of Discrimination in America*, ed. by Michael Fix and Raymond J. Struyk. Washington, D.C.: Urban Institute Press.

Heimer, Karen, Kecia R. Johnson, Joseph B. Lang, Andres Rengifo, and Don Stemen. 2012. "Race and Women's Imprisonment: Poverty, African American Presence, and Social Welfare." *Journal of Quantitative Criminology* 2: 219–44.

Henderson, Loren, Cedric Herring, Hayward Derrick Horton, and Melvin Thomas. 2015. "Credit Where Credit is Due?: Race, Gender and Discrimination in Credit Scores of Business Startups." *Review of Black Political Economy* 42: 459–79.

Hernandez, Tanya Kateri. 2010. "Employment Discrimination in the Ethnically Diverse Workplace." *The Judges' Journal* 49: 33–7.

Herring, Cedric, Hayward D. Horton, and Melvin E. Thomas. 2002. "Is Inner-city Entrepreneurship a Cure for Poverty?" pp. 89–111 in *The New Politics of Race: From DuBois to the 21st Century*, ed. by Marlese Durr. Westport, CT: Praeger.

Hersch, Joni. 2008. "Profiling the New Immigrant Worker: The Effects of Skin Color and Height." *Journal of Labor Economics* 26(2): 345–86.

Hersch, Joni. 2011. "Skin Color, Physical Appearance and Perceived Discriminatory Treatment." *The Journal of Socio-Economics* 40: 671–78.

Hiramatsu, Gloria. 2013. "Making the Best of Workplace Stereotypes." *GoldSea: Asian American Careers.* http: //goldsea.com/Text/index.php?id=2266.

Hirsch, Barry T. 2008. "Sluggish Institutions in a Dynamic World: Can Unions and Industrial Competition Coexist?" *Journal of Economic Perspectives* 22: 153–76.

Hirsh, C. Elizabeth and Sabino Kornrich. 2008. "The Context of Discrimination: Workplace Conditions, Institutional Environments, and Sex and Race Discrimination Charges." *American Journal of Sociology* 113: 1394–1432.

Hochschild, Arlie Russell. 2003. *The Managed Heart: Commercialization of Human Feelings.* Berkeley: University of California Press.

Hochschild, Arlie. 2016a. *Strangers in Their Own Land: Anger and Mourning on the American Right.* New York: The New Press.

——2016b. "I Spent 5 Years With Some of Trump's Biggest Fans. Here's What They Won't Tell You." *Mother Jones.* September/October. http: //www.motherjones.com/politics/2016/08/trump-white-blue-collar-supporters.

Hodson, Randy. 2001. *Dignity at Work.* New York: Cambridge University Press.

Hofferth, Sandra. 2002. "Did Welfare Reform Work?: Implications for 2002 and Beyond." *Contexts* 1(1): 45–51.

Holt, Thomas C. and Elsa Barkley Brown. 2000. "Major Problems in African American History: From Freedom to Freedom Now, 1865–1990s." Belmont, C.A.: Wadsworth.

Hondagneu-Sotelo, Pierrette. 2001. *Doméstica: Immigrant Workers Caring and Cleaning in America.* Berkeley: University of California Press.

——2002. "Families on the Frontier: From Braceros in the Fields to Braceras in the Home." pp. 259–73 in *Latinos: Remaking America*, ed. by Marcelo M. Suarez-Orozco and Mariela M. Paez. Berkeley: University of California Press.

Hochschild, Jennifer L. and Velsa Weaver. 2007. "The Skin Color Paradox and the American Racial Order." *Social Forces* 86:643–70

Hu, Yue, Long Liu, Jan Ondrich, and John Yinger. 2011. "The Racial and Gender Interest Rate Gap in Small Business Lending." Presented at Economic Seminar, Tulane University. March 21. http: //www.tulane.edu/~economic/ seminars/OndrichIntRate Gap.pdf.

Huffman, Matt L., and Philip N. Cohen. 2004. "Racial Wage Inequality: Job Segregation and Devaluation across U.S. Labor Markets." *The American Journal of Sociology* 109: 902–36.

Hum, Tarry. 2000. "A Protected Niche?: Immigrant Ethnic Economies and Labor Market Segmentation." pp. 279–314 in *Prismatic Metropolis: Inequality in Los Angeles*, ed. by Lawrence Bobo, Melvin L. Oliver, James H. Johnson Jr., and Abel Valenzuela Jr. New York: Russell Sage Foundation.

Hurtado, Aida. 1989. "Relating to Privilege: Seduction and Rejection in the Subordination of White Women and Women of Color." *Signs* 14: 833–55.

Hyun, Jane. 2005. *Breaking the Bamboo Ceiling: Career Strategies for Asians.* New York: HarperCollins.

——2006. *Breaking the Bamboo Ceiling: Career Strategies for Asians.* New York: HarperCollins.

Ibarra, Herminia. 1995. "Race, Opportunity, and Diversity of Social Circles in Managerial Networks." *The Academy of Management Journal* 38(3): 673–703.

Ignatiev, Noel. 1996. *How the Irish Became White.* New York: Routledge.

Jaspin, Elliot. 2007. *Buried in the Bitter Waters: The Hidden History of Racial Cleansing in America.* New York: Basic Books.

Johnson, Kecia and Jacqueline Johnson. 2012. "Racial Disadvantage and Incarceration: Sources of Wage Inequality among African American, Latino and White Men." pp. 217–98 in *Reinventing Race, Reinventing Racism*, ed. by John Betancur and Cedric Herring. Boston: Brill Academic.

Jones, Jacqueline. 1998. *American Work: Four Centuries of Black and White Labor.* New York: W.W. Norton.

Jorgensen, Joseph G. 2000." Gaming and Recent American Indian Economic Development" pp. 96–107 in *Indian Gaming: Who Wins?*, ed. by Angela Mullis and David Kamper. Los Angeles: UCLA American Indian Studies Center.

Jung, Moon-Kie. 2006. *Reworking Race: The Making of Hawaii's Interracial Labor Movement.* New York: Columbia University Press.

Kalev, Alexandra, Frank Dobbin, and Erin Kelly. 2006. "Best Practices or Best Guesses?: Assessing the Efficacy of Corporate Affirmative Action and Diversity Policies." *American Sociological Review* 71: 589–617.

Kalleberg, Arne L. 2007. *The Mismatched Worker.* New York: W.W. Norton.

Kalleberg, Arne L., Barbara F. Reskin, and Ken Hudson. 2000. "Bad Jobs in America: Standard and Nonstandard Employment Relations and Job Quality in the United States." *American Sociological Review* 65(2): 256–78.

Kang, Sonia K., Katherine A. DeCelles, András Tilcsik, and Sora Jun. 2016. "Whitened Résumés: Race and Self-presentation in the Labor Market." *Administrative Science Quarterly* 61(3): 469–502.

Kanter, Rosabeth Moss. [1977] 1993. *Men and Women of the Corporation.* 2nd edn. New York: Basic Books.

Kaplan, Steven N. and Joshua Rauh. 2010. "Wall Street and Main Street: What Contributes to the Rise in the Highest Incomes?" *Review of Financial Studies* 23: 1004–50.

Katz, William Loren. 2005. *Eyewitness: A Living Documentary of the African American Contribution to American History*. Revised edn. New York: Simon & Schuster.

Katznelson, Ira. 2005. *When Affirmative Action Was White: An Untold History of Racial Inequality in the Twentieth Century*. New York: W.W. Norton.

Keister, Lisa A. 2014. "The One Percent." *Annual Review of Sociology* 40: 347–67.

Keller, John F. 1983. "The Division of Labor in Electronics." pp. 346–73 in *Women, Men and the International Division of Labor*, ed. by June Nash and Maria Patricia Fernandez-Kelly. Albany: State University of New York Press.

Kelley, Robin D. G. 1993. "'We are Not What We Seem': Rethinking Black Working-class Opposition in the Jim Crow South." *The Journal of American History* 80(1): 75–112.

Kennelly, Ivy. 1999. "That Single Mother Element: How White Employers Typify Black Women." *Gender and Society* 13: 168–92.

Keoke, Emory Dean and Kay Marie Porterfield. 2002. *Encyclopedia of American Indian Contributions to the World: 15,000 Years of Inventions and Innovations*. New York: Facts on File.

Kessler-Harris, Alice. 2003. *Out to Work: A History of Wage-Earning Women*. New York: Oxford University Press.

Khosrovani, Masoomeh and James W. Ward. 2011. "African Americans' Perceptions of Access to Workplace Opportunities: A Survey of Employees in Houston, Texas." *Journal of Cultural Diversity* 18(4): 134–41.

Kim, ChangHwan and Arthur Sakamoto. 2010. "Have Asian American Men Achieved Labor Market Parity with White Men?" *American Sociological Review* 75: 934–57.

Kim, Claire Jean. 1999. "The Racial Triangulation of Asian Americans." *Politics and Society* 27: 105–38.

Kim, Marlene. 2012. "Unfairly Disadvantaged?: Asian Americans and Unemployment During and After the Great Recession (2007–10)." *Economic Policy Institute*. Briefing Paper #323. Washington, D.C.: EPI.

Kim, Marlene and Don Mar. 2007. "The Economic Status of Asian Americans." pp. 148-84 in *Race and Economic Opportunity in the 21st Century*, ed. by Marlene Kim. New York: Routledge.

King, Martin Luther Jr. 1968. *Where Do We From Here: Chaos or Community?* Boston: Beacon Press.

Kirschenman, Joleen and Kathryn Neckerman. 1991. "'We'd Love to Hire Them, But . . .' The Meaning of Race for Employers." pp. 203–32 in *The Urban Underclass*, ed. by C. Jencks and P. E. Peterson. Washington, D.C.: The Brookings Institution.

Kochhar, Rakesh and Richard Fry. 2014. "Wealth Inequality Has Widened along Racial, Ethnic Lines Since end of Great Recession." Pew Research Center. http: //www.pewresearch.org/fact-tank/2014/12/12/racial-wealth-gaps-great-recession/.

Kochhar, Rakesh, Richard Fry, and Paul Taylor. 2011. "Wealth Gaps Rise to Record Highs Between Whites, Blacks, Hispanics." Pew Research Center. Social and Demographic Trends. http: //www.pewsocialtrends.org/2011/07/26/wealth-gaps-rise-to-record-highs-between-whites-blacks-hispanics/.

Kohn, Melvin and Carmi Schooler. 1983. *Work and Personality: An Enquiry into the Impact of Social Stratification.* Norwood, N.J.: Ablex Publishing Corporation.

Kovel, Joel. 1984. *White Racism: A Psychohistory.* 2nd edn. New York: Columbia University Press.

Kushnick, Louis. 1996. "The Political Economy of White Racism in the United States." In *Impacts of Racism on White Americans,* ed. by Benjamin P. Bowser and Raymond G. Hunt. Thousand Oaks, C.A.: Sage.

Lach, Alex. 2012. "5 Facts About Overseas Outsourcing: Trend Continues to Grow as American Workers Suffer." *Center for American Progress.* https: //www.american progress.org/issues/labor/news/2012/07/09/11898/5-facts-about-overseas-outsourcing/.

Lakota People's Project. 2015. "Native Lives Matter." https://www.lakotalaw. org/resources/native-lives-matter.

Landry, Bart. 2000. *Black Working Wives: Pioneers of the American Family Revolution.* Berkeley and Los Angeles: University of California Press.

Leach, Colin Wayne. 2002. "Democracy's Dilemma: Explaining Racial Inequality in Egalitarian Societies." *Sociological Forum* 17: 681–96.

Lebsock, Suzanne. 1984. *The Free Women of Petersburg: Status and Culture in a Southern Town, 1784–1860.* New York: W.W. Norton.

Lefkowitz, Joel. 1994. "Race as a Factor in Job Placement: Serendipitous Findings of 'Ethnic Drift.'" *Personnel Psychology* 47: 497–513.

Leidner, Robin. 1991. "Serving Hamburgers and Selling Insurance: Gender, Work, and Identity in Interactive Service Jobs." *Gender and Society* 5: 154–77.

Lerner, Gerda. 2004. *The Grimké Sisters from South Carolina: Pioneers for Women's Rights and Abolition.* 3rd edn. Chapel Hill: The University of North Carolina Press.

Lieberson, Stanley. 1980. *A Piece of the Pie: Blacks and White Immigrants Since 1880.* Berkeley: University of California Press.

Light, Ivan and Carolyn Rosenstein. 1995. *Race, Ethnicity, and Entrepreneurship in Urban America.* Hawthorne, N.Y.: Aldine DeGruyter.

Light, Ryan, Vincent J. Roscigno, and Alexandra Kalev. 2011. "Racial Discrimination, Interpretation, and Legitimation at Work." *The ANNALS of the American Academy of Political and Social Science* 634: 39–59.

Lipsitz, George. 1998. *The Possessive Investment in Whiteness: How White People Profit from Identity Politics.* Philadelphia: Temple University Press.

Liu, Cathy Yang and Jason Edwards. 2012. "Immigrant Employment through the Great Recession: Individual Characteristics and Metropolitan Contexts." W.J. Usery Workplace Research Group Paper Series. Working Paper 2012–41. https: //pdfs.semanticscholar.org/ae1b/00c7b37328c8064580b0631d203817e d26c7.pdf.

Livers, Ancella B. and Keith A. Carver. 2002. *Leading in Black and White: Working Across the Corporate Divide in Corporate America.* San Francisco: Jossey-Bass.

Livers, Ancella. 2006. "Black Women in Management." pp. 205–21 in *Gender, Race and Ethnicity in the Workplace: Issues and Challenges for Today's Organizations,* Vol.1 ed. by Margaret Foegen Karsten. Westport, CT: Praeger.

Loewen, James W. 1988. *The Mississippi Chinese: Between Black and White.* 2nd edn. Long Grove, IL: Waveland Press.

——1995. *Lies My Teacher Told Me: Everything Your History Textbook Got Wrong.* New York: Touchstone.

Loscocco, Karyn. 1989. "The Instrumentally Oriented Factory Worker: Myth or Reality?" *Work and Occupations* 16: 3–25.

——2009. "White Ethnics and White Privilege." pp. 245–55 in *Uncertainty and Insecurity in the New Age*, ed. by Vincent N. Parrillo. New York: John D. Calandra Italian American Institute.

Loury, G. 2006. "Racial Stigma: Toward a New Paradigm for Discrimination Theory." pp. 401–8 in *Understanding Poverty*, ed. by A. Banerjee, R. Benabou, D. Mookherjee. New York: Oxford University Press.

Lowe, Lisa. 1996. *Immigrant Acts: On Asian American Cultural Politics*, Durham and London: Duke University Press.

Lumumba-Kasongo, Mana. 2006. "My Black Skin Makes My White Coat Vanish." *Newsweek* 147(14): 20. http: //www.newsweek.com/my-black-skin-makes-my- white-coat-vanish-107511.

Lundquist, Jennifer Hickes. 2008. "Ethnic and Gender Satisfaction in the Military: The Effect of a Meritocratic Institution." *American Sociological Review* 73: 478–96.

McCall, Leslie. 2001. "Sources of Racial Wage Inequality in Metropolitan Labor Markets: Racial, Ethnic, and Gender Differences." *American Sociological Review* 66(4): 520–41.

Macartney, Suzanne, Alemayehu Bishaw, and Kayla Fontenot. 2013. *Poverty Rates for Selected Detailed Race and Hispanic Groups by State and Place: 2007–2011*. American Community Survey Brief. Washington, D.C.: U.S. Census Bureau. https: //www.census.gov/prod/2013pubs/acsbr11–17.pdf.

McCall, Leslie and Christine Percheski. 2010. "Income Inequality: New Trends and Research Directions." *Annual Review of Sociology* 36: 329–47.

Macdonald, Cameron L. and David Merrill. 2009. "Intersectionality in the Emotional Proletariat: A New Lens on Employment Discrimination in Service Work." pp. 113–35 in *Service Work: Critical Perspectives*, ed. by Marek Korczynski and Cameron MacDonald. New York: Routledge.

Macdonald, Cameron L. and Carmen Sirianni. 1996. "The Service Industry and the Changing Nature of Work." In *Working in the Service Society*, ed. by C. L. Macdonald and C. Siranni. Philadelphia: Temple University Press.

McGuire, Gail. 2002. "Gender, Race and the Shadow Structure: A Study of Informal Networks and Inequality in a Work Organization." *Gender and Society* 16: 303–22.

McDonald, Steve. 2011. "What's in the 'Old Boys' Network?: Accessing Social Capital in Gendered and Racialized Networks." *Social Networks* 33: 317–30.

McIntosh, Peggy. 1990. "White Privilege: Unpacking the Invisible Knapsack." *Independent School* 49(2): 31–6.

McKay, P. F. and M. A. McDaniel. 2006. "A Reexamination of Black-White Mean Differences in Work Performance: More Data, More Moderators." *Journal of Applied Psychology* 91: 538–54.

MacLeod, Jay. 2009. *Ain't No Makin' It: Aspirations and Attainment in a Low-Income Neighborhood*. 3rd edn. Boulder, CO: Westview Press.

Madrid, Arturo. 1988. "Missing People and Others: Joining Together to Expand the Circle." *Change* 20: 55–9.

Maldonado, Marta Maria. 2009. "'It is in Their Nature to do Menial Labor': The Racialization of Latino/a Workers by Agricultural Employers." *Ethnic and Racial Studies* 32(6): 1017–36.

Mankiller, Wilma and Michael Wallis. 1993. *Mankiller: A Chief and Her People*. New York: St. Martin's Press.

Marable, Manning. 2015. *How Capitalism Underdeveloped Black America: Problems in Race, Political Economy and Society.* 2nd edn. Chicago: Haymarket Books.

Mason, Patrick L. 2004. "Annual Income, Hourly Wages, and Identity among Mexican-Americans and Other Latinos." *Industrial Relations* 43: 817–34.

Massey, Douglas S. 2007. *Categorically Unequal: The American Stratification System.* New York: Russell Sage.

Mather, Mark and Beth Jarosz. 2014. "The Demography of Inequality in the United States." *Population Bulletin* 69(2): 1–16

Maume, David J. Jr. 1999. "Class Ceilings and Glass Escalators: Occupational Segregation and Race and Sex Differences in Managerial Promotions." *Work and Occupations* 26: 483–509.

Milkman, Ruth and Stephanie Luce. 2015. *The State of the Unions 2015: A Profile of Organized Labor in New York City, New York State, and the United States.* New York: Joseph S. Murphy Institute for Worker Education and Labor Studies. https: //www.gc.cuny.edu/CUNY_GC/media/CUNY-Graduate-Center/PDF/Communications/1509_Union_Density2015_RGB.pdf.

Mills, Charles M. 1997. *The Racial Contract.* Ithaca, N.Y.: Cornell University Press.

Mink, Gwendolyn. 1995. *The Wages of Motherhood: Inequality in the Welfare State, 1917–1942.* Ithaca, N.Y.: Cornell University Press.

Mishel, Lawrence. 2006. "CEO-to-Worker Pay Imbalance Grows." Economic Snapshot. June 21. http: //www.epi.org/publication/webfeatures_snapshots_20060621/.

Mong, S. and Vincent Roscigno. 2010. "African American Men and the Experience of Employment Discrimination." *Qualitative Sociology* 33: 1–21.

Montford, Christina. 2014. "6 Interesting Things You Didn't Know About 'Black Wall Street.'" *Atlanta Black Star.* http: //atlantablackstar.com/2014/12/02/6-interesting-things-you-didnt-know-about-black-wall-street/.

Moore, Robert B. 1988. "Racism in the English Language" pp. 269–79 in Rothenberg, Paula S. Ed. Racism and Sexism: An Integrated Study. N.Y.: St. Martin's Press.

Moore, John H. 1996. "Cheyenne Work in the History of U.S. Capitalism." pp. 122–43 in *Native Americans and Wage Labor*, ed. by Alice Littlefield and Martha C. Knack. Norman and London: Oklahoma University Press.

Morales, Maria Cristina. 2008. "The Ethnic Niche as an Economic Pathway for the Dark-Skinned: Labor Market Incorporation of Latina/o Workers." *Hispanic Journal of Behavioral Science* 30: 280–98.

——2009. "Ethnic-Controlled Economy or Segregation?: Exploring Inequality in Latina/o Co-Ethnic Jobsites." *Sociological Forum* 24: 589–610.

Morgan, Edmund S. 1975. *American Slavery, American Freedom: The Ordeal of Colonial Virginia.* New York: W.W. Norton.

Morris, Edward W. 2005. "'Tuck in that Shirt!' Race, Class, Gender and Discipline in an Urban School." *Sociological Perspectives* 48: 25–48.

Morris, Monique. 2016. *Push Out: The Criminalization of Black Girls in Schools.* New York: The New Press.

Morrison, Elizabeth Wolfe. 2002. "'Newcomers' Relationships: The Role of Social Network Ties During Socialization." *Academy of Management Journal* 45(6): 1149–1160.

Moskos, Charles C. 1986. "Success Story: Blacks in the Military." *The Atlantic.*

https: //www.theatlantic.com/magazine/archive/1986/05/success-story-blacks-in-the-military/306160/.

Moskos, Charles C. and John Sibley Butler. 1997. *All That We Can Be: Black Leadership and Racial Integration the Army Way*. New York: Basic Books.

Moss, Philip and Charles Tilly. 1996. "'Soft Skills' and Race: An Investigation of Black Men's Employment Problems." *Work and Occupations* 23: 252–76.

Moss, Philip and Chris Tilly. [2001] 2003. *Stories Employers Tell: Race, Skill and Hiring in America*. New York: Russell Sage Foundation.

Mouw, Ted. 2002. "Are Black Workers Missing the Connection?: The Effect of Spatial Distance and Employee Referrals on Interfirm Racial Segregation." *Demography* 39(3): 507–28.

Mouw, Ted and Arne L. Kalleberg. 2010. "Occupations and the Structure of Wage Inequality in the United States, 1980s to 2000s." *American Sociological Review* 75(3): 402–31.

Myers, Barton and Chris Dobbs. [2005] 2016. "Sherman's Field Order No. 15." *New Georgia Encyclopedia*. http: //www.georgiaencyclopedia.org/articles/ history-archaeology/ shermans-field-order-no-15.

Myrdal, Gunnar. 1944. *An American Dilemma*. N.Y. and London: Harper and Brothers.

Nash, Gary B. 1974. *Red, White and Black: The Peoples of Early America*. Englewood Cliffs, N.J.: Prentice Hall

National Research Council. 2014. *The Growth of Incarceration in the United States: Exploring Causes and Consequences*. Committee on Causes and Consequences of High Rates of Incarceration, Jeremy Travis, Bruce Western, and Steve Redburn, Editors. Committee on Law and Justice, Division of Behavioral and Social Sciences and Education. Washington, D.C.: The National Academies Press.

Newman, Dorothy K. 1978. *Protest, Politics and Prosperity: Black Americans and White Institutions, 1940–1975*. N.Y.: Pantheon Books.

Newman, Katherine S. 1999. *No Shame in My Game: The Working Poor in the Inner City*. New York: Knopf.

Ngai, Mae M. 2004. *Impossible Subjects: Illegal Aliens and the Making of Modern America*. Princeton, N.J.: Princeton University Press.

Nir, Sarah Maslin. 2015. "The Price of Nice Nails." *New York Times*. http: //www.nytimes.com/2015/05/10/nyregion/at-nail-salons-in-nyc-manicurists-are-underpaid-and-unprotected.html.

Norton, Michael I. and Samuel R. Sommers. 2011. "Whites See Racism as a Zero-Sum Game That They are Now Losing." *Perspectives on Psychological Science* 6: 215–18.

Nunez-Smith, M., N. Pilgrim, M. Wynia, M. Desai, B. Jones, C. Bright, and H. Krumhoiz. 2009. "Race/ethnicity and Workplace Discrimination: Results of a National Survey of Physicians." *Journal of General Internal Medicine* 24: 1198–1204.

Okihiro, Gary Y. 1994. *Margins and Mainstreams: Asian American History and Culture*. Seattle: University of Washington Press.

——2000. "Is Yellow Black or White?" In *Asian Americans: Experiences and Perspectives*, ed. by Timothy P. Fong and Larry H. Shinawaga. Upper Saddle River, N.J.: Prentice Hall.

Oliver, Melvin L. and Thomas M. Shapiro. 2006. *Black Wealth/White Wealth: A New Perspective on Racial Inequality*. New York: Taylor & Francis.

——2007. "Creating an Opportunity Society." *The American Prospect* 18: A27–A28.

Omi, Michael and Howard Winant. 2014. *Racial Formation in the United States: From the 1960s to the 1990s*. 3rd edn. New York: Routledge.

Ong, Paul and Suzanne Hee. 1994. "Economic diversity." pp. 31–56 in *The State of Asian Pacific America: Economic Diversity, Issues, and Policies*, ed. by Paul Ong. Los Angeles: LEAP Asian Pacific American Public Policy Institute and University of California at Los Angeles Asian American Studies Center.

Ortiz, Susan Y. and Vincent J. Roscigno. 2009. "Discrimination, Women, and Work: Processes and Variations by Race and Class." *The Sociological Quarterly* 50: 336–59.

Osajima, Keith. 1999. "Asian Americans as the Model Minority: An Analysis of the Popular Press Image in the 1960s and 1980s." pp. 165–74 in *Reflections on Shattered Windows: Promise and Prospects for Asian American Studies*, ed. by Gary Y. Okihiro, Shirley Hune, Arthur A. Hansen and John M. Lui. Pullman: Washington State University Press.

Pager, Devah. 2003. "The Mark of a Criminal Record." *American Journal of Sociology* 108(5): 937–75.

——2007. "The Use of Field Experiments for Studies of Employment Discrimination: Contributions, Critiques and Directions for the Future." *Annual American Academy of Academic Political and Social Sciences* 609: 104–33.

Pager, Devah and Hana Shepherd. 2008. "The Sociology of Discrimination: Racial Discrimination in Employment, Housing, Credit, and Consumer Markets." *Annual Review of Sociology* 34: 181–209.

Pager, Devah and Lincoln Quillian. 2005. "Walking the Talk? What Employers Say Versus What They Do." *American Sociological Review* 70: 355–80.

Pager, Devah, Bruce Western, and Bart Bonikowski. 2009. "Discrimination in a Low-Wage Labor Market: A Field Experiment." *American Sociological Review* 74: 777–99.

Parks, Virginia. 2010. "Gendering Job Competition: Immigration and African American Employment in Chicago, 1990–2000." *Urban Geography* 31(1): 59–89.

Parks-Yancy, R. 2006. "The Effects of Social Group Membership and Social Capital Resources on Careers." *Journal of Black Studies* 36: 515–45.

Parkin, Frank. 1979. *Marxism and Class Theory: A Bourgeois Critique*. New York: Columbia University Press.

Parrillo, Vincent N. 2009. *Strangers to These Shores*. 9th edn. Boston: Allyn & Bacon.

Passel, Jeffrey S. and D'Vera Cohn. 2009. *A Portrait of Unauthorized Immigrants in the United States*. Washington, D.C.: Pew Hispanic Center.

Pearson, Adam R., John F. Dovidio, and Samuel L. Gaertner. 2009. "The Nature of Contemporary Prejudice: Insights from Aversive Racism." *Social and Personality Psychology Compass* 3: 314–38.

Pedraza-Bailey, Sylvia. 1985. *Political and Economic Migrants in America: Cubans and Mexicans*. Austin: University of Texas Press.

Perdue, Theda and Michael D. Green. 2007. *The Cherokee Nation and the Trail of Tears*. New York: Penguin Group.

Peterson, Trond and Ishak Saporta. 2004. "The Opportunity Structure for Discrimination." *American Journal of Sociology* 109: 852–902.

Petersen, Trond, Ishak Saporta, and Marc-David L. Seidel. 2000. "Offering a Job: Meritocracy and Social Networks." *American Journal of Sociology* 106(3): 763–816.

Pettit, Becky and Bruce Western. 2004. "Mass Imprisonment and the Life-course: Race and Class Inequality in U.S. Incarceration." *American Sociological Review* 69: 151–69.

Pfaelzer, Jean. 2007. *Driven Out: The Forgotten War Against Chinese Americans.* Berkeley: University of California Press.

Pickens, Josie. 2013. "The Destruction of Black Wall Street." Ebony. May 31. http://www.ebony.com/black-history/the-destruction-of-black-wall-street-405#axzz4aQYjJmgN.

Pincus, Fred L. 2003. *Reverse Discrimination: Dismantling the Myth.* Boulder, CO: Lynne Rienner Publishers.

Portes, Alejandro. 1969. "Dilemmas of a Golden Exile: Integration of Cuban Refugee Families in Milwaukee." *American Sociological Review* 34(August): 505–18.

Portes, Alejandro and Robert Bach. 1985. *Latin Journey.* Berkeley: University of California.

Posadas, Barbara M. 1982. "The Hierarchy of Color and Psychological Adjustment in an Industrial Environment: Filipinos, the Pullman Company, and the Brotherhood of Sleeping Car Porters." *Labor History* 23(3): 349–73.

Prison Policy Initiative 2010. "Racial and Ethnic Disparities in Prisons and Jails." https://www.prisonpolicy.org/profiles/US.html

Puleo, Stephen. 2007. *The Boston Italians.* Boston: Beacon Press.

Putnam, Robert. 2015. *Our Kids: The American Dream in Crisis.* New York: Simon & Schuster.

Quillian, Lincoln. 2006. "New Approaches to Understanding Racial Prejudice and Discrimination." *Annual Review of Sociology* 32: 299–328.

Reagan, Ronald. 1990. *An American Life.* New York: Simon & Schuster.

Regan, Shawn. 2014. "Unlocking the Wealth of Indian Nations: Overcoming Obstacles to Tribal Energy Development." *PERC Policy Perspective* 1(February). http: //www.perc.org/sites/default/files/pdfs/IndianPolicySeries%20HIGH.pdf.

Reich, Michael. 1981. *Racial Inequality: A Political-Economic Analysis.* Princeton, N.J.: Princeton University Press.

Reich, Robert. 2015. "The Rise of the Working Poor and the Non-Working Rich." *Huffington Post.* http: //www.huffingtonpost.com/robert-reich/ working-poor-non-working-rich_b_6973822.html.

Reskin, Barbara F. 1998. *The Realities of Affirmative Action.* Washington, D.C.: American Sociological Association.

——2003. "Including Mechanisms in our Models of Ascriptive Inequality." *American Sociological Review* 68: 1–21.

——2012. "The Race Discrimination System." *Annual Review of Sociology* 38: 17–35.

Reskin, Barbara and Patricia Roos. 1990. *Job Queues, Gender Queues.* Philadelphia: Temple University Press.

Rich, Nathaniel. 2016. "Inside the Sacrifice Zone" *New York Review of Books.* http: //www.nybooks.com/articles/2016/11/10/american-right-inside-the-sacrifice-zone/.

Ridgeway, Cecilia. 1997. "Interaction and the Conservation of Gender Inequality: Considering Employment." *American Sociological Review* 62: 218–35.

Risso, Francisco 2010. "Immigrant Workers at Non-union Chicken Plant Stop Work Over Dangerous Conditions." *LaborNotes.* http://www.labornotes.

org/2010/07/immigrant-workers-non-union-chicken-plant-stop-work-over-dangerous-conditions.

Ritter, Joseph A. and Lowell J. Taylor 2011. "Racial Disparity in Unemployment" *The Review of Economics and Statistics* 93(1): 30–42.

Ritzer, George. 2010. *The McDonaldization of Society.* 6th edn. Newbury Park, C.A.: Sage.

Rivera, Marcia. 1986. "The Development of Capitalism in Puerto Rico and the Incorporation of Women into the Labor Force." In *The Puerto Rican Woman: Perspectives on Culture, History and Society,* ed. by Edna Acosta-Belen. New York: Praeger.

Rodgers, W. M. III. 2008. "Understanding the Black-White Earnings Gap." *The American Prospect.* http: //prospect.org/article/understanding-black-white-earnings-gap.

Rodgers, Ward H. 1935. "Sharecroppers Drop Color Line." *The Crisis* June: 168–78.

Roediger, David R. 1991. *The Wages of Whiteness.* London: Verso.

Rollins, Judith. 1985. *Between Women: Domestics and Their Employers.* Philadelphia: Temple University Press.

Roscigno, Vincent J. 2007. *The Face of Discrimination: How Race and Sex Impact Work and Home Lives.* Lanham, MD: Rowman & Littlefield.

Roscigno, Vincent J., Lisette M. Garcia, and Donna Bobbitt-Zeher. 2007. "Social Closure and Processes of Race/Sex Employment Discrimination." *The Annals of the American Academy of Political and Social Science* 609: 16–48.

Rosensteil, Annette. 1983. *Red and White: Indian Views of the White Man, 1492–1982.* New York: Universe Books.

Rosette, Ashleigh Shelby, G. J. Leonardelli, and K. W. Phillips. 2008. "The White Standard: Racial Bias in Leader Categorization." *Journal of Applied Psychology* 93: 758–77.

Rosette, Ashleigh Shelby and Robert W. Livingston. 2012. "Failure is Not an Option for Black Women: Effects of Organizational Performance on Leaders with Single Versus Dual-Subordinate Identities." *Journal of Experimental Social Psychology* 48: 1162–7.

Rospenda, Kathleen M., Judith A. Richman, and Stephanie J. Nawyn. 1988. "Doing Power: The Confluence of Gender, Race and Class in Contrapower Harassment." *Gender and Society* 15: 879–97.

Roth, Philip L., Allen I. Huffcutt, and Philip Bobko. 2003. "Ethnic Group Differences in Measures of Job Performance: A New Meta-Analysis." *Journal of Applied Psychology* 88:694–706.

Royster, Deirdre. 2003. *Race and the Invisible Hand: How White Networks Exclude Black Men from Blue-Collar Jobs.* Oakland: University of California Press.

Rumbaut, Rubén G. 2009. "Pigments of Our Imagination: On the Racialization and Racial Identities of 'Hispanics' and 'Latinos.'" pp. 15–36 in *How the U.S. Racializes Latinos: White Hegemony and its Consequences,* ed. by José A. Cobas, Jorge Duany, and Joe R. Feagin. Boulder: CO: Paradigm Publishers.

Saez, Emmanuel and Gabriel Zucman. 2016. "Wealth Inequality in the United States since 1913: Evidence from Capitalized Income Tax Data." *The Quarterly Journal of Economics* 131(2): 519–78.

Schor, Juliet. 1991. *The Overworked American: The Unexpected Decline of Leisure.* New York: Basic Books.

Schulte, Brigid. 2014. *Overwhelmed: Work, Love, and Play When No One Has the Time.* New York: Sarah Crichton Books.

Schwalbe, Michael. 2007. *Rigging the Game: How Inequality is Reproduced in Everyday Life.* 5th edn. New York: Oxford University Press.

Schwalbe, Michael, Sandra Godwin, Daphne Holden, Douglas Schrock, Shealy Thompson, and Michele Wolkomir. 2000. "Generic Processes in the Reproduction of Inequality: An Interactionist Analysis." *Social Forces* 79(2): 419–52.

Shaefer, H. Luke and Kathryn Edin. 2013. "Rising Extreme Poverty in the United States and the Response of Federal Means-Tested Transfers" *Social Service Review* 87: 250–68.

Shaefer, H. Luke, Kathryn Edin, and Elizabeth Talbert. 2015. "Understanding the Dynamics of $2-a-Day Poverty in the United States." *RSF: The Russell Sage Foundation Journal of the Social Sciences* 1: 120–38.

Shapiro, Thomas M., Tatjana Meschede, and Sam Osoro. 2013. "The Roots of the Widening Racial Wealth Gap: Explaining the Black-White Economic Divide." *Research and Policy Brief.* Institute on Assets and Social Policy, Heller School for Social Policy and Management, Brandeis University.

Sharkey, Patrick. 2008. "The Intergenerational Transmission of Context." *American Journal of Sociology* 113(4): 931–69.

Shelby, Tommie. 2003. "Ideology, Racism, and Critical Social Theory." *The Philosophical Forum* 34(2): 153–88.

Sherman, Erik. 2014. "America is the Richest, and Most Unequal, Country." *Fortune.* http: //fortune.com/2015/09/30/america-wealth-inequality/.

Slack, T. and L. Jensen. 2002. "Race, Ethnicity, and Underemployment in Nonmetropolitan America." *Rural Sociology* 67(2): 208–33.

Smith, Cheryl A. 2006. "This is How We Do It: Black Women Entrepreneurs. Management Styles and Strategies." In *Gender, Race and Ethnicity in the Workplace: Issues and Challenges for Today's Organizations*, ed. by Margaret Foegen Karsten. Westport, CT: Praeger.

Smith, Ryan A. 2002. "Race, Gender, and Authority in the Workplace: Theory and Research." *Annual Review of Sociology* 28: 509–42.

Smith, Sandra Susan. 2005. "'Don't Put My Name on It': Social Capital Activation and Job-Finding Assistance among the Black Urban Poor." *American Journal of Sociology* 111: 1–57.

Snipp, C. Matthew. 2003. "Racial Measurement in the American Census: Past Practices and Implications for the Future." *Annual Review of Sociology* 29: 563–88.

Spear, Allan H. 1967. *Black Chicago: The Making of a Negro Ghetto 1980–1920.* Chicago and London: The University of Chicago Press.

Stainback, Kevin and Donald Tomaskovic-Devey. 2009. "Intersection of Power and Privilege: Long-term Trends in Managerial Representation." *American Sociological Review* 74: 800–820.

Steele, Claude M. 2010. *Whistling Vivaldi: How Stereotypes Affect Us and What We Can Do.* New York and London: W.W. Norton.

Stepick, Alex and Guillermo Grenier. 1993. Cubans in Miami. pp. 79–100 in *In the Barrios: Latinos and the Underclass Debate*, ed. by Joan Moore and Raquel Rivera. New York: Russell Sage Foundation.

Stepick, Alex and Carol Dutton Stepick. 2002. "Power and Identity: Miami Cubans." pp. 75–92 in *Latinos: Remaking America*, ed. by Marcelo Suarez-Orozco and Mariela Paez. 2008. Berkeley: University of California Press.

Sterks, H. E. 1972. *The Free Negro in Ante-Bellum Louisiana*. New Jersey: Farleigh Dickinson University Press.

Stern, Ithai and James D. Westphal. 2007. "Flattery Will Get You Everywhere (Especially If You are a Male Caucasian): How Ingratiation, Boardroom Behavior, and Demographic Minority Status Affect Additional Board Appointments at U.S. Companies." *Academy of Management Journal* 50: 267–88.

Sue, Derald Wing. 2003. *Overcoming Our Racism: The Journey to Liberation*. San Francisco: Jossey-Bass.

——2006. "The Invisible Whiteness of Being." pp. 15–30 in *Addressing Racism: Facilitating Cultural Competence in Mental Health and Educational Settings*, ed. by Madonna G. Constantine and Derald Sue Wing. Hoboken, N.J.: John Wiley & Sons.

Sumler-Lewis, J. 1981. The Forten-Purvis Women of Philadelphia and the American Anti-Slavery Crusade. *The Journal of Negro History*. 66: 281–88. doi: 10.2307/2717236.

Sweeney, Megan H. 2011. "'We'd Love to Match Them But . . .' How Temporary Agencies Understand and Use Race and Ethnicity." *Connecticut Public Interest Law Journal*. Paper 5: 51–91.

Tafoya, Sonya M. 2005. "Shades of Belonging: Latinos and Racial Identity." *Harvard Journal of Hispanic Policy* 17: 58–78.

Takaki, Ronald. 2008. *A Different Mirror: A History of Multicultural America*. 2nd edn. Boston: Little Brown.

Takei, Isao and Arthur Sakamoto. 2008. "Do College-Educated, Native Born Asian Americans Face a Glass Ceiling in Obtaining Managerial Authority?" *Asian American Policy Review* 17: 73–85.

Tamura, Eileen. 1994. *Americanization, Acculturation, and Ethnic Identity: The Nisei Generation in Hawaii*. Chicago: University of Chicago Press.

Tang, Chiung-Ya and Shelley MacDermid Wadsworth. 2008. *The 2008 National Study of the Changing Workforce: Time and Workplace Flexibility*. New York: Families and Work Institute.

Texeira, Mary Thierry. 2002. "'Who Protects and Serves Me?': A Case Study of Sexual Harassment of African American Women." *Gender and Society* 16: 524–45.

Thomas, Ward. 2003. "The Meaning of Race to Employers: A Dynamic Qualitative Perspective." *The Sociological Quarterly* 44(2): 227–42.

Thrupkaew, Noy. 2002. "The Myth of the Model Minority" *The American Prospect*. http: //prospect.org/article/myth-model-minority.

Thurm, Scott. 2012. "U.S. Firms Add Jobs, but Mostly Overseas." *The Wall Street Journal*. http: //www.wsj.com/articles/SB10001424052702303990604 57736788197 2648906.

Tilly, Charles. 1998. *Durable Inequality*. Berkeley: University of California Press.

Tilly, Nannie M. 1948. *The Bright-Tobacco Industry, 1860–1929*. Chapel Hill: University of North Carolina.

Tindall, George Brown. 1967. *The Emergence of the New South, 1913–1945: A History of the South*. Volume 10. Baton Rouge: Louisiana State University Press.

Tinker, George E. and Loring Bush. 1991. "Native American Unemployment: Statistical Games and Cover-ups." pp. 119–44 in *Racism and the Underclass*, ed. by George W. Shepard Jr. and David Penna. Westport, CT: Greenwood.

Tomaskovic-Devey, Donald. 1993. *Gender and Racial Inequality at Work: The Sources and Consequences of Job Segregation.* Ithaca, N.Y.: ILR Press.

Tomaskovic-Devey, Donald and S. Skaggs. 1999. "An Establishment-level Test of the Statistical Discrimination Hypothesis." *Work and Occupations* 26(4): 422–45.

Tomaskovic-Devey, Donald, Melvin Thomas, and Kecia Johnson. 2005. "Race and the Accumulation of Human Capital across the Career: A Theoretical Model and Fixed Effects Application." *American Journal of Sociology* 111: 58–89.

Torlina, Jeff. 2011. *Working Class: Challenging Myths about Blue Collar Labor.* Boulder, CO and London: Lynne Rienner Publishers.

Trimble, Lindsey and Julie Kmec. 2011. "The Role of Social Networks in Getting a Job." *Sociology Compass* 5: 165–78.

Trumpbour, John and Elaine Bernard. 2002. "Unions and Latinos: Mutual Transformation." pp.126–45 in *Latinos: Remaking America*, ed. by Marcelo M. Suarez-Orozco and Mariela M. Paez. Berkeley: University of California Press.

Tuan, Mia. 1998. *Forever Foreigners or Honorary Whites?: The Asian Ethnic Experience Today.* New Brunswick, N.J.: Rutgers University Press.

Turner, Lesley J., Sheldon Danziger, and Kristin S. Seefeldt. 2006. "Failing the Transition from Welfare to Work: Women Chronically Disconnected from Employment and Cash Welfare." Social Science Quarterly 87(2): 227–49.

Uhler, Sherman. 1951. *Pennsylvania's Indian Relations to 1754.* Allentown, Pa.: Donecker.

United Way of Greater Los Angeles. 2009. *LA County 10 Years Later: A Tale of Two Cities, One Future.* Los Angeles: United Way of Greater Los Angeles.

U.S. Bureau of Labor Statistics, Employment Projections. 2014a. "Employment, Wages and Projected Change in Employment by Typical Entry-level Education." http: //www.bls.gov/emp/ep_table_education_summary.htm.

——2014b. "Occupations with the Most Job Growth, 2014 and Projected 2024." http: //www.bls.gov/emp/ep_table_104.htm.

U.S. Bureau of Labor Statistics, U.S. Department of Labor. 2014. "Foreign-born Workers: Labor Force Characteristics- 2014." News Release. http: //www.bls. gov/news.release/pdf/forbrn.pdf.

——2015. "Union Members 2015." https: //www.bls.gov/news.release/union2. toc.htm.

U.S. Department of Labor. 2012. "The African American Labor Force in Recovery." https: //www.dol.gov/_sec/media/reports/BlackLaborForce/Black LaborForce.pdf.

——2015. "Occupations with the Most Job Growth." Occupational Employment Statistics Program. U.S. Bureau of Labor Statistics. http: //data.bls.gov/cgi-bin/ print.pl/emp/ep_table_104.htm.

U.S. Equal Employment Opportunity Commission. 2016. "Farmers Insurance Exchange to Pay $225,000 to Settle EEOC Race Discrimination Suit Involving Two Hmong – American Workers and Another Worker For Retaliation." October 27. http: //www.pressreleasepoint.com/print/1068169.

Vaisey, Stephen. 2006. "Education and its Discontents: Overqualification in America, 1972–2 002." *Social Forces* 85(2): 835–64.

Vallas, Steven P. 2003. "Rediscovering the Color Line within Work Organizations: The 'Knitting of Racial Groups' Revisited." *Work and Occupations* 30: 379–400.

——2012. *Work.* Cambridge and Malden, M.A.: Polity.

Walby, Sylvia, Jo Armstrong, and Sofia Strid. 2012. "Intersectionality: Multiple Inequalities in Social Theory." *Sociology* 46(2): 224–40.

Waldinger, Roger. 1997. "Black/Immigrant Competition Re-Assessed: New Evidence from Los Angeles." *Sociological Perspectives* 40: 365–86.

Waldinger, Roger, Howard Aldrich, and Robin Ward. 1990. "Opportunities, Group Characteristics, and Strategies." In *Ethnic Entrepreneurs: Immigrant Business in Industrial Societies*, ed. by Roger Waldinger, Howard Aldrich, and Robin Ward. Newbury Park, C.A.: Sage.

Walker, Juliet E. K. 1998. The History of Black Business in America. Woodbridge, CT: Macmillan.

Wander, Philip C., Judith N. Martin, and Thomas K. Nakayama. 1999. "Sociohistorical Foundations of Whiteness." In *Whiteness: The Communication of Social Identity*, ed. by Thomas K. Nakayama and Judith N. Martin. Newbury Park, C.A.: Sage.

Warhurst, Chris, Paul Thompson, and Dennis Nickson. 2009. "Labor Process Theory: Putting the Materialism Back into the Meaning of Service Work." pp. 91–112 in *Service Work: Critical Perspectives*, ed. by Marek Korczynski and Cameron MacDonald. New York: Routledge.

Waters, Mary C. 1990. *Ethnic Options: Choosing Ethnic Identities in America*. Berkeley: University of California Press.

Watkins-Hayes, Celeste. 2009. "Race-Ing the Bootstrap Climb: Black and Latino Bureaucrats in Post-Reform Welfare Offices." *Social Problems* 56: 285–310.

Weatherford, Jack. 1988. *Indian Givers: How the Indians of the Americas Transformed the World*. New York: Random House.

Weber, Brandon. 2016. "Ever Heard of Black Wall Street?" http://progressive. org/dispatches/ever-heard-black-wall-street/

Wellman, David T. 1993. *Portraits of White Racism*. Cambridge, England: Cambridge University Press.

Western, Bruce. 2007. *Punishment and Inequality in America*. New York: Russell Sage.

Western, Bruce, Deirdre Bloome, Benjamin Sosnaud, and Laura Tach. 2012. "Economic Insecurity and Social Stratification." *Annual Review of Sociology* 38: 341–59.

Western, Bruce, Anthony A. Braga, Jaclyn Davis, and Catherine Sirois. 2015. "Stress and Hardship after Prison." *American Journal of Sociology* 120(5): 1512–47.

Western, Bruce and B. Pettit. 2005. "Black-White Wage Inequality, Employment Rates, and Incarceration." *American Journal of Sociology* 111: 553–78.

Western, Bruce and Jake Rosenfeld. 2011. "Unions, Norms, and the Rise in U.S. Wage Inequality." *American Sociological Review* 76(4): 513–37.

White, Deborah Gray. 1999. *Too Heavy a Load: Black Women in Defense of Themselves, 1894–1994*. N.Y.: W.W. Norton.

Williams, Christine L. 2006. *Inside Toyland: Working, Shopping, and Social Inequality*. Berkeley: University of California Press.

——2013. "The Glass Escalator Revisited: Gender Inequality in Neoliberal Times." *Gender and Society* 27(5): 609–29.

Williams, Christine L., Chandra Muller, and Kristine Kilanski. 2012. "Gendered Organizations in the New Economy." *Gender and Society* 26(4): 549–73.

Williams, Robert W. 2005. "W. E. B. Du Bois and His Social-Scientific Research: A Review of Online Texts." *Sociation Today* 3(2). http: //www.ncsociology. org/sociationtoday/v32/williams.htm.

Willis, Paul. 1977. *Learning to Labor*. Farnham, United Kingdom: Gower.

Wilson, Donald and Jane Wilson. 2003. *The Pride of African American History* Bloomington, IN: 1st Book Library.

Wilson, George and David Maume. 2014. "Men's Mobility into Management from Blue Collar and White Collar Jobs: Race Differences across the Early Work-Career." *Social Science Research* 46: 117–29.

Wilson, George and Debra McBrier. 2005. "Race and Loss of Privilege: African American/White Differences in the Determinants of Job Layoffs from Uppertier Occupations." *Sociological Forum* 20: 301–21.

Wilson, William Julius. 1997. *When Work Disappears: The World of the New Urban Poor*. New York: Random House.

——2009. *More Than Just Race: Being Black and Poor in the Inner City*. New York: W.W. Norton.

Winant, Howard. 2000. "Race and Race Theory." *Annual Review of Sociology* 26: 169–85.

——2004. *The New Politics of Race: Globalism, Difference, Justice*. Minneapolis: University of Minnesota Press.

Wingfield, Adia Harvey. 2007. "The Modern Mammy and the Angry Black Man: African American Professionals' Experiences with Gendered Racism in the Workplace." *Race, Gender and Class* 14: 196–212.

——2009. "Racializing the Glass Escalator: Reconsidering Men's Experiences with Women's Work." *Gender and Society* 23: 5–26.

——2010. "Are Some Emotions Marked 'Whites Only'?: Racialized Feeling Rules in Professional Workplaces." *Social Problems* 57: 251–68.

——2012. *No More Invisible Man: Race and Gender in Men's Work*. Philadelphia: Temple University Press.

Witz, Anne, Chris Warhurst, and Dennis Nickson. 2003. "The Labour of Aesthetics and The Aesthetics of Organization." *Organization* 10: 33–54.

Wolters, Raymond. 1970. *Negroes and the Great Depression*. Westport, CT: Greenwood.

Woo, Deborah. 2000a. *Glass Ceilings and Asian Americans: The New Face of Workplace Barriers*. Walnut Creek, C.A.: Altamira.

——2000b. "The Inventing and Reinventing of 'Model Minorities': The Cultural Veil Obscuring Structural Sources of Inequality." pp. 193–211 in *Asian Americans: Experiences and Perspectives*, ed. by Timothy P. Fong and Larry H. Shinagawa. New York: Pearson.

Wooten, L. P. and E. H. James. 2004. "When Firms Fail to Learn: The Perpetuation of Discrimination in the Workplace." *Journal of Management Inquiry* 13(1): 23–33.

Wright, J. Leitch Jr. 1981. *The Only Land They Knew*. New York: The Free Press.

Wu, Frank. 2002. *Yellow: Race in America: Beyond Black and White*. New York: Basic Books.

Yang, Song. 2007."Racial Disparities in Training, Pay-raise Attainment, and Income." *Research in Social Stratification and Mobility* 25: 323–35.

Yoder, Janice D. and Patricia Aniakudo. 1997. "'Outsider Within' the Firehouse: Subordination and Difference in the Social Interactions of African American Women Firefighters." *Psychology of Women Quarterly* 25: 27–36.

Yosso, Tara J. 2006. *Critical Race Counterstories along the Chicana/Chicano Educational Pipeline*. New York: Routledge.

Young, Alford and Donald Deskins. 2001. "Early Traditions of African-American Sociological Thought." *Annual Review of Sociology* 27: 445–77.

Yount, Kristen. 2004. "Sexualization of Work Roles among Men Miners." pp. 65–91 in *In the Company of Men: Male Dominance and Sexual Harassment*, ed. by James E. Gruber and Phoebe Morgan. Boston: Northeastern University Press.

Zamudio, Margaret and Michael Lichter. 2008. "Bad Attitudes and Good Soldiers: Soft Skills as a Code for Tractability in the Hiring of Immigrant Latina/os over Native Blacks in the Hotel Industry." *Social Problems* 55: 571–89

Zavodny, Madeline. 2003. "Race, Wages, and Assimilation among Cuban Immigrants." *Federal Reserve Bank of Atlanta*. Working Paper #2003–10.

Zinn, Howard. 1995. *A People's History of the United States: 1942-present*. New York: Harper Collins.

——2004. *Voices of a People's History of the United States*. New York: Seven Stories Press.

Zwerling, Craig and Hilary Silver. 1992. "Race and Job Dismissals in a Federal Bureaucracy." *American Sociological Review* 57: 651–60.

Index